Praise for

'*Chess Queens* is a meditation ... [...] ... [...] ... n so under-represented in the [...] ... of those who played on against t [...] e, thoughtful and inspirational book by a person who has seen it all from the inside.'

Angela Saini, author of *Inferior*

'Like *The Queen's Gambit*, this isn't really about chess, but power . . . Shahade wants to provoke discussion and show how chess is just a starting point for wider liberation.'

The Sunday Times

'Jennifer's book gives readers an insider look into the complex realities of being a female chess player, while also showcasing the badass women knocking down these barriers. Highly recommended!'

Alexandra Botez, chess champion and Twitch streamer

'The fascinating true stories of the lives of champion chess players. All women should take up the challenge and pick up a board!'

Yoko Ono

'Shahade gives us a tour of the history, geography and gender politics of chess, accompanied by the uplifting stories of chess heroines, of triumph after triumph over stunning misogyny and stifling cultural expectations. *Chess Queens* is an exhilarating read for anyone interested in the highs and lows of competitive games, especially those who are told they don't belong!'

Gina Rippon, author of *The Gendered Brain*

'I really enjoyed *Chess Queens* and reading about the triumphs and struggles of women in chess. Jennifer Shahade does an amazing job'

Eric Rosen, International Chess Master

'There is little technical analysis or jargon. She writes for the general reader . . . in a droll and conversational style, with a sharp eye for character quirks'

The New Humanist

'An inside look at feminism and sexism in the chess world – a riveting, page-turning read'

Nell McShane Wulfhart, author of *Off-Menu*
and *The Great Stewardess Rebellion*

'*Chess Queens* is brutally honest – that is, sometimes shocking and revealing – well researched, and highly entertaining. It is at times glamourous but overall it is an instructive work that confronts the reader with the darker sides of a chess player's complex reality. It does so with a generous dose of sarcasm and good humor . . . an excellent advertisement for chess itself'

ChessBase.com

JENNIFER SHAHADE

Chess Queens

*The True Story of a Chess Champion
and the Greatest Female Players
of All Time*

HODDER

First published in Great Britain in 2022 by Hodder & Stoughton
An Hachette UK company

This paperback edition published in 2023

1

A CIP catalogue record for this title is available from the British Library

Paperback ISBN 9781399701389

Typeset in Plantin Light by Palimpsest Book Production Limited,
Falkirk, Stirlingshire

Printed and bound in Great Britain by Clays Ltd, Elcograf S.p.A.

Hodder & Stoughton policy is to use papers that are natural,
renewable and recyclable products and made from wood grown in
ustainable forests. The logging and manufacturing processes are expected
to conform to the environmental regulations of the country of origin.

Hodder & Stoughton Ltd
Carmelite House
50 Victoria Embankment
London EC4Y 0DZ

www.hodder.co.uk

To my father, Mike Shahade, for making me a chess player, my mother, Sally Solomon, for making me a writer and in memory of my coach, Victor Frias, for making me a champion.

And to Daniel and Fabian, for making me happy.

Contents

Contents

Introduction

Recently I conducted a poll: I asked hundreds of aspiring chess girls what they liked about the game. Most of them gave multiple answers: winning, meeting friends, the intrinsic beauty of checkmate. Some had practical reasons, like scholarships. But one twelve-year-old girl's response stuck out the most: 'Love to whip obnoxious boys.'

Beth Harmon, the hero of the book and TV series *The Queen's Gambit*, embodied that ruthless spirit. In her seafoam silk dress, with a withering stare, Beth seduced hundreds of millions of viewers into the power of the Sicilian Defense and the joy of smothered mate. Grandmaster Harmon showed how dangerous it is to underestimate a woman's mind, because she will checkmate those obnoxious boys.

The chess in *The Queen's Gambit* was more accurate than anything I've ever seen on screen, from the intensity of a chess staredown to the globetrotting glamour of a top grandmaster on tour. The popularity of the show caused a worldwide shortage of chess sets, and inspired new devotees from all over the world, of every age and gender. Chess champion streamers like Anna Rudolf, Qiyu Zhou and the Botez sisters saw their viewerships multiply in the frenzy, leading to sponsorship deals and a richer era for chess. Content creators studied Beth Harmon's games for each nuance and tactic, from opening finesses to endgame artistry.

But the TV show was fiction.

Chess Queens is the true story of the women and girls who broke down barriers to become chess champions. They resisted federations that barred them from playing against men. They protested the skewed prize funds that offered female chess players ten times less than men. They shot back at organizers who asked if they were 'rated 2550 for women.' They conquered minds on the board, and changed minds off of it.

Chess Queens is also my story – I spent my teens and early twenties travelling the world, battling on the chessboard, while coming of age. I celebrated my sixteenth birthday between chess games in Iceland, and chased the International Master title while crashing at hostels in Hungary. I explored Turkish baths and nightclubs at my first Chess Olympiad and played a World Championship at the Kremlin in Moscow.

Connecting with people of all different backgrounds, ages and genders over the chessboard reminded me that while a few of games of chess could tell us which player was better, in life nobody was better than me, and nobody was worse than me. As the Italian proverb goes, at the end of the game, the king and the pawn go into the same box.

I totally lose myself when engrossed in a chess position. As a teen and young adult, this was precious. Wrapped up in a middlegame, I didn't care about what a guy thought about me, how popular I was, or if I was going to ace or fail a test. Those pure flow experiences taught me that true happiness was not just about avoiding pain and seeking pleasure, but also about deliberate focus.

It wasn't all joy, friendships and checkmates. I encountered sexism and old-fashioned attitudes, and came up hard against some of my own weaknesses in the game itself, which ranged from a lack of confidence to impatience. The chessboard became a mirror for my mind, and I had to learn to like what I saw, even when it wasn't perfect.

Chess Queens has a precursor: *Chess Bitch*. I wrote that earlier

version of the book in 2005, just after I had won my second
US Women's Chess Championship. On a bus in Atlantic City,
I told my dad that the racy title of my first book aggravated
some chess fans. It was even censored on many platforms,
including the *New York Times*. My dad thought for a minute
and then said I should rename it 'Checkmate, Asshole!' *Chess
Bitch* was a fitting title at the time – I wrote about things in
the chess world that were unfair and sexist but that I sometimes
felt too agreeable to shout out. The title was my call to action:
a reminder to tap into my own rage.

And that flame lives on. *Chess Queens* honors the growing
number of female champions all over the world, while maintaining the fiery spirit of the first edition. This is an important
time for all chess queens. While women have more power in
chess than we've ever had before, we are still vastly outnumbered. And we're also outnumbered in many other arenas, from
politics to coding to the boardroom.

I believe that chess is a gateway for women into other fields
where we're underrepresented. When I started playing poker
seriously, I was often the only female at the table. I preferred
to see other women but I also knew I could handle being the
only one. Chess, like poker, is all about making decisions over
and over again, even when uncertain, even when pressed for
time. I believe in the power of women and gender minorities
to make those choices on and off the board and the importance
of cultivating and celebrating those decisions.

Resistance to female aggression in chess dates back to the
15th century, when the queen turned from the weakest piece
on the board, only able to move one square diagonally, to the
strongest, sweeping the board in one stroke. That game was at
first referred to as the madwoman chess's game, mocking the
powerful queen as crazy. Once the game was widely adopted,
the 'mad' and the 'woman' were dropped and now it's just

'chess'. The potent queen changed the game for the better, but her credit was quickly removed.

There is still plenty to be mad about in chess, from the relentless sexualization of female players to discourse erasing trans and non-binary identities. Shallow questions about women's supposed inferiority persist, while systemic issues like childcare, racism and safety are minimized.

Bitch may have been dropped from the title, but the chess queen was mad centuries ago and she's still mad today. The book has changed in far more than title. It has been significantly reshaped, with updates on each chapter. Opinions are revised by new evidence and experiences, and players are added to the roster of impressive queens. You'll learn about the Holocaust survivor, Isabelle Choko, who was rescued from the concentration camp Bergen-Belsen when she weighed just 55 pounds – she made a full recovery and later became the French Women's Champion. Lyudmila Rudenko, the second Women's World Champion, will inspire you with her wins, but even more with her heroism in World War II. Koneru Humpy, the Indian star who broke the record for the youngest female to earn the Grandmaster title, tells us why she feels freer when playing Open events. You'll meet the Ugandan chess star, Phiona 'Queen of Katwe' Mutesi, who became an international symbol for resilience.

At its best, chess can be an aspirational model for our culture – what would it be like if we focused more on what people think and the decisions they make, and less on how they look, how old they are, or how much money they have? At its worst, chess can magnify the problems that come with a chess culture so dominated by one gender, and by one type of mindset, no matter how magnificent those minds are.

In the past decade, I've seen far more chess events for women, girls and gender minorities, including workshops, camps and tournaments. I have supported and led many such spaces. As one student from my US Chess girls club said, 'It's inspiring to know that there are other girls out there who love chess, and that I'm not just crazy.'

I want to see new passionate chess players all over the world pick up the pieces and checkmate without apology. And I want for them to be accepted with open arms by a chess world with no place for harassment or elitism. Because while this book may be filled with chess queens, there is always room for more.

I

Playing Like A Girl

'I am a woman who plays a man's game, so I balance feminine emotions with masculine logic to become the strongest player possible.'

Zhu Chen, ninth Women's World Champion

I was angry, overwrought, and couldn't control my aggression and desire to win at any cost. It was the first time I had felt such intense killer instincts, and when I went to the bathroom to splash water on my face, I looked in the mirror and wondered, is this what it means to play like a man?

It was Christmas in Las Vegas and I was twenty-two years old. Accompanied by my father, Michael, a now inactive chessmaster, I was there playing in a chess tournament. As we walked through the hotel, the Paris Las Vegas, with its wide-carpeted boulevards, sky-painted ceilings, and beret-wearing waiters with fake French accents, my cheerful father ironically declared in a booming voice, 'This is so authentic!' I was less enthusiastic. I didn't like gambling or even poker back then,* and I was baffled by the slot machine junkies and sad-eyed big-money losers.

* Soon after the original publication of this book, I learned to play poker from my brother. I learned that poker was also a mindsport and could be approached like chess: as a game to study and master, and as a vehicle to travel the world, empower women and understand myself and other people better.

The hectic tournament schedule was set at two games a day. Each game would likely last between three to six hours. I was already exhausted and running on caffeine, sandwiches bolted in transit, and the adrenaline rush that accompanies an encounter as intense as a chess game.

The games were played far from Paris, in a sterile ballroom in Bally's Casino and Resort. I'd had a lukewarm tournament so far, winning two games against masters I was favored to beat, and losing two to grandmasters.* My last-round opponent was an affable, completely inoffensive master. I wasn't playing for any prize, so the source of my aggression was not lust for cash. Maybe it was the sharp attacking position that aroused my killer instinct. In any case, I was angry and playing like a man – or playing violently, which – for me – were the same. I was also playing badly: too many aggressive, but ineffective, moves. I sacrificed a Queen in a position where I saw that my opponent's best response – rejecting my Queen sacrifice and fortifying his own position – would lead to a winning game for him. With just one minute on my clock, I was going to lose! My opponent offered me a draw. Riled up with all that masculine fire, I had the nerve to decline. With the next move, I came to my senses and renewed the draw offer: luckily my opponent, who by now had a clear advantage on the board, shook my hand in agreement. Did his lack of ruthless courage mean that he was playing like a girl?

From open-air chess parks to professional tournament halls, 'playing like a girl' has negative connotations, while 'playing like a man' is a standard to be admired and emulated. It is no surprise that 'playing like a boy' or 'playing like a woman' are rarer phrases. Men and girls are on opposite ends of a

* In order to earn the title of grandmaster, a player needs to reach a minimum rating of 2500 and score three especially stellar results, called 'Grandmaster norms.'

continuum of strength and power. Boys and women, in between, are less-apt categories for generalizing skill level.

The stereotype that female players are naturally weaker chess players is widespread, stretching from the world's top players to total beginners. But I wondered if this concept was a foregone conclusion: we explained why women are weaker than men at chess without interrogating whether the opposite could also be true.

So I started asking women chess players if there were any feminine qualities that contributed to their chess skill. Former European women's champion Almira Skripchenko responded after a pause. 'I don't know. No one has ever asked me that before,' admitting that, to her, 'The male standard is the highest standard.' Many women named advantages in being a chess-world minority: 'I receive more invitations and recognition as a woman' or 'Some men play badly against women.' Biology is often used to explain the supposed inferiority of women in chess, but the women I asked only named advantages peripherally related to being female.

At the moment of writing, the rate of female chess participation, especially at the adult level, is astonishingly low. In the United States, around 5% of competitive adult-rated players are women.* When you include youth players, the statistics are somewhat more promising. From 2010 to 2020 the percentage of female participation in US chess hovered between 11 and 15%, a massive increase from 2000, when it was just 8%. In the worldwide ranking system of FIDE (Fédération Internationale des Échecs) the situation is similar. There, about 10% of active players are female.[1] Countries with high rates of female participation ranging from 25–40% include Vietnam, Georgia, China,

---

* These numbers are based on classical over the board games, not online or blitz ratings. The FIDE statistics listed are based on January 2020 classical ratings.

Mongolia and Ecuador. Russia, Indonesia and Kenya also rank
well above average between 17–25%. Some of the lowest figures
come from Denmark, Ireland, Norway, the Netherlands and
Sweden with 5% or lower.

Interpreting the data in such a male-dominated group is
complex, but a good place to start is with Elo ratings, named
after Professor Arpad Elo. In the 1960s, Elo developed the
rating system now used by FIDE to estimate the relative strength
of chess players based on previous results. After each tournament, ratings are revised to reflect a player's performance. A
master player's rating ranges from 2200 to 2400, and an international master or a grandmaster is usually rated between 2400
up to 2882, the highest rating of all time earned by Magnus
Carlsen in 2014.[*]

It is typical to confuse the low rate of participation with
poor performance. The percentage of top female players has
to be compared to the percentage of active female chess players,
and to the number of games that women and girls play. The
top female player of all time, Judit Polgar, reached a career
high of number 8 in the world in 2005. In the United States,
there are currently three women in the top 100 players[†] in the
country: not an encouraging stat on its own, but pretty close
to the percentage of women players. There is no clear evidence
that women play worse than men. There are, however, clearly
fewer women who play and those who play, play fewer games
on average.

Explanations abound as to why women are rarely drawn to
competitive chess, including Freudian theories, studies on the

---

[*] Garry Kasparov held the previous record, achieving a high of 2851 in
1999, the stat published in the first edition of this text.
[†] This stat is based on the October 2021 US Chess rating list, and the three
players in the top 100 are Irina Krush (68), 2021 US Women's Champion
Carissa Yip (88) and Anna Zatonskih (96).

importance of testosterone, and evolutionary theories. Garry Kasparov, who held the World Champion title from 1985 till 2000, now supports women and girls in chess. But in his early career he dismissed female chess talent, explaining that the ability to concentrate is the most important quality in a chess player. He argued that women are more easily distracted: 'A woman's train of thought can be broken more easily by extraneous events, such as a baby crying upstairs.' Kasparov said that women are more sensitive to external stimuli, so that even a childless woman has maternal impulses that make it harder for her to focus. To test Garry's theory, I propose that a tournament with one hundred female and one hundred male participants be held underneath a baby nursery. It would then be possible to see how men and women react and adapt their play to the distracting cries of babies.

The Male Variability Hypothesis is another theory that's frequently tossed out. This is based on the idea that men have more variable IQs, on both the high and low end. It's often nicknamed as the 'More Idiots, More Geniuses' theory. That one irritates me most of all. Partly because from the data I've seen, male IQs may have more variability, but when I see this theory mentioned, it's ableist, exaggerated and used in bad faith to make strange logical leaps, often by non-scientists trolling successful women.

Presented in inappropriate contexts, this discourages females. I should know. I first heard about these ideas as a preteen at a chess camp, where a psychologist was invited to talk about gender and chess. With no understanding of statistics at that age, all I remember is seeing charts showing why my own potential was limited: the last thing I needed to hear at such an impressionable age.

Even if the theory were valid, it's a leap to use this to explain why women play less chess than men. The link between genius

IQ scores and chess skill is unclear, and the value of IQ itself is under constant scrutiny. Author and science journalist Angela Saini told me she wasn't sure what men were trying to achieve by citing such studies and, as she pointed out in her book *Inferior*, 'The scientific picture emerging now is that there may be very small biological differences (between men and women), but that these can be so easily reinforced by society that they appear much bigger as a child grows.'[2]

American Grandmaster Reuben Fine, a World Championship contender, professor and author of many books on psychology, links the desire to play chess with latent, unspeakable desires. In his 1956 treatise 'Psychoanalytic Observations on Chess and Chess Masters', Fine writes, 'The unconscious motive actuating the players is not the mere love of pugnacity but the grimmer one of father-murder.' Women are less inclined to pick up the game, argues Fine, since they lack a 'subconscious urge to kill their father(s).' Fine believes that the King attracts boys to the game because the piece is important (if it is trapped, the game is over), yet impotent (it can only move one square at a time.) He argues that adolescent males are in a similar state, because they are unable to express their budding social and sexual powers. In his view, the rules of chess mirror for boys the rules of sex. 'Don't touch your piece until you're ready to move it' encodes to 'Don't masturbate.'

This outrageous Oedipal model is just one of many possible ways to decode the symbolism of chess. I prefer to think of chess in the spirit of Carl Jung, as a system of opposites, from the black and white colors of the pieces and squares to knowing when it is time to attack and when to defend.

A good chess player also strives to balance overconfidence and fear, practice and rest, and – in the game itself – tactical and strategic thinking. Tactics are short operations that force checkmate or a quick win of material (pieces or pawns) and require proficiency in calculating. When a good player calculates, she considers her possible moves, taking into account her opponent's possible responses, and how she would play against each, and so on, until she is reasonably satisfied with her choice. Though many nonplayers and amateurs are fascinated by how many moves ahead a chessmaster can see, it can sometimes be easy to see twelve moves ahead if there are few pieces on the board, but extremely difficult to see three moves ahead if the opponent has a variety of responses, which lead to a dense web of variations. Strategic thinking requires long-term planning and maneuvering: when there are no tactics to watch out for or employ, masters play moves based on their intuition and experience, waiting for the time when the position reveals more concrete answers. Even the very best players have difficulty with the tension, as Russian-American Grandmaster Gregory Kaidanov said to me: 'I can play well tactically, I can play well strategically, but I have difficulty switching quickly between one mode of thinking to the other.'

During a tournament game, balancing intense concentration with relaxation is crucial, to save energy for critical moments. Many players get up between moves to pace, eat an energy bar, or glance at friends' games. It is easy to go too far with this practice, slip into daydreams, and totally lose concentration – and the game. Some men claim that thinking about sex diverts their focus. A twenty-two-year-old male amateur told me jokingly, 'I would be a grandmaster if only I could stop thinking about sex during the game for more than fifteen minutes. I think it would be easier if I were a woman.' According to the four-time US Champion Alexander Shabalov, professionals have not overcome that obstacle: he said that most men, regardless of their strength, are thinking about sex for most of the game. With characteristic humor, the Latvian-born grandmaster jokes, 'In most games, I am thinking about women for about fifty to seventy-five percent of the time, another fifteen percent goes to time management, and with what's left over I am calculating.' When I mention that twenty-five percentage points is a big range, Alexander agrees. 'You can tell if it's closer to fifty or seventy-five percent by the quality of the game. Fifty percent is great chess, seventy-five percent I can play okay, but where it is really dangerous is when it slips up to ninety percent.'

Learning the rules of chess takes a few hours, but gaining competence in its intricacies and developing a personal style takes years of work. Playing a highly focused board game for four to six hours is difficult, and neither men nor women nor non-binary players are born with the concentration and motivation to excel at it. For that reason, I find the emphasis on women's biological inferiority absurd: when it comes to chess, we are all born inept.

The desire to find gender-based stylistic differences is based on a belief that if women and men are different, they ought to play chess differently as well. Indeed, women and men do tend to have different chess careers and get started in the game for different reasons. In my usage, the category of women's chess does not refer to some intrinsically female way of playing chess but rather to being a minority in the chess world, which can affect the way women or gender minorities play.

The development of my own style was affected by being one of the few girls in chess. My brother, Greg, and father, Michael, were both masters by the time I became serious about chess, in high school. My father has a sedate style. He is an excellent calculator, but his tendency to choose solid, positional set-ups, such as the English opening (starting the game with the c-pawn, commonly thought as the safest first-move option), surprises some people in the chess world. English Grandmaster Tony Miles, after taking in my dad's iron-man physique, loud voice, and commanding presence, and after watching several of his games, said, 'I thought you would play more like a thug!' My brother has a balanced style, which favors tactics but is also flexible. He does employ solid systems against opponents when he thinks they will be uncomfortable with long strategic battles. Impressed by Greg's psychological awareness, one master told me, 'Greg has the most pragmatic style I've ever seen.'

Jennifer and her dad Michael (Shahade family collection)

As a teenager, I played the most dynamic openings in the family, and tended to win by executing ruthless attacks. I improved rapidly between the ages of fourteen and sixteen. Just before I turned sixteen in 1996, I entered the Insanity Tournament, an all-night chess marathon that began at nine at night and ended at nine the next morning. I won the tournament and also gained enough rating points to join my brother and father as national masters. I was euphoric. My father, who took the train with me to the tournament and stayed to watch my games, joked gleefully on the ride home, 'No one could ever say you play like a girl.' At the time, I considered it a compliment. I didn't see any reason for my violent style except that I liked attacking chess. However, I was aware of the stereotype that women were more patient and passive when men were supposedly braver, and I wanted to be a hero too. In retrospect, I see my chess style was loaded with meaning – to be aggressive was to renounce any stereotype of my play based on my gender. I was also emulating the attacking style of the top woman player in the world, Hungarian Judit Polgar.

Jennifer and her brother Greg
(photo by Eric Rosen)

For a while, I played recklessly, and at first I lost many games because of my one-dimensional style. Many opponents altered their strategies when playing against me, choosing quiet systems – such as the English opening – in order to de-rail the tactical melees at which I excelled. This resulted in my progress pursuing a zigzag course: I dipped below master, and back up again, and then under again. I realized that I needed to learn other aspects of the game, so I began to study strategy manuals and endgame theory to improve my standard of play.

I needed to curb my desire to subvert stereotypes by playing violently. By the time I was nineteen, I started to mingle in the higher ranks of international chess, playing in world championships and the biennial chess Olympiads. I realized that to play like a girl did not have the same meaning at the top as it did in parks and scholastic tournaments. It turned out that to play like a girl meant to play too aggressively! This was most vividly demonstrated to me when a Russian coach looked at some of my boldest games and said derisively, 'I see women's chess hasn't changed. Women have no patience; they always want to attack immediately.'

Even women players sometimes join the chorus. The first German woman to earn the grandmaster title, Elisabeth Paehtz, once told me: 'Women are mostly of the more aggressive category. They don't want to sit for six hours, so they attack and try to get the game over with. Probably this is because men in the Stone Age had the more focused goal of hunting, while women had a variety of tasks.'

Grandmaster Susan Polgar also believes that women have difficulties in strategic thinking, although her reasoning is based on more recent history: 'Women are rarely given the freedom to think abstractly. Men are often afforded the luxury of having their basic tasks, like laundry and cooking, taken care of. Women are usually compelled to focus on the details of life.' Susan concludes, 'This is the root of why women are equal to men in tactics, but still lag behind men in strategy.'

Paehtz and Polgar attempt to explain aggressive female play by referencing female characteristics, naturally and culturally. I think we need to consider the conditions of the contemporary chess world. A feature of the present standard of women's chess is excessive aggression, a playing trait that may just be more common for masters rated 2300-2500 Elo, the range in which professional women fall. Grandmasters tend to have more balanced styles. To determine whether women are more aggressive than men, one would have to compare the games of the top female players with the games of randomly selected male players rated 2300-2500. In determining a feminine style, the conclusions are rarely based on statistical analyses of games. Playing like a girl, whether it is supposed to refer to passive or aggressive play, is usually intended as an insult. This devaluing of the feminine in chess dates back to the 1300s and the birth of modern chess rules.

The Queen is the most powerful piece on the chessboard, shuttling across ranks and files, checkmating lone Kings, and grabbing loose pieces on an open board. This was not always so. In the Persian versions of the game, there was no Queen. The piece that stood by the King was the Ferz, or the adviser. Replacing this male counselor with the Queen, the romantic partner of the King, occurred after Persian, Byzantine and Arabian traders transported the game to Europe circa AD 1000. Chess historian H. J. R. Murray thinks that this change came about because of 'the general symmetry of the arrangement of the pieces, which pointed to the pairing of the two central pieces.'

The Queen began as one of the weakest pieces on the board and her presence was not revered. In 1345, when the Queen could only inch along the diagonals, a medieval writer described her force: '[Her] move is aslant only because women are so

The chess queen's early movements (illustration by Megan Lee)

greedy that they will take nothing except by rapine and injustice.'[3] Diagonal lines were then seen as sinister and sneaky, in contrast to the honesty of straight lines. The connotation lingers in English phrases such as 'crooks' or 'straight-up'. In Go, a game which originated in China, the pieces do not connect on the diagonals. In chess, blundering on diagonals is more common than on the straight lines of the ranks or files, as I've often discovered when playing against the very sinister opening called the London.*

The old chess was slower, with each game taking far more moves. It was hard to deliver checkmate without the mighty

---

* This popular and very solid opening involves an early development of the bishop to f4, which is often tucked in to that diagonal for a long time, so long that it's easy to forget about it.

Queen of today. Games were rarely recorded, and to quicken the pace, players often began the games with *tabiyas*, midgame starting positions.

Around 1500 the rules of chess underwent a sudden metamorphosis, and the Queen was given much greater powers. The bishop acquired greater mobility at this time also. These changes made the play of chess quicker and set up a balance between strategy and tactics, or intuition and calculation, which makes the game tantalizing to this day. The alterations occurred during the time of Columbus's bloody voyages and Queen Isabella's reign of Spain. No single individual is given credit for the changes; probably they were initiated as a result of collective experimentation, brought on by dissatisfaction with the old game. Chess literature spread the new rules, which were rapidly standardized with the contemporaneous advent of the printing press. Chess with its radical new rules was at first called 'The madwoman's chess game.'

Emory Tate, one of America's most legendary and talented senior masters, often displayed his ambivalence toward powerful women as embodied by the Queen. Emory had a spectacular style, and at open tournaments he was known for his impromptu performances, his muscled body writhing as he shouted out the moves of his games. Emory reeled off his accomplishments in rapid-fire diction, punctuated with profanities. In one of these so-called post-mortems, I was among several dozen onlookers when Emory exclaimed, 'And now I made a triple-force postal move – Bitch to g5!' The first part of this is nonsensical rhetorical flourish – there is no such thing as a triple-force postal move. As for calling the Queen a 'bitch', she is central to the inspired checkmating attacks Emory loved. The reception of the potent sixteenth-century Queen also showed a negative association with female aggression. The new Queen was not described in a positive way as the super queen or power queen, but rather pathologized as the mad, crazy queen.*

Women are too docile, claimed English Grandmaster Nigel Short, to enjoy the highest levels of chess competition. 'They just don't have the killer instinct,' he said, 'men and women's brains are hardwired differently.'[4] Reuben Fine was straight-forward in defining chess as 'quite obviously a play-substitute for war.' But is chess really so like war? In chess, both players begin with armies of precisely the same strength and use only their intellects to express their aggression; in this way, chess is antithetical to war. Women's World Champion Susan Polgar said that when she was four years old, she pictured chess as a 'fairy tale' because her father told her dramatic stories involving the King, the Queen, castles, and romance. If chess is a meta-phor for war, it is not war as hell, but war where fairness, females, and rules matter above all.

The power of the Queen foreshadows the strength of the women champions in this book, but it also hints at something more sinister. Author and historian Marilyn Yalom writes that the queen is an 'ultimate female status, but one which is played out in life as in chess on a predominantly male playing field.' Empowered women are often called bitches, or mocked for their lack of femininity. Nearly every up-and-coming female in the history of women's chess has had her femininity minimized, complimented not for being a strong woman but for 'playing like a man.' Many great women players have been called Amazons, which means literally 'without one breast'.† In chess

---

* In a 2017 art piece, *Not Particularly Beautiful*, that I created with my husband, Daniel Meirom, we showcased misogynistic insults toward female chess players on an oversized chessboard. The piece referenced insults to the 'madwoman's chess queen' game from the sixteenth century, tracing a 500-year lineage of anger and resentment toward female power in chess.

† Not that we'd take it as an insult. In 2021, I co-hosted a tournament titled

variants, an 'Amazon' refers to an even more powerful queen that also possesses the movements of the knight.[*]

As much hate as the mad queen got when she gained her new powers, she made a better game. The 'madwoman's chess' became chess, as we know it now.

In February of 2003 I received a call from Susan Polgar, the eldest of the legendary Polgar trio from Hungary. She wanted to get together. I was excited, because Susan was one of my childhood heroines. Susan, along with her sisters Sofia and Judit, was a child prodigy, trained from infancy in chess tactics and strategies as most children are taught the alphabet. Susan is one of a handful of women to hold the overall grandmaster title and is a former World Women's Champion. Born in Budapest, Susan moved to New York in 1995, where she moved to be with her husband. She started a family and took a hiatus from competitive play.

Susan and I met in a bookstore in Manhattan, where I found her flipping through a cookbook. She greeted me warmly, but moved quickly onto business, telling me that she was distraught by the lowly status of chess in the United States. In Europe, chess is a respected sport. It occurred to Susan that the top women players in the United States, with some training, would be strong enough to compete with the best women's Olympic teams in the world. She hoped that this would promote chess in the United States. Susan would come out of retirement in order to train the team and play board one (where the strongest players from each team face off) during the next Olympic games, set for Mallorca, Spain, in 2004.

'Amazon's Pride' with chess champion and streamer Dina Belenkaya.

[*] A chess variant is any form of chess with different rules, from slight tweaks like replacing a Queen with an 'Amazon' to dramatically different formats, like 'crazyhouse' in which captured pieces become your own army.

Susan Polgar (photo by Bill Hook, courtesy of the
World Chess Hall of Fame)

Four months after our meeting, along with three other young
women, I was invited for a one-week training session to be held
at the Susan Polgar Chess Authority, a one-level community
chess center and chess bookshop that Susan founded. The club
is in Rego Park, deep in Queens where English is often a third
language. It was to be the first of eight official training meetings
for what team publicist Paul Truong termed The Dream Team.

Anna Zatonskih was the only non-New Yorker on the
squad, so she stayed with me in my Brooklyn apartment.
Anna, an international master who was twenty-five-years-old
at the time, arrived at my place and shyly presented me with
a box of chocolates from Ukraine, where she had been born
and raised. Anna has a wide jawbone, silky, dark hair and legs

so long that she seems overwhelmed by her own stature. Anna was not yet fluent in English, so the first few hours between us were awkward, until we sat down at the chessboard set up in my living room. Anna quickly opened up and showed me one of her best games, giggling with childlike glee as she replayed the moves: 'And now I sacrificed another piece!'

The next morning Anna and I took the long subway ride to Rego Park for our first session. We were excited and nervous about training with the famous Susan Polgar. Anna and I were early, and we chatted awkwardly with Susan about her club and our upcoming tournaments as the other members arrived.

Irina Krush entered the club next, brown hair back in a ponytail, wearing a jean jacket, eating an apple. Irina became an international master at sixteen, and was the youngest player to win a US championship as a fourteen-year-old. At the time of this session, Irina was enrolled as a full-time student at NYU, but her devotion to chess is constant. 'For me every game of chess is a character test – such intense situations arise so rarely in real life.' Irina approaches life as she does chess, with a contagious intensity. Though chess is her first and deepest love, Irina cultivates what she calls 'mini-passions', such as ones for the French language and tennis.

Rusudan Goletiani, an energetic and rail-thin woman in her twenties, completed the squad. Rusudan is from the ex-Soviet Republic of Georgia, where the first great women's chess tradition originated. In boring moments of endgame lectures, I sometimes stared at Rusa's snazzy high-top sneakers and imagined her jumping over tall buildings. Rusudan's buoyant presence belies a serious character. In 2000, Rusudan fled a grim economic situation in post-communist Georgia. Upon her arrival in the United States, she spent most of her time coaching chess to support herself – this also enabled her to send money back to friends and family in Georgia. Consequently, her chess activity abated, and she was the lowest-rated person on the team. However, by common consensus she may be the most talented player, often reeling off long variations (long strings of projected moves) and finding surprising ideas in analysis.

The training program was exhausting. Each day began at ten in the morning and ran until seven at night: grandmaster guests came, taught, and left. Conversations and lectures were conducted in a swirl of English, Russian, and chess. We analyzed complex endgames, investigated the weaknesses in our play by showing our worst games, and played training games against each other. This grueling work was rewarding for me as a chess player. But one afternoon, my peaceful progress was punctured by a sexist discussion.

Michael Khodarkovsky, a Russian trainer who works closely with Garry Kasparov, is a sturdy, balding man with piercing blue eyes, kind mannerisms and confident diction. Michael began his session with us by saying, 'I know that feminism is popular in the United States, but in Russia we understood that women and men play differently.' Michael advised us: 'With this in mind, you should never be ashamed to tell your trainers most intimate details . . . or when you may not be able to play one hundred percent.' Paul Truong, a fuzzy-haired ball of energy with a tittering laugh, clarified Michael's statement for the team: 'Does everyone know what Michael is talking about? . . . Menstruation!'

I thought I had entered the twilight zone, an impression that was furthered when Susan Polgar, one of my childhood heroines, joined forces with Michael: 'Now, menstruation may not require that someone take a day off, but it might affect, for instance, the choice of opening.' Michael mentioned a computer program that a Soviet friend of his had developed, which would determine how, at any given day, the menstrual cycle would affect play. I was too shocked to say much, though later that afternoon, I could not resist joking – after suggesting a poor move in analysis – that 'It's that time of month; can't think straight.' The laughter that ensued made me hopeful that no one took the issue too seriously.

Periods were happily left undiscussed until a few days later when the whole team took a break from our formal training to visit the IBM headquarters in New Jersey. IBM, a sponsor of our team, generously donated computers to us, and allowed us to play against Deep Blue, the computer developed by IBM in 1997 that made history by defeating Kasparov in a match. Susan Polgar gave a talk about her career and lifestory to a group of computer programmers, many of whom were amateur chessplayers and many who had feminist views. Then Susan grappled with the question: 'Why is only one woman, my sister Judit, among the top one hundred chessplayers in the world?' Susan argued that although many of the causes were social, 'the "monthly problem" gets in the way of the full development of many women chessplayers, since women may be menstruating during a crucial game.'

Other strong women chess players, such as Irina Krush, prefer not to play while menstruating. Even if I could not relate, never having had problems playing when bleeding, how could I contest the testimonies of my peers? Susan's argument was not that all women suffer during menstruation. Indeed, she was quick to point out that 'though many women cite no special problems playing during these times, others are barely able to get out of bed.' Susan often felt faint while playing on her period, and even fell off a chair once. As Susan told *Psychology Today*, 'In a game where every point is precious, even one minute of discomfort could jeopardize a woman's score', though the article's author Carlin Flora counters: 'Mother Nature may have equipped female chess players with a compensatory measure, however: the extra estrogen surging through a woman's body during menstruation aids concentration.'[5]

Susan's argument is dangerously circular. When a strong, powerful woman such as Susan is vocal in describing the deficiencies of the female body, she promotes such discourse as legitimate. Such statements could make female players more conscious of their periods, who would otherwise not even consider menstruation as an obstacle. In her doctoral dissertation from the California School of Professional Psychology, Los Angeles, psychologist and amateur chess player Linda Carol Gilbert details the sloppy methodology of previous writing on gender and chess. In her work, *Chessplayers: Gender Expectations and the Self-Fulfilling Prophecy*, she argues that the way we talk about women in chess influences the reality of women in chess. 'A vicious cycle emerges when world-caliber chess celebrities voice their opinions on why women "don't play as well as men" and cite "science", perpetuating a disastrous self-fulfilling cycle that results in females being unfairly labeled as inferior.'

Talking about menstruation as a problem perpetuates menstruation as a problem. The argument is also reminiscent of doubting women's capabilities in politics and business: 'How could we elect a female president, what if she had her period during a war?' The cultural depiction of menstruation is still oppressive – even the casual labeling of the natural female cycles as a 'problem' is an example of how the female body is considered substandard. The way that pads and tampons are advertised – ''cause you're the only one who has to know' – associates bleeding with a shameful secret. When I was a teen, magazines had special sections in which girls wrote in to tell humiliating stories of bleeding excessively in front of 'hotties' or in a pool. Instead of shaming girls for their natural bodily rhythms, we could instead celebrate the power it represents and the gorgeousness of red, my favorite color.

Susan is a pioneer in chess, the first woman ever to compete

at the highest level as a Grandmaster alongside male professionals. Her life had shown that with the same work ethic, women
could be the players that top men could, but now she was
doubting that women had equal potential. Such a contradiction
between a woman chess player's words and accomplishments
is not atypical partly because, as five-time British women's
champion Harriet Hunt notices, 'Most of the best female
chessplayers just play, without knowing too much about feminist
theory. Most feminists in chess don't have enough time to work
on the game.'

I was happy to train with the top female players and coaches
in America, but I was offended by the discussion of menstruation.* That week symbolized my ambivalence toward the larger
chess world, which is the driving force behind this book. I love
the passion, diversity and intelligence in the chess world, but
am often frustrated by the sexist views I encounter there.

One IBM employee shared my feelings on the speech: 'I

---

* In 2020, I started a cross-cultural program with US Chess Women (a
division of US Chess that I run). In cooperation with the Lighthouse Chess
Club in Mombasa, Kenya, and Business Meets Chess & Kids, we introduced
girls in Kenya (later growing to other African countries) and USA using
online chess as a medium. After one of our sessions, a Kenyan member of
the club sent me a message explaining that menstrual inequality prevented
many girls from going to school or playing in chess tournaments. That
student reminded me that menstruation can indeed be an impediment for
some girls, and all over the world, because of the expense and unavailability
of the products themselves. In the context of this chapter, I now think that
topics like menstruation or pregnancy should not be taboo, but be tackled
with a positive approach, rather than as an explanation for inferiority. For
example, a coach could advocate to get all bathrooms at a tournament hall
stocked with a variety of products and even provide equipment like increasingly popular 'period underwear'. This super absorbent underwear adds a
secondary layer of protection for menstruating people who have heavy flows
but can't take hourly bathroom breaks.

loved the talk till she brought up periods. Why? Why did she have to go there?' Focusing on supposed impediments such as menstruation distracts us from the fact that there are many women for whom chess is a profession and still others for whom it is an important and essential part of their lives. I reject the negative tone that wraps itself around women's place in chess. Instead, I will turn my attention to the variety of strong and passionate women who have broken the glass chessboard.

War-Torn Pioneers:
Vera Menchik and Sonja Graf

'Vera Menchik was the first woman to play chess like a
man.'   Grandmaster Salo Flohr

'Sonja Graf has written a book! We must be in the presence
of something singular.'

Roberto Grau, Argentinian chess writer

Vera Menchik and Sonja Graf played in the first head-to-
head match for the world women's chess title in the summer
of 1937, in Semmering, a winter sports resort in Austria. The
contrast in their chess styles predicted exciting games: Sonja
attacked with ruthless abandon, while Vera excelled in positional
play. Physically, they differed even more radically. Sonja was
an expressive blond with a confident stride, while Menchik had
a sweet round face and was impassive and modest. A British
reporter wrote, 'Sonja smokes without end, and during breaks
eats candies. Between moves, she paces and talks with observers.
Menchik is heavy-set and sits all game with her hands in front
without even moving a muscle in her face.'[1]

Vera Menchik defeated Sonja Graf, ending up with 11.5
points out of a possible 15. Vera's overwhelming victory was
not surprising. Just over thirty at the time of her victory over
Sonja, Vera had already won six world titles. It was the last

time the two would face off in a match. World War II altered
the trajectory of both their lives, and the history of women's
chess.

Vera Menchik and Sonja Graf at the Bloomsbury Hotel
in London, 1936 (Topical News Agency)

In photographs, Vera Menchik is pictured smiling sweetly with
nary a mean bone in her body. But her tournament records
and game scores depict a different Vera – beneath this gentle
veneer was a trailblazer who raised the bar for women's chess.
Vera Menchik was the first woman to compete seriously against
top male professionals.

Born in Moscow in 1906 to a Czech father and a British
mother, Vera learned chess from her father when she was nine
years old. Early on she played in a club tournament among
boys and finished in third place, which she later said 'gave
birth to my sporting spirit.' Despite this early show of chess

talent, Vera's main passions were for literature and theater, not chess.

Vera came from a comfortable family and shared a six-room apartment with her father, mother, and sister, Olga. Vera was eleven years old at the time of the 1917 Russian Revolution after which Vera and her family were forced to share their ample space with neighbors. A friend of Vera's described what happened: 'People from below came up, bringing their goats and fowls with them. Below was a forbidden land to her sister and herself and of course extra fascinating on that account . . . people lived in these basements in great poverty; they had earth floors and the children were terribly dirty and ill-cared for.'[2]

Unhappy with these changes in lifestyle, the Menchik family decided to emigrate. The family settled in Hastings, a seaside city in England. Teenaged Vera, shy by nature and struggling to become fluent in English, found her interest in chess flourishing as her loneliness deepened. 'Chess is a quiet game,' she pointed out, 'a perfect activity for someone who does not speak the language.' Vera began to play regularly, in spite of the critics who were concerned that 'the deep silence and smoke is not appropriate for a young woman.'

Hastings was a lucky place for Vera to settle. The Hastings Chess Club was one of the most well established in England, founded in 1882. International tournaments were held there each year, attracting some of the best players on the continent and in England. Vera joined the club in 1923 and soon caught the attention of a Hungarian player, Géza Maróczy (1870–1951). Maroczy began to train her. It was a good match and Vera improved rapidly, developing a patient style similar to Maroczy's.

Unlike Vera, most women players were not systematically trained at the time; Vera Menchik soon became dominant among women. By 1925 she was unquestionably the strongest female

Vera Menchik at the 1932 London International vs Géza Maróczy,
next to 4th World Champion Alexander Alekhine
(Hulton Archive)

player in England, having defeated the second-best player, Edith
Price, in two matches.

In 1927 she got a chance to test herself on the world stage.
The first-ever Women's World Championship was to be held
in London. Sixteen women from seven countries would participate in the round-robin (everybody plays everybody) event,
which was scheduled in conjunction with the first men's world
team competition. Vera swept through the tournament, ceding
only one draw. She won the next six Women's World
Championships held in Hamburg, Prague, Folkestone, Warsaw,
Stockholm and Buenos Aires. Out of the sixty-nine games she
played in these championships, she won sixty-four, drew four,
and lost only one. Vera was miles ahead of the competition in

women's chess, but thirsty for more distinctions: 'Victories over women don't satisfy me anymore. I want to drink men's blood.'

Chess Review celebrates Menchik's life, shown here after
she won the first women's world title in 1927
(courtesy of US Chess)

Vera Menchik's first chance to prove herself against men came in 1929 in a tournament in Ramsgate, an English seaside resort. Menchik represented Czechoslovakia on a team composed entirely of foreigners, giving her an opportunity to play against the best male players in England. The Englishmen were trounced, most notably by Vera, who shared the second highest score with Pole Akiba Rubinstein (1882–1961). The winner by half a point was the Cuban World Champion Jose Capablanca (1888–1942). Vera's own coach, one of the strongest masters in the world, Géza Maróczy, also played with the foreign team under the flag of Hungary. Training Vera helped her more than coach Géza could have counted on – his young pupil finished ahead of him. Her result was described as 'outstanding', and her ability 'to come out unscathed' against such opposition astounded the chess world, particularly in view of Vera's youth.

After Ramsgate, Vera was welcomed into the elite chess arena and given opportunities to compete against the top men in the world in tournaments all over Europe. During the summer of 1929, Vera was invited to a particularly strong round-robin event in Carlsbad, a small town in Czechoslovakia. An Austrian participant, Albert Becker, was so shocked by her inclusion that he devised a humiliating plan. Anyone who lost to her would receive a lifetime membership in the Vera Menchik Club. In comic retribution, he was the first to lose to Menchik, and thus became a charter member of the club. Aside from that satisfying incident, Menchik's overall performance in the tournament was not good. She came in last, scoring just three points out of a possible fifteen.

Also in 1929, Menchik traveled to Paris for her first international tournament. She didn't fare well there either, scoring only three points out of twelve. One notable opponent was Marcel Duchamp, the celebrated conceptual artist and painter, who for some time gave up art to pursue his passion for chess. Born in France, Marcel spent most of his life in New York City, as well as a year in Buenos Aires when his interest in chess was most intense. Marcel's position in the chess world was similar to Vera's. Both were superstars when they played world-class events – Duchamp because of his fame as an artist, and

Vera because of her gender – even though they were weaker than most of their opponents.

The most famous game played between Duchamp and a woman remains the one chronicled in a much-celebrated photograph; in it he is playing against a completely naked Eve Babitz, an American writer. Babitz had just started taking birth-control pills, which made her breasts swell to the size of bowling balls. Not sure at first if they were going to just pose or also play, Babitz later wrote: 'Marcel – whose obsession with chess made him give up not only art but girls – was waiting for me to make the first move.'[3] She was a novice in chess and Duchamp won the first game in four moves. This piece has been recreated by many artists over the years, but always with a naked woman vs. a clothed man. In 2009, I made a new version: I faced a naked man.* The chess set used for this game was also composed of carved nudes, and I used the Queen to execute a frontal checkmate.

When Vera and Marcel played, both clothed, Marcel found a tactic, netting two pawns for nothing. With careful play, he should have easily won, but after a few mistakes by Duchamp, Menchik fought back to earn a draw. Menchik ended in eleventh place in the tournament, with Duchamp right behind in twelfth place.

In the next decade Menchik played in tournaments with the world's top players, sometimes defeating the best in the world. The Vera Menchik Club grew, adding two particularly distinguished members to its ranks: future World Champion Max

---

* This piece, *Naked Chess*, was created by me and my now husband Daniel Meirom in 2009, partly to celebrate the release of a book about Marcel Duchamp and chess, which I co-authored along with Dr Bradley Bailey and art gallerist and author Francis Naumann. *Naked Chess* has been featured in the World Chess Hall of Fame and the Boston Sculptors Gallery, and a spin-off was featured in Amsterdam, where I played against three nude people simultaneously.

Euwe (1901–1981) and future US Champion Samuel Reshevsky (1911–1992).

Jennifer Shahade vs Jason Bretz from *Naked Chess*
(photo by Daniel Meirom and Jennifer Shahade)

However, the cold numbers of the scorecards revealed that Vera's percentages against the world elite were generally poor. In Moscow in 1935, she played in a tournament attended by luminaries such as World Champions Jose Capablanca, Emanuel Lasker and Mikhail Botvinnik. Some Soviet organizers, who worried that her standard of play was too weak, had discouraged Menchik's participation. It was finally decided that Vera could play since she might provide a positive example for rising Soviet women players.

Unfortunately, Vera was not to be a vampire this time. She finished last with just three draws, giving her a horrendous score of 1.5 out of 19. She wrote, 'I felt helpless to be a weak woman who has nothing with which to oppose my adversaries.' In a rare bright spot of the tournament, she held a draw in her game against the tournament runner-up, Salo Flohr. Spectators gave her an ovation.

Vera was active in British chess politics and journalism. She met Rufus Stevenson, editor of the *British Chess Magazine* and later secretary of the British Chess Federation. Rufus married Vera in 1937 and the couple moved to London. From then on, coverage on women's chess was expanded in the magazine. Annual updates on the state of women's chess in addition to frequent coverage of women's events now filled the previously male-dominated pages. Vera later became the games editor and opening columnist for another British publication, the monthly magazine *Chess*. Vera also gave lessons and, according to one student, was a 'splendid and pleasant teacher.'

People rarely had an ill word against Vera. Three-time British chess champion and war-time codebreaker Harry Golombek suggested that she was kind to a fault, choosing the word complacent to describe her – not exactly a compliment for a chess player or any intellectual for that matter. Golombek, speculating that Vera's kindness and modesty held back her chess results, proposed that 'the defect in her play was the inevitable reflection of her character.'

In my opinion, this conclusion is oversimplified. The styles of many chess players clash with their personalities, such as that of top woman player Ketevan Arakhamia, a slight, quiet woman with a hyperactive chess style. Judging from Vera's approach and erratic results, she suffered from mythologizing stronger players as unbeatable, a judgment that reduced her already-small chances to win. I am often victim to this debilitating lack of confidence against certain players. I considered rated masters and experts out of my league until I began to participate in all-night-marathon blitz (chess games played at extremely fast time limits, usually five minutes per player) sessions after tournaments. I remember playing dozens of games with two expert – the category just beneath master – players, one a female blackjack dealer and the other a middle-aged businessman. At first, I lost every game, but by the third day, I won several games in a row, and as the night went on I continued to hold my own. It was an important step on my road to becoming an expert and beyond.

Jennifer and Greg at two and four years old
(Shahade family collection)

But there was one player, no matter how often I played him, who remained stubbornly in the category of the unbeatable: Greg. In the many blitz games we played, I would, from time to time, get a winning position, but then my brother would pound the moves down faster and start to trash-talk. A spectator might find Greg's behavior confusing as he would act out in inverse proportion to the strength of his position. If he were up a Knight, he would calmly defeat me, but if his King were in danger of being checkmated, he would bang down the moves and chatter about how bad my pawn structure was.

As a fourteen-year-old, in a tournament at the end of a summer chess clinic in central Pennsylvania, I had a breakthrough tournament by beating one of the coaches, veteran Grandmaster Arthur Bisguier. Then I was paired against my brother. He was playing white. At the master level, having the white pieces and playing the first move is a big edge. I responded strongly against his relatively tame opening choice, and as lots of pieces were quickly traded off, the position was equal. Greg offered me a draw. Nowadays I would think little of such a game, but at the time it was key to breaking a myth – my brother and coaches were somehow fallible, as we all are. To this day Greg continues to use intimidation tactics when I achieve better positions against him in blitz. It's a running joke.

Remnants of my childhood chess inferiority complex creep up even today: I am still sometimes struck in disbelief for some seconds when gaining a winning position against a grandmaster. These self-doubts are balanced, though, by another force from an even deeper source, which I suspect many chess players share. When I sit down to play, there is a visceral level at which I believe I should win because I am who I am. When this physical confidence comes, and it tends to come in waves when I'm under pressure, it trumps all.

Like me, Vera also struggled with these issues, never completely solving them. 'In chess it is far better to err on the side of overconfidence than underconfidence,' as

Grandmaster Gregory Kaidanov told me in a training session. The danger in being overconfident is that a player will not scrutinize her weaknesses closely enough, but underconfidence is even more perilous because a player risks being paralyzed, playing slowly, and/or shying away from critical variations. Women who show brazen self-confidence are sometimes criticized for behavior that would be seen as normal for boys. After a quick victory, talented eighteen-year-old junior champion from Georgia, Nana Dzagnidze, glowed with self-assurance. 'She won in twenty moves with black and thinks she is a great player,' one spectator noted, puffing out his chest with an exaggerated look of arrogance, 'and now she is walking around like a man.'

Vera was often too passive against strong opposition. Chess writer Reuben Fine used a particularly uninspiring showing by Menchik against World Champion Jose Capablanca to criticize her for not paying attention to the maxim 'When playing for a draw, play for a win!' Vera played against Capablanca nine times, losing each and every game. In one of these games, held in Hastings in 1930, Vera seemed particularly determined to hold Capablanca to a draw. She traded off all the pieces, hoping that Capablanca would not have enough firepower left to defeat her. However, he calmly converted his small advantage into a win. Vera's spineless strategy was ineffective.

Against weaker players, Vera was much more aggressive, often showing off a tactical flair. In a match game against Sonja Graf, Vera Menchik placed a Rook on an empty square. Sonja took it with her Queen, and Vera sacrificed her own Queen. The game was over. If Sonja accepted this second sacrifice, she would be mated instantly. The brilliant combination is still published in tactic books around the world.

Vera was the first woman to play consistently against, and sometimes defeat, the best players in the world. She may have exceeded the standards of her time by an even larger margin if she had used against men the fearless, confident style she exhibited against women.

Vera Menchik's nearest female rival was Sonja Graf. Sonja was born in December 1908 in Munich, Germany. (She claimed that her birthyear was 1914, and historians repeated this date. However, her passport was recently unearthed in Germany, confirming the 1908 birthyear.) A copious source for details of Sonja's life is the hundreds of pages from her two books. *Impressions of a Woman Chessplayer* deals mainly with Sonja's chess career and concepts of the game. The second is a memoir, recalling Sonja's life in and outside of chess. This autobiographical account focuses on a character 'Susann', whom Sonja reveals to be herself by titling the book *I Am Susann*.[4] This tactic allowed for a more self-aggrandizing tone, evident by glancing at the book cover, in which a muscular woman with clenched fists stands victoriously on top of the globe.

As revealed in *I Am Susann*, Sonja had a traumatic childhood. According to her impressionistic book, her father was a priest in Russia, but when he fell in love with Sonja's mother, the two eloped to Munich, Germany, where Sonja's father became a painter. He was moderately successful, but didn't earn enough to feed his large family. While Sonja respected her father's artistic talent, she abhorred his sentimental but selfish character, telling how 'an injured parrot brought tears to his eyes, but he had no sympathy for his hungry children.' She pitied and disliked her mother, a woman Sonja saw as confined to the home and blindly devoted to her husband. The first sentence of Sonja's memoir is, 'My mother's destiny was, undoubtedly, housework,' a fate that the young Sonja would avoid at all costs.

Yo soy Susann (*I am Susann*) book cover
(Royal Library of the Netherlands)

In *I Am Susann*, there are harrowing accounts of parental abuse, both physical and emotional. In one case, Sonja receives a toy car as a present from a neighbor. Curious as to the mechanics of the gift, she takes it apart. Her mother calls her ungrateful for destroying a present and her father beats her mercilessly in punishment. Another time, her mother wakes up in the morning and loudly recounts a dream she had the night before in which God demands that she give up one of her daughters. Her mother is adamant in her decision to sacrifice Susann, calling her 'ugly and stupid'. After describing each such incident, Susann repeats, 'I don't understand the world.'

Sonja directs rare words of praise to her father for teaching her the rules of chess at a young age. She started by playing casually with her brothers. When she began to sneak away to a chess café at twelve years old, she fell in love with the 'insomnia brought on by the chaos of variations. [Chess] is happiness, deep emotion, a full and intimate vibration of all our being.'

She became a regular at the chess cafés of Munich, where her talent for the game impressed a tournament player, who arranged for her to meet Grandmaster Siegbert Tarrasch (1862–1934). He had a gang of admirers who would watch as he analyzed variations for hours. Sonja was transfixed by Tarrasch, describing him as funny, indefatigable, and also reflective. And like Sonja he had a way with words. His ode to chess is often quoted: 'Chess, like love, like music, has the power to make men happy.' He was eloquent and funny on lighter subjects, like his berating of gambiteers (players who favor gambit openings, in which players give up material, usually pawns, in the hopes of winning with a quick attack), whose ambition he said was 'to acquire a reputation of being a dashing player at the cost of losing a game.' Tarrasch's personality and play appealed to Sonja, who admitted that before meeting Tarrasch, 'my play was rather primitive.'

Sonja vividly recalled the day she decided that she would transfer her love for the game into a career and become a professional chess player. She was seventeen and had just become the female champion of Munich. Pointing out 'without false modesty' that she had 'strength in many areas', she decided to dedicate her life to chess, 'glimpsing through to a future interesting life: a panorama of travels, independence, magnificent liberty . . . and a means to know well this large, cruel, and beautiful world.'

From Sweden to Poland, Sonja travelled all over Europe with

chess. Sonja's euphoric reaction upon receiving an invitation to Ireland was typical: '. . . to have the joyous opportunity to visit a new country. Fantastic!' Curious and brave, Sonja records her impressions of people, parties and drinks, always on the lookout for an amusing anecdote or character portrayal. She was wide-eyed and optimistic, even when initially disenchanted, as on her first trip to England. At first frustrated with reserved British manners, Sonja's impression of coldness is reversed on a train trip, when she pulls out a cigarette, rummages in her bag for a light, then looks up to see that half the men in the car are offering her a match.

There was another reason Sonja traveled so much. Her hometown, Munich, had become a headquarters of the Nazis, a regime that Sonja was strongly opposed to. For a while, she relocated to the more liberal city of Hamburg, but for the most part, Sonja lived as a 'gypsy fated to roam the world', jumping on and off trains, staying until she ran out of money (which Sonja once called 'a vile metal'), and pursuing one love affair after another.

Sonja enjoyed her burgeoning fame as one of the few strong females in the chess world. Of one large crowd of admirers she wrote, 'Public applause infiltrated each part of my body like honey.' Giving autographs years later, 'just like a movie star', made her feel 'famous and loved'. Sonja's high opinion of herself comes up in her books again and again. She has a sixth sense, her presence is magical, and her teachers proclaim her poetry as the work of a genius. She even writes 'her kisses ranked among the best possible.'

The outlandish boasting is funny, but jeopardizes her credibility. Was Graf not self-aware enough to realize how arrogant she may appear? Another possibility, which I began to accept as I delved more deeply into her works, is that for Sonja to live as freely as she did, she needed a shell of confidence harder than I could imagine.

Sonja loved to shock men who underestimated her. In cafés all over Europe, Sonja would humiliate unsuspecting coffeehouse players (invariably men) by winning game after game before revealing that she was a professional player. Sonja describes her first serious game against a man memorably: 'From this moment I had played only with women. How my poor heart beat remembering all the things I had heard about the stronger sex! I began to feel a bit . . . overwhelmed.' But Sonja soon concluded that in chess, gender was all in the mind: 'The complications of the fight dissipated all my fears. And as the game went on, I began to forget the difference between the strong and weak sex. Here I was obliged to play like a man, although, to the majority, I was only a little girl. I really felt like a man. And in this hard fight, I found strengths that were hidden inside me, and I won.'

1948 US Champion Herman Steiner with Sonja Graf
(courtesy of the World Chess Hall of Fame)

Sonja sought after moments of heightened intensity in her personal life as well as her chess career. 'To have experiences is to have lived,' Sonja wrote. She wanted 'all life's stimuli', rejecting the ideal that women should abstain from sex until marriage and questioning the rigid gender binaries. In Barcelona, she went to a costume party as a man, wearing a suit and donning a fake goatee. Sonja danced with several of the ladies at the party and chuckled to herself about tricking them. Then, a male friend of hers recognized her face. He asked her for a dance. Sonja consented. The guests were outraged, informing her that 'here, two men are not permitted to dance together.' Sonja stopped dancing with him and, not to horrify the women she had danced with earlier, 'I continued acting as a man for the rest of the night.'

Sonja portrayed in detail the alcoholic delights and nightlife at each place she visited in Europe. But she grappled with balancing fun with serious chessplay, pointing out that 'alcohol is a great enemy of chess.' Post-match bar-hopping is common among even top Grandmasters. The intensity of tournament play, as well as the erratic lifestyle of a professional player, has driven more than a few to alcoholism. The capacity of some great players is so formidable that the joke goes there should be a publication *Drink Like a Grandmaster*, a pun on the popular classic *Think Like a Grandmaster*, by Russian GM Alexander Kotov. Other top players have more athletic approaches, avoiding alcohol, or at least abstaining until after a tournament. Some players can party and play well, but for most, like Sonja, there is a stark choice between bringing her A-game and enjoying herself. As my coach Victor Frias advised me, 'You have a choice, Jen: either have fun at a tournament or play well.' In my experience, this advice rings true. I often extend my stays at tournaments in faraway destinations so that I can have the time to explore and enjoy the place without the demands of competition. Sonja did the same but was still convinced that her zest for life interfered with reaching her full chess potential. Sonja used chess to set up a good life, rather than setting up her life to maximize her chess results.

Sonja had a particular passion for Spain, which she explored at the beginning of 1936, just a couple of months before the Spanish Civil War would have prevented such an adventure. Sonja was immediately infatuated with the free-wheeling, nocturnal lifestyle she encountered there. Rhapsodizing about Spanish food, bullfights, and nightlife, Sonja was convinced that in Spain 'the sun shines brighter and more intensely than anywhere else in the world.' The late hours suited her zest for nightlife; Sonja described giving simultaneous exhibitions (in which a strong player is invited to take on many opponents at once) that began at eleven in the evening and didn't end until dawn.

Frequent travel left Sonja little time to style her hair, so she chopped most of it off. When walking through the streets in Burgos, a city in northern Spain, she writes that bystanders were shocked by 'my hair cut very short, my sex appeal, my frankness, the vigorous line of my features, my strong profile, and my impulsive gestures. Many times, I had to contain myself from making faces when listening to the absurd expressions and commentaries from people who could not be pointed out for their intellectual qualities.'

Despite her confident prose, presence, and style, Sonja was still intimidated by the top players in the world. She was invited to play in a strong round-robin tournament in Prague. She scored only 2.5 of 11, but her tournament still had some bright spots, including a draw against the great Estonian Grandmaster Paul Keres. Sonja's writings give the impression of a brilliant, egotistic woman who was proud of her intelligence, rather than her looks. Sonja believed that her presence transcended physical beauty. She was intolerant of women who obsessed over make-up and clothing. 'I have never felt shame not to be an exceptional beauty, like so many women who live with this as their only preoccupation, because I consider physical beauty secondary.'

By all accounts Sonja was beautiful in a more conventional sense than she describes. Photographs of Sonja show a svelte woman with striking eyes and classic features. Sonja was nonchalant, even defiant, about her good looks, but fiercely proud of her mental qualities. To this day her message is subversive.

In late July 1939, the *Piriapolis* set sail from Antwerp, Belgium, for Buenos Aires. The Chess Olympiad and Women's World Championship was set for the first time ever in the Americas. Several dozen chess players were among the passengers, including Vera Menchik, Paul Keres, and Mojsze Najdorf. The three-week-long voyage was great fun, with constant game-playing and socialization on board along with tourist stops in Montevideo and Rio. According to British editor B. H. Wood, 'The masters take their responsibility with a light heart. In fact, one might assume it is a bridge tournament they are to play!' Upon docking in Buenos Aires, Wood noted an aggressive racist practice, perhaps a sinister omen: 'We were all assaulted by an official who twisted back our eyelids in search for Negro blood. The reactions of various members of our team to this ordeal are entirely unprintable.'[5]

Sonja set sail on the *Highland Patriot* a few days later and was the sole chess player on her boat. Sonja was characteristically thrilled to cross the Atlantic for the first time, dismissing racist comments by Europeans who warned her of so-called primitive, savage customs of South Americans. Sonja, vocal against the Nazi regime, espoused the virtues of equality and liberty. Upon arriving in Buenos Aires, she was promptly punished for her views. Sonja was told that Joseph Goebbels, Nazi minister of propaganda, had removed her from the list of German participants. She played anyway, switching allegiance to the international flag of Liberty. Her new flag was not contested by the organizers or her opponents.

Germany declared war on Poland on the first of September, midway through the tournament. Play went on, despite agony and panic among the participants. The flags of all the nations except Argentina were taken down in order to ward off disputes. Some players returned immediately to Europe, including the British men's team. Sonja described how some players from the Axis nations stopped speaking with Allied players. The top two scoring teams, Germany and Poland, refused to play their match, so they agreed to a 2–2 forfeit/draw.

The women's games were uninterrupted. Sonja Graf and Vera Menchik played nineteen games each, with no forfeits. They both strung together victories: Sonja won sixteen games; Vera, seventeen. But while Vera drew her two remaining games, Sonja suffered three losses. In the crucial encounter between the two women, Sonja played excellently, gaining a position she could have won in various ways. But she collapsed. She played two terrible moves in a row, first throwing away the win, and then also the chance to salvage a draw. Once again, Vera Menchik was champion of the world. Sonja Graf was second. The two women never met again. World War II interrupted the organization of Women's World Championships for an entire decade.

Vera Menchik played in one tournament in Montevideo, Uruguay, a fundraiser for the British Red Cross, before returning to London, where she and her husband oversaw the National Chess Centre. During the war years Vera remained active in chess, though international tournaments were infrequent. She earned money and passed the time by playing, teaching, and writing. Vera scored a prestigious match victory against Jacques Mieses, a Jewish chess champion. In 1938, after Kristallnacht, Mieses fled Nazi Germany to the UK. He lived to the age of eighty-eight and became the first British player to be awarded the FIDE Grandmaster title.

The first in a series of calamities for Vera Menchik came in 1940, when the Chess Centre was bombed. Luckily, the bombing took place at night, so the building was empty. A fund was set up to raise money for what was lost, but little was donated. The Menchiks survived the London Blitz (1940–1941) in the basement of their large house on Gauden Road. Menchik's husband, Rufus, fell ill in 1940, and his health was never very good until his death in 1943. The loss almost debilitated Vera. 'It was the bravest thing she could do to go on with her life,' said a friend of Vera's.

On 26 June 1944, a crumbling Nazi regime dropped bombs over London. Vera, along with her sister and mother, hid out again in their basement, which was instantly demolished by a direct hit. All three died. Their home, which contained Vera's papers, letters, and game scores, was destroyed. Chess players in Britain were devastated by Vera's death, calling it 'an unspeakable tragedy', and 'a robot action taken by a robot people.'[6] Another friend, Thomas Olsen, wrote, 'That she who faced the blitz undaunted should now, in the last days of the war, be struck down, is a catastrophe for British chess and a heavy blow to her friends.'[7]

Menchik was only thirty-eight years old when she died. The most important move of her life turned out to be an unlucky one. Across their street was a subway bomb shelter, which remained intact. Had they decided to run for that shelter, they would have likely survived. Unlike chess, life gives us incomplete information. The eight-time World Champion couldn't have known that she'd have time to cross the street.

Isabelle Choko in 1956
(courtesy of Isabelle Choko and Benjamin Portheault)

The odds were stacked against survival for another chess heroine of the era, also by the hands of Nazis. Isabelle Choko was born in Lodz, Poland in 1928, an only child of loving parents. They owned a pharmacy and doted on their talented and kind-hearted child. When Germany invaded Poland on 1 September 1939, life changed quickly for Isabelle. The Jewish family of three was sent to the Lodz ghetto and their pharmacy was confiscated.

'Mother, with tears in her eyes, handed the store keys to two men I had never seen before . . . . The fruit of over twenty years' labor had been relinquished to strangers who had only to hold out their hands for the keys to a Jewish business.'[8]

Isabelle's dad died of illness in the ghetto. Isabelle and her mother were then sent to the infamous Auschwitz concentration camp, and later they were moved to another death camp, Bergen-Belsen. In Bergen-Belsen, Isabelle saw her own beloved mother die. Isabelle was also withering away from starvation. In April 1945, she was down to just 55 pounds when British soldiers liberated the camp. She later told me she believes she was within hours of her death.

After she was nursed back to health, Isabelle moved to France. That's when she discovered her passion for chess and began to play in Parisian clubs. Her talent was spotted by the legendary Jewish Grandmaster and writer Savielly Tartakower, who predicted she would become a chess champion. Tartakower was a former member of the Polish chess team and was also in Buenos Aires in 1939. He returned to France to fight in the resistance movement, as an intelligence officer, under the pseudonym 'Lieutenant Cartier'. His intelligence was prescient in the case of Isabelle's talent: Isabelle won the 1956 French Women's Chess Championship and went on to represent France in the 1957 Olympiad.

In an interview with me, Choko, now in her nineties, urged me to never forget 'the horror if we do not fight for peace, for respect for human beings and especially for children, for solidarity, friendship. There are so many beautiful things, let's throw the others in the garbage.'

Sonja stayed in Buenos Aires after the 1939 Olympiad, rather than return to the continental bloodbath. She had become smitten with Argentina upon seeing the Argentinean coat of arms with its two hands clasped in a decidedly anti-war gesture. Sonja was enamored with the culture of Buenos Aires, which she compared to that of Spain. It was 'not only for the style of the buildings, but for the ways of the people' that she had affection. The Spanish language suited Sonja's romantic tongue, and she loved the Argentinean zest for life. The only thing she couldn't comprehend was the Argentinean 'mania for make-up', which, according to Sonja, afflicted many of the women. It must have been overwhelming for a chess trip to turn into a permanent relocation. I can only suspect, from her writings, that the vivacious Sonja took it all in her stride. She certainly mastered the Spanish language quickly, even publishing books in her new language.

Sonja was not the only chess player to make such a drastic life decision. Many great European players stayed in Argentina after the event, like Grandmaster Najdorf, a Polish Jew, who escaped the Holocaust by staying on in Argentina. In the hopes of contacting his family still in Poland, Najdorf performed blindfold exhibitions, in which he played many opponents at once, without sight of the board. In 1943, he broke the former world record by playing forty at once. He hoped that this outstanding feat would gain international press and that his family in Poland would contact him. After the war had ended, he discovered the terrible news: his entire family (wife, parents, child, and four brothers) had died in concentration camps. He then repatriated to Argentina, changed his name from Mojsze to Miguel, remarried, and made Buenos Aires his home for the rest of his life.

Some of the best tournaments held during the forties were hosted in Buenos Aires, due to the influx of strong Jewish European players. Graf played, usually finishing at the bottom of the cross-table, with Najdorf often at the top.

During the spring of 1947, FIDE president and former World Champion Max Euwe was in Buenos Aires to play in the yearly Mar Del Plata round-robin. In placing a phone call, he got misconnected to a Mr Vernon Stevenson, an American sailor. Stevenson happened to be fascinated by chess and in this misdirected phone call arranged a meeting that same afternoon with Euwe, who already had an appointment with his old friend Sonja Graf.[9] According to Euwe, there were sparks right away between Vernon and Sonja, who fell in love and shortly made plans to marry. The two moved to Hollywood, California, and Sonja became Mrs Graf-Stevenson (coincidentally, Sonja and Vera both married Mr Stevensons).

Sonja disappeared from the chess world for several years while she raised her son Alexander. She came out of retirement with a bang in 1957 by winning the US Women's Chess Championship. Sonja had not lost her dramatic flair, and New Yorker Allen Kaufman, who was a rising young player at the time, remembers playing casual games with her. 'Sonja used to enter tournaments with two bulldogs. She would play chess with me, banging down the pieces and shouting, "It's your move, boobee." You could tell that Sonja had made a decision to present a masculine persona.'

Sonja and her family later moved to New York City, and in 1964 she won her second US Women's Chess Championship. Shortly thereafter, in an interview with *The New Yorker*, Sonja spoke of her regrets over her world championship game twenty-five years earlier against Vera Menchik. 'I had a won game . . . I played the three stupidest moves.' Less than a year later, on 7 March 1965, Sonja died of a liver ailment. She was fifty-six years old. In Sonja's own words, she was 'an artist of life'.

The lives of Menchik and Graf show the very different ways chess can help women. Chess allowed the shy Menchik the opportunity to come out of her shell, to achieve greatness, and to make a name for herself. It gave Graf a chance to express her passion for life, while affording her the freedom to travel the world. Sonja Graf was drawn to the intensity of the game,

observing that chess players have 'their gazes locked to the board
. . . hypnotized, forgetting the world.' 'To the chessplayer, of
what importance is World War I, Hitler's regime, or the League
of Nations?' As it happened, Hitler's regime and World War II
were of major importance to Sonja Graf, resulting in a whirlwind
life in which she would live on three different continents. For
Vera Menchik and her family, the war brought tragedy.

The chess world values, above all, quantifiable achievements.
Vera is still (and rightly) hailed as a chess pioneer. By comparison the free-thinking bon vivant Sonja Graf who rejected the
Nazi regime has faded into obscurity. Her books are scarcely
available and have never been translated into English or
German. Likely Sonja would be remembered much more if
she had won her game against Vera Menchik in Buenos Aires
along with the crown of Women's World Champion.

It was Vera Menchik who served as the inspiration for women
players worldwide: she was the first to be called the queen of
women's chess. The Vera Menchik cups are awarded to the
winning women's teams at the biennial Chess Olympiads.

Though Menchik lived and played mainly in England,
because she was born in Moscow and spoke Russian, the Soviet
Union claimed Vera as their own – a Soviet champion, both
by birth and inclination. Mikhail Botvinnik, a patriotic Soviet
who won the first world title after World War II, said of Vera:
'This Czech woman playing under the English flag is in her
essence . . . Russian.'

Soviet chess would not wait long for a citizen of the USSR
to claim the crown, as a trio of middle-aged Russian women
dominated post-World War II chess.

Born in Ukraine in 1904, Lyudmila Rudenko learned chess
at age ten from her father, but she focused on swimming in
her early years and became a champion in breaststroke. In her
twenties and thirties she won numerous Moscow and Leningrad

Chess Championships but had to wait till after the war to play for the ultimate crown.

The first Women's World Championship after Vera Menchik's death began on 19 December 1949, in Moscow with a packed opening ceremony in the Central House of the Red Army, concurrent with celebrations for Stalin's seventieth birthday.[10] Rudenko, forty-five at the time, was one of sixteen players in the one-month-long event, which stretched into the new year.

Rudenko began the event with a shocking first-round loss to American champion Gisela Gresser. Soviet coaches Rimma Bilunova and Sergei Rosenberg wrote that this horrified the Soviet authorities, who threatened to send Rudenko to Siberia.

Lyudmila Rudenko vs Gisela Gresser
(Russian State Film and Photo Archive)

Rudenko composed herself and won nine games in the subsequent rounds to claim the crown.

Rudenko was much more than a hero on the chessboard. Her biggest life accomplishment was from one of the worst humanitarian atrocities in World War II history, the Nazi siege of Leningrad. Rudenko was working in an armament factory, which, in advance of the siege, was evacuated to Ufa, a city over 2000km from Leningrad. But hundreds of children of factory workers were left behind, including Rudenko's own son, Vladimir. Rudenko was given a passage mandate by the factory director and returned to St Petersburg to arrange a train for the children to escape before Nazis completely closed in on the city. The twelve-carriage train journeyed to Ufa in nineteen days, saving 300 children. Manuel Azuaga Herrera, in writing for *Diario Sur*, called Rudenko 'The World Champion Who Emulated Schindler'. 'Rudenko made every effort to ensure that the children ate with clean hands and did not fall ill. A few boxes of aspirin were the only first-aid kit.' They all arrived safely in Ufa.

The Nazi siege of Leningrad led to over 600,000 deaths, with some estimates reaching over a million, mostly of starvation. In 2018, Google celebrated Rudenko's heroism by featuring her on its homepage as its 'Google Doodle' of the day, where hundreds of millions of visitors could read about both her chess and humanitarian feats.

A student and later friend of Rudenko, Ekaterina Bishard, remembered her warmly as a multi-talented woman who was devoted to friends and family, and loved chess, bridge, literature and art.[11] 'She loved people, received guests hospitably and kept an open table. When chess players from other cities came and had no place to stay, she spread a big carpet on the floor so that everybody could sleep.'

In 1952, Moscow hosted the first ever Candidates Tournament, which would produce a challenger for Rudenko, aligning it more closely with the Overall World Championship. This tweak made it harder for a challenger. They had to win twice: once against many other contenders, and only then against the champion.

The winning score was again 11.5 points, secured by Elizaveta Bykova ahead of fifteen other players, including five Soviets and two Americans. This earned Bykova the right to play Rúdenko in a head-to-head match in 1953, which she won, with a narrow 8-6 victory.

Elizaveta Bykova (Olimpiu G. Urcan collection)

Bykova was born a peasant in the Russian village Bogolyubovo on 4 November 1913, and was an ideal symbol for the intellectual victory of the working class. She lived through a turbulent era, from the Russian Revolution to World War II. Learning chess from her older brother at a young age, she was taken in by the game in 1935, inspired by the same international tournament that brought Vera Menchik to Moscow. An excellent student, Bykova studied and played frequently, often competing in open competitions as well as women's events. Her work ethic was legendary, and mandatory. She'd spend almost ten years losing, regaining and defending the coveted title.

The 1955 Women's Candidates tournament, again in Moscow, expanded to twenty players. This edition saw the return of Sonja Graf Stevenson, now playing for the USA and ending in the middle of the pack. It was competitive at the top, as Olga Rubtsova edged out her nearest rival, Larissa Volpert, by just half a point.

Instead of a head-to-head match, FIDE structured a triangle match for the crown, where Rubtsova would face both Bykova and Rudenko for the title. Each woman played each other eight times. Rubtsova and Bykova both trounced Rudenko, so it came down to Rubtsova's better performance against Bykova, awarding her the much-earned title: Olga ended up prevailing over twenty-two contenders.

Rubtsova only held the World Championship title for two years, when she handed it back to Bykova in 1958. And yet, Rubtsova, known for her 'endless desire to play and analyze games', had many other laurels to rest her head on. She won the Soviet Women's Championship five times. She was also the Women's World Correspondence Champion, becoming the only player ever to be both the World and World Correspondence Champion. Correspondence chess, which used to also be known as postal chess,* is the slowest form of chess competition, in which players take days, and sometimes even a week, to plan a move, before dropping a postcard in the mail, with the

---

* Such slow games are still a popular style of chess, but it's usually done via email or 'Daily games' on popular chess websites.

intended play. It allows for deep research into each position, and rewards hard work more than steady nerves.[12]

Olga Rubtsova (Olimpiu G. Urcan collection)

Rubtsova had five children, one for each of her Soviet Women's Chess Championships. One of her children, Elena Fatalibekova, became women's Soviet chess champion, adding a sixth title to the family mantle. Birthing so many children while winning so many championships is awe-inspiring. The modern chess player travels constantly, with peak play years spanning from eighteen to forty, which makes it hard to combine large families with professional chess. How did she manage it? It helped that Rubtsova won the Women's World Championship title at forty-seven, after all of her children were already born.

The longevity of Rubtsova's career led to the formation of the 'Rubtsova Club'. Unlike the Vera Menchik Club, this was definitely one you wanted to be a member of. It was for anyone who earned 100 victories in the Soviet Women's Championship, named after Olga, because she was the first to do it.

Bykova was able to win back her title from the prodigious Rubtsova in 1958, and she again defended it successfully in 1960.* Bykova was multi-faceted in her chess career: a writer and television producer, she was chosen to write a biography of Vera Menchik to reflect glory onto the Soviet Union. Published in 1957, the book outlines the triumphs of Vera's career and attempts to extend the Russian champion tradition to the beginnings of professional women's chess. Bykova also wrote two other books, about Soviet women chess players and the Women's World Championship, and worked on TV shows and magazines about chess in the USSR.

Bykova's devotion to communism gives a propagandistic tone to her biography on Vera. Bykova dwells on Vera's trip to Moscow. She conjectures that Menchik may have played badly in Moscow because she was awestruck by the utopian conditions and the kindness of the people. 'In the West, a person who doesn't succeed professionally is nobody. Despite all my failures I still feel warm attention here. This is only possible in the USSR.' Menchik had loved to go to the theater as a young girl, and marveled at the improvements: 'What a pleasure to sit in a wonderful theater, to see a happy and content crowd, and remember that in 1919, I sat here shivering.' According to Bykova, Menchik left with an overwhelmingly positive impres-

---

* The 1960 victory was against the Soviet player Kira Zvorykina, who won the 1959 Candidates tournament in Plovdiv, Bulgaria to challenge Bykova.

sion of Moscow: 'You couldn't recognize the city – the change was too huge and great.'

Despite Soviet women's post-war dominance of World Women's Championships, authorities were not happy with the state of women's chess. A paper published in 1953, 'On the State of Chess Work in Physical Culture Organization and Means of Improving It', stated: 'The All-Union Committee considers the state of work in chess among women to be unsatisfactory. The number of women regularly playing chess is insignificant.'[13] Unlike Vera Menchik, the Soviet women rarely competed against men in major events. British writer John Graham, author of *Women in Chess*, dismissed the playing standard of the Soviet champions: '[Rudenko, Bykova, and Rubtsova] were curators of the title, making no strides toward equality.'[14] Even more negative was British Grandmaster Nigel Short, writing in 2015 that, 'What struck me . . . was just how mediocre many of these players were' calling the rise of the Soviet veterans, a 'particularly fallow' period.[15]

Such interpretations leave out important historical perspective. Rudenko won her Women's World Championship at the age of forty-five, Bykova at forty and Rubtsova at forty-seven. I can only imagine the greater heights the trio may have reached if their peak playing years weren't interrupted by tumult of war, from its horrors and deprivations to its call for heroism.

The players who took women's chess to the next level were indeed from the USSR. Unsurprisingly, they were younger than the trio of Russian legends but from farther south than anyone would have predicted.

3

Building a Dynasty:
The Women of Georgia

'Georgian women have such difficult characters! They
don't ever listen to men.'

Georgian Master Varlam Vepkhvishvili

It is two o'clock in the morning, and five-time Women's World
Champion Georgian Nona Gaprindashvili has been at the
blackjack table for hours, her dark eyes still focusing intently
on the cards. It is the autumn of 2002, and the thirty-second
biennial Olympiad is being held in Bled, Slovenia, a picturesque
mountain resort town in the former Yugoslavia. Outside the
casino in Bled, the view across Lake Bled is a stunning backdrop
of a castle situated in mountains. During breaks from the tournament, chess players, coaches and officials stroll the perimeter
of Lake Bled, resplendent with turning leaves of autumn. Sixty-
one-year-old Nona Gaprindashvili prefers the confines of the
casino to the mountain scenery. 'Fierce, strong, and obsessive',
said one fan. 'For Nona it doesn't matter what else is going on.
She won't stop, she'll keep studying, keep throwing dice.'

Forty years earlier, Nona won her first World Championship
match, bringing her fame and unprecedented accolades, while
galvanizing a women's chess revolution in Georgia. Georgia, a
small country with about four million inhabitants, lies in the
Caucasus Mountains on the south-eastern shores of the Black
Sea. The tiny Eurasian country dominated women's chess for

nearly thirty years, producing two world champions, winning four Olympiads,* and training dozens of talented young girls to be masters.

Female chess talent in Georgia exploded in an environment where traditional values were the norm. Georgian women usually got married between the ages of seventeen and twenty-two. Rusudan Goletiani, the Georgian-born women's grand-master now living in the US, told me, 'If you are a twenty-five-year-old girl in Georgia and not yet married, it is very strange.' Dowries of Georgian women included chess sets, because Georgian women were encouraged to play chess as a hobby. Gennady Zaitchik, a Georgia-born grandmaster who now lives near Philadelphia, told me, 'In Georgia it was the job of the man to do work and put bread on the table. It was good for women to cook, clean, and play chess at home.'

Nona Gaprindashvili was born in the spring of 1941 in Zugdidi, a small town near the Black Sea, where she grew up among five older brothers. Her intense brown eyes, dark hair, and strong features give her a confident presence that can be witnessed even in photographs of her as a young girl. Nona's father taught her the rules of chess when she was five. In family tournaments her brothers beat her regularly, and it is likely that this youthful competition shaped her tough, fearless character and promoted her high standard of play. Vakhtang Ilyich Karseladze, a renowned chess trainer visiting Zugdidi, spotted Nona's talent immediately and persuaded her parents to allow their twelve-year-old daughter to move to the capital, Tbilisi, where she could live with her aunt and train with experienced coaches. Throughout her teens, various Georgian grandmasters were called upon to instruct her. One of

* In addition to the gold medals the Georgian team won in 1992, 1994, 1996 and 2008, Georgian women also starred in many of the Soviet victories in the 60s–80s with Nona earning eleven gold team medals in total. The post USSR Georgian team also took one silver and three bronze medals.

them, Gennady Zaitchik, describes how difficult it was to train her. 'She wanted me to analyze some hopeless opening variation for hours. She was always so stubborn. She wouldn't respect my opinion as a grandmaster.'

Nona Gaprindashvili (Olimpiu G. Urcan collection)

Nona's competitive character was also witnessed by players: Nona had a reputation as a sore loser. A talented young Georgian girl joked to me that she hoped not to be paired against Nona because she was afraid of an angry reaction if Nona were to lose. After a crucial victory against Nona, one British grandmaster told me that he'd made the mistake of complimenting Nona by mentioning that a friend of his had named his daughter in her honor. Unimpressed by this story, Nona walked off in an angry huff.

In 1961 Nona won the Women's Candidates Tournament held in Vrnjacka Banja, a mountain town then in Yugoslavia.

With this victory, Nona earned the right to challenge the reigning World Champion, Russian Elizaveta Bykova, a year later. Nona was merciless in Moscow. She amassed nine points to Bykova's two – a landslide victory. Many players might have thrown a few draws in the mix, in order to rest a little and prepare for the next game, but this was not in Nona's aggressive, fearless character. According to one of her fans, 'Nona always plays for one result: Win.'

After winning her first world title, the young Nona became an instant celebrity in Georgia. Salo Flohr, a candidate for the World Championship in the 1930s, described her return home: 'Young and old, great and small, mobbed to see her, shake her hand, embrace her, and kiss her.'

John Graham, in *Women in Chess*, suggests that Nona's reception 'as a conquering hero' may have been partly rooted in patriotism piqued by regional racism. He writes that Georgians were often 'the victim[s] of cruel ethnic jokes.' Georgian people tend to have dark complexions and strong features, like neighboring Armenian and Azerbaijani people. Their looks have often incited racism from Russia, where the blond, blue-eyed, fair-skinned Russians were idealized. Estonian Grandmaster Jaan Ehlvest joked in an interview that, above all qualities, he values 'blonde hair and blue eyes.'[1]

In Moscow I saw two darker-skinned women being denied admission to a rock show. The girls were told that they were too drunk to enter, even though they looked and smelled perfectly sober to me. Extremist racism intersected with chess in 2007. Outside a soccer game, beloved International Chess Master Sergey Nikolaev was beaten to death with baseball bats by a racist gang of teenagers. A year later, CNN reported on the sentencing trial.[2] The murderers were 'Influenced by ideas on exclusivity of people of Russian ethnicity and inferiority of non-Slavic individuals' and the criminals 'formed organized groups to kill people coming from former Soviet republics located in the Asian and Caucasus regions.' Disheartened by such hate crimes, Garry Kasparov, born in the Azerbaijani capital Baku, decried the violent racism in Russia.[3] In a 2009 speech, he lambasted the Russian government for doing little to stop it: 'Genocide doesn't just appear out of nowhere.'

During the sixties and seventies, as Nona was winning championships, national pride in the ancient country of Georgia was never greater. From 1921 until 1991, when Georgia was an official republic of the Soviet Union, the Georgian people studied Russian in school, but continued to speak Georgian, which has a thirty-three-character alphabet and is a unique language unrelated to any other in the world. In 1978, massive public protests struck down Soviet attempts to establish Russian as the official language of the Republic of Georgia. More than being a woman champion or a Soviet champion, Nona Gaprindashvili was a Georgian champion.

Nona spent her twenties and thirties winning one World Championship match after another, including three in a row against Moscow-born Alla Kushnir, her major competitor at the time. By 1975 her influence on women's chess in Georgia was at its peak. Her next challenger, Nana Alexandria, was another Georgian. Alexandria, born in 1952 in the port city of Poti, worked with Karseladze, the same coach who had noticed the young Nona years earlier. The 'in-house' World Championship match thrilled the Georgian public. A perfumery even developed a scent – Nona and Nana – to celebrate the event. Patriotic camaraderie between the two combatants disappeared quickly over the board, where a brutal slugfest unfolded. Of the twelve games, Nona won eight; Nana, only three. There was just one draw. The final 8.5-3.5 score was a great triumph for Nona, who, at thirty-four, was at the top of her game.

Nona played less frequently, but successfully, against male opposition. According to International Master Victor Frias, 'Nona was the first woman who could sit down against anyone and play.' Nona's most impressive result among men was in 1976 in a tournament held in Lone Pine, a mountain resort town in California. She tied for first, defeating four male grandmasters. Nona's strength of character must have helped her endure unflattering comments, such as the one in *The Lone Pine Bulletin* that wrote Nona was 'constructed more like a bricklayer than a woman.' This ludicrous description implies that Nona is not a woman and that a woman can't win a tournament.

Nona Gaprindashvili playing twenty-eight men simultaneously in the UK, 1965 (Olimpiu G. Urcan collection)

Despite such sexist slurs, Nona was widely respected in the chess world as a pioneer in women's chess. The FIDE Congress, held in Buenos Aires in conjunction with the 1978 Olympiad, decided to award Nona the title of grandmaster based on her result in Lone Pine, her overall high level of play, and her sixteen-year reign as world champion. She was the first woman to hold this title, the most prestigious in chess, for which many players strive their entire lives. The decision to make her a grandmaster was not without controversy. Nona had not strictly met the requirements that would normally merit a grandmaster title. To become a grandmaster, a player must earn three norms, meaning that they have to perform over the 2600 level at three different events while maintaining an overall minimum rating of 2500. Grandmaster Pal Benko wrote at the time, 'She is the only woman ever to have deserved it [the title]. It is regrettable that she did not earn the title in the regular way. In my opinion, this historic occasion should not have been allowed to carry even this slight tarnish.'[4]

The timing of Nona's acquiring the GM title was bittersweet. Nona had just encountered the first major disappointment of her chess career, one from which she would never bounce back. In October of 1978, Nona was scheduled to defend her title against another Georgian, the seventeen-year-old Maia Chiburdanidze.

Maia learned chess from her eldest brother when she was a child of six or seven. She improved rapidly at her local club, catching the eye of Grandmaster Eduard Gufeld. Eduard played a few casual games with Maia and was immediately impressed by the focus and passion of the child: 'Before me sat a girl of nine who was not in the least perturbed by an international grandmaster. I remember her resourcefulness, surprising for someone of her age, with which she tried to reorganize her reduced forces after she had lost a pawn in the middlegame. We played another game, and it was clear that she had great natural chess talents and an all-absorbing love for our ancient game.'[5] Between the opening (the first phase of the game in which the pieces are developed) and the endgame (where the material is reduced and the result often settled) is the middle-game. Professional players have usually spent countless hours studying their opening set-ups prior to the game and memorizing the most common endgames. Middlegames are the least theoretical phase of the game, where a player must rely on creativity, intuition and calculating abilities.

Maia Chiburdanidze (photo from TAR-TASS Archive, courtesy of Olimpiu G. Urcan collection)

Maia is often called the first prodigy of women's chess. Prodigies are common to chess, math and music, all abstract endeavors in which competence does not require adult experience. In chess, the energy of youth often balances the wisdom of older players. The young are also more likely to have the time and inclination to spend countless hours studying and weeks competing in tournaments.

When Maia was ten, her family moved to Tbilisi, where Maia would be able to improve her skills and face better competition. She played incessantly. As an eleven-year-old, she competed in twelve different week-long events in one year. The intensive training and playing program were effective. At just sixteen years old, Maia won the Soviet Women's championship. She also qualified for the Candidates Final, where she beat former World Champion candidate Alla Kushnir in a match. This gave Maia invaluable experience, and the opportunity to challenge Nona two years later.

The World Championship match was held in 1978 in Pitsunda, Georgia, a resort town on the coast of the Black Sea. Despite Chiburdanidze's obvious talent, the experienced, determined Nona was still the favorite. Three tense draws began the match. In the fourth round, Maia won in thirty-four moves with the black pieces, punishing Nona harshly for an ineffective opening strategy followed by very poor middlegame decisions. Nona was shell-shocked. An energized Maia won the next game as well. In the latter half of the match, Nona narrowed Maia's lead by winning three games to Maia's two. In the final game Maia had the white pieces and needed only a draw to dethrone Nona. The course of the last-round game could not have been more dramatic. Maia, under tremendous pressure, played too passively and Nona won a pawn and simplified into an endgame. After a ninety-four-move struggle, Nona was forced to yield a draw to Maia's determined defensive fortress, bringing to an end the reign of Nona, de facto Queen of Georgia.

By defeating Nona, Maia became, at the age of seventeen, the youngest world champion in history, too young to fully understand her victory. One observer remarked, 'Maia was pure genius. She just loved the game but had no idea of the historical import of what she had done. After she won the match, she went to her room to play with dolls.'

There is no prototype for the temperament of a champion. Maia and Nona are very different from each other. While Nona's energy emanates outward, Maia's is more introspective, giving her a meditative glow. She is deeply religious. Like many Georgian Orthodox Christians, she often wears a headscarf. Romanian International Master Corina Peptan admires Maia's modest demeanor: 'She is not concerned with her image and prefers to stay in the corner. She is a star in chess, but she does not need or want attention.'

The personalities of the two women carry over into their chess styles. Nona is aggressive, even ruthless, while the mysterious Maia is patient and strategically minded. 'You could never predict Maia's moves,' said one contemporary, 'Nona – you could be sure she would choose the most aggressive option.' Nona pushed too hard in the Pitsunda match, and it was her overwrought decisions that cost her points. Judging from the style of the games, a master would surely guess that Maia was the veteran and the impetuous, aggressive Nona the youngster.

Maia defended her title four times. In 1981 she played against Nana Alexandria, who'd previously lost in the battle of the Georgians, Nana versus Nona. This time Alexandria played very well and managed to tie the match. But the rules state that in the case of a tie, the champion retains her title. Maia's next successful defense was against Irina Levitina from Russia, who now lives in the United States and is a professional bridge player. With two rounds to go the women were even, then Maia rallied and won both games. Her third and fourth World Championship victories – in 1986 against Siberian Elena Akhmilovskaya and in 1988 versus compatriot Nana Ioseliani – went more smoothly.

Elena had dismal memories of her games against Maia. 'When I first played Maia, I was fourteen years old, and she was just a chubby little girl of eleven years old who stared at the ceiling for most of the game. But staring at the ceiling, she began to make spectacular moves and it became clear to me immediately that she was a genius. I could never get over this young loss to her, and my lifetime record against her has been horrendous. The match was a catastrophe.'

Maia's own reign finally ended in 1991, in a surprise upset at the hands of the Chinese player Xie Jun. According to Maia, losing her world title made her hungry to reclaim it. She came close, but failed to regain her title in six attempts. In the documentary, *Glory to the Queen*, Maia also spoke about the flip side of losing, explaining that after 1991 she 'was free to play differently because I wasn't obliged to win. The quality and the creativity of my games increased.'

Nona Gaprindashvili and Maia Chiburdanidze were the only two Georgian women to achieve the ultimate women's title of World Champion. Nona and Maia inspired many players, and the Georgian women's chess culture grew. Nana Alexandria and Nana Ioseliani both lost World Championship matches by narrow margins. Although they never enjoyed the fame or success that Maia and Nona did, they helped to establish the great tradition and international reputation of women's chess in the tiny country of Georgia.

Every two years players and fans look forward to the most prestigious chess team event, the Olympiad. The first Olympiad was held in London in 1927, but fielded only male teams, while women played individually in the first ever Women's World Championship. Starting from 1957, the Women's World Championship was organized separately, and women's teams entered the Olympiad. Each participating nation selects four players for its women's Olympic team, three of whom play at any given time while the fourth sits out.[6] The team result is derived from the individuals' combined records. Georgian women were selected most often for the Soviet team, but there were talented contenders from other parts of the USSR, including Elena Akhmilovskaya, who played for the 1986 world title, losing to Maia.

Elena was born in Leningrad, in 1957. Although chess was not popular in Siberia, Elena's mother, Lidia, was a strong player and taught her eight-year-old daughter the rules. Elena says, 'My mom was everything in my chess development. We played blitz every day and I got mad when I lost.' When she turned twelve, Elena had the opportunity to be introduced to the wider chess community. Twice a year, the most talented young players in the USSR met in Moscow to spend a week at a special training academy, run by World Champion Mikhail Botvinnik. Among the students at the school was a future champion, Garry Kasparov, who later wrote glowingly of his experiences there. Elena's own experience was abruptly interrupted. At the age of sixteen, she was not invited back, because of her recent mediocre results.

Temporarily disenchanted with chess, Elena turned her attention to her university studies, which were biophysics and mathematics. She did continue to play, however, and to her surprise, had a breakthrough tournament in the 1975 Soviet Women's Championship. Elena gave up biophysics and math and switched to law in order to devote more time to studying and playing chess. 'Chess never came easily to me. I always had to train very hard for good results.'

Elena's renewed confidence and personal motivation gave her the strength she needed to confront the Georgians. To them, Elena was something of an outsider, and was not readily welcomed into their circle. At the Candidates Tournament in

1978, held in Tbilisi, the Georgians went to extraordinary lengths to slow Elena's progress. A Georgian man, 'incredibly gorgeous' by all accounts, showed up at the tournament. The man, Vladimir Petukhov, showered Elena with flowers and presents. Elena suspected he was a plant to distract her from her games, so that the Georgian women would prevail. 'It may have been a distraction,' noted an observer, 'but they fell in love and got married, and Elena ended up playing Maia for the World Championship anyway, so it must have been a positive distraction!' Vladmir lived in Tbilisi. Elena transferred to the university there and married him. She divorced him after seven years of marriage and one child, Dana.

Another romance would soon burgeon for Elena, with American John Donaldson, an intelligent and affable international master and author from Seattle. They met at a tournament in 1985 in Cuba, where Elena was playing and John was coaching. Their contact should have been limited because of the scrutiny of the Soviet authorities; however, 'As luck would have it,' John recalled, 'Soviet security was very lax.' The two spoke cautiously about uncontroversial topics such as opening variations. 'We felt severely constrained in saying what we wanted to say,' John explained. 'We didn't want to attract a lot of attention.'[7]

Elena and John continued to see each other at tournaments around the world. At the 1986 Olympiad in Dubai, they met at a disco every night. Their meetings were noted by the Soviet authorities, one of whom gave Elena an official censure for associating with a Westerner. Elena was warned that if it happened again, she would be barred from playing outside the Soviet Union.

In the 1988 Thessaloniki Olympiad, Elena's romantic and professional ambitions were destined to collide. The Soviet team had to contend with a formidable Hungarian team's rising stars: Susan, Judit, and Sofia Polgar. Maia Chiburdanidze was first-board on the Soviet squad, the sole Georgian on the team – the first time in years that the Soviet team was not dominated by Georgian women. The contest between the Hungarian and Soviet teams was tight throughout the event. Judit Polgar and Elena Donaldson were the high-scoring stars of their respective teams. With three rounds to go, both women were playing at the grandmaster level with staggering performance ratings of more than 2600. On the day of the eleventh round, Elena failed to appear for her game. That morning she left her team to elope with John Donaldson, who was there as captain of the United States team. American players cheered on the couple, and it became the fairy tale of the tournament. But Elena's sudden departure wounded her team. She had performed brilliantly, earning 8.5 points from nine games. In the final three rounds, the now-weakened Soviet team lost to Hungary by just half a point.

This loss was symbolic of the end of Soviet domination of women's chess. Elena's abrupt departure foreshadowed a great migration of Soviet players to various corners of the world, especially that of Russian Jews to the United States and Israel. Fifteen years later, remarried to International Master Georgi Orlov and still living in Seattle, Elena regretted her decision to leave in the middle of the tournament: 'I cried when I read the news that the Polgars ended up winning the gold medals. Now, it is clear that with the disintegration of the Soviet Union soon after the Thessaloniki Olympiad, I could have left the country easily without abandoning my team. But at the time, there were still KGB spies traveling with us, and I had no idea whether I would get another chance to escape the country.'

After the break-up of the Soviet Union in 1991, Georgia suffered enormously as a result of corruption, damaged infrastructure, and an economy that relied heavily on imports from other Soviet republics. In 1994 the unemployment rate was estimated at 1.5 million, nearly half of the Georgian working-age population. As a result, one million Georgians, almost a fifth of the population, emigrated. The situation for Georgian sportspeople, who were well supported under the Soviets, deteriorated, and among the one million émigrés are several prominent chess players. This exodus loosened Georgia's stronghold in women's chess. In the 1992, 1994, and 1996 Olympiads, Georgia won each Olympiad impressively – the same players who had dominated a decade earlier, including Maia and Nona, were still playing successfully. It helped that the stellar Hungarian team dominated by the Polgars had dissolved as Judit stopped playing in women's events after 1990, and Susan moved to the United States in 1994. But countries such as China and Russia, with younger squads, were closing in on the Georgian dominance.

The economic problems in Georgia have resulted in the departure of some of the most talented young players – those who had fewer personal and professional roots in Georgia. Among those who emigrated are youth champions Tea Lanchava and Rusudan Goletiani, who moved to the Netherlands and the United States, respectively.

I became friendly with Rusudan throughout our meetings as members of the US Women's Olympic Team. Rusudan calmly told me about her dramatic childhood. She grew up in Abkhazia, a region in north-west Georgia where civil war erupted in 1992. Tipped off by a KGB agent of the upcoming civil chaos, Rusa and her family fled the region for Tbilisi with only the clothes on their backs. 'It was awful; the plane was crammed full of people, and everyone was crying.' Rusudan was one of more than 200,000 ethnic Georgian refugees to flee from Abkhazia in the years 1992–1993. Rusa and her family slowly built up a life in Tbilisi, but making money in Georgia was difficult, and in 2000, Rusa jumped at a chance to move to the United States.

Rusudan Goletiani on the February 2009 edition of
Chess Life Magazine (courtesy of US Chess)

Friendly and magnetic, Rusudan had no problem fitting in in
New York, especially not in Brooklyn, where she first landed: 'I
was shocked to see how many Georgians are living in New York.
When I first moved here to Brighton Beach, I would constantly
hear people speaking Georgian.' Her heart is with Georgia, but
the economic situation keeps her in the United States. 'Ever since
the break-up of the Soviet Union, there has been no government
support for chess players. So, if you want any money to play in
tournaments, you have to go to private sponsors and you have
to self-promote, and this is not for me.' Rusudan told me that
she sent a large part of her monthly take-home pay back to
family and friends in Georgia: 'I would rather that a friend has
money for food than to have a new pair of jeans.'

Rusa began her life in the United States living in Coney Island and babysitting. When her English improved, she moved to Westchester, New York, where she began to teach chess. Rusa could make in an hour what she could in a month in Georgia by giving lessons in posh homes, but she does not feel that Americans respect chess. 'In Georgia, if I was training for a tournament, the teacher would allow me to concentrate all my efforts on chess, but here in America nobody takes chess seriously. They see it just as a game, whereas for me it is like a small model of life – the middlegame in chess is like being middle-aged and you have to decide on the right plan.'

Rusa's life and career blossomed in New York, where she lives with her husband and three kids. After winning the 2005 US Women's Championship, she transitioned out of the pro-circuit. She has a business degree and now works in finance, still winning chess tournaments in her spare time. Rusa also volunteers to speak and inspire young chess girls, where she emphasizes the importance of fighting spirit and confidence.

Tea Lanchava shares Rusa's ambivalence about leaving her beloved Georgia. Tea's first years as a chess player were like those in a fairy tale. Her role model, Nona Gaprindashvili, discovered her at the age of nine when she was brought by her uncle to play against Nona in a simultaneous exhibition. Nona recognized Tea's talent and instructed her parents that she should move to Tbilisi in order to train. Tea describes those days as the best of her life. 'Nona and I would train for hours, and she would tell me stories until I would look at the window and notice that it was getting dark. I would forget hunger, time, thirst.' Tea won two World Youth Championships for the Soviet Union. 'I'm really nostalgic for the Soviet days. I was lucky to see the last days of how much support you could get as a Soviet sportsperson.'

Now Tea lives in Holland with her husband and child; she still plays chess, insisting that she will never quit 'because it is in my blood. Everyone is always asking me about how frequently I travel, when I have a husband and child. Sometimes I feel like telling them to shut up and allow me to live my life. I love chess and I can't quit.'

Most of the older players have remained in Georgia, including Nona and Maia, who still enjoy celebrity status. Nona Gaprindashvili has lost a couple of hundred rating points since her peak, but she keeps playing with an undying competitive spirit. At a European Women's Championship in Istanbul, she would play Yahtzee for hours. I hung around the table watching her play for a while, hoping to ask her a few questions, but Nona was totally wrapped up in the dice. In *Glory to the Queen*, Nona, exuding a larger-than-life personality, said that 'Chess makes you live longer.'

In the 2002 Olympiad in Bled, Slovenia, the Georgian team was poised to recapture the gold medals, which had fallen into Chinese hands for the past four years. After ten rounds Georgia was ahead by three full points and, under normal conditions, would be able to glide gracefully into first place. But disaster struck. Ketevan Arakhamia had 'never seen anything like it. It was as if nobody could win a single game.' The terrible performance of the Georgian women in the last few rounds left them off the podium and allowed the Chinese to gain top honors for the third time in a row. Judging only by the Olympic team members, three of whom were over thirty-five, you'd think that Georgian women's chess was a tradition of the past.

In reality, Georgia's female chess talent crosses generations. Nana Dzagnidze won the 2003 World Girls Championship and became the third Georgian woman to earn the grandmaster title. Bela Khotenashvili and Nino Batsiashvili also earned GM titles. Nino, Nana and Bela were all born within a year of each other (1987–1988). However, young Georgian stars often had to take a backseat to the more experienced Georgian women at tournaments like the Olympiad. But the energy of youth can trump higher ranking, especially at long and exhausting tournaments. Nino Gurieli, former president of the Georgian Chess Federation and past member of winning Georgian women's Olympic teams, is dedicated to promoting the younger generation: 'From now on we need to support the team of the twentieth-first century.'

In the fall of 2003 I called Nana Alexandria, the former World Championship candidate turned chess politician. She answered her phone in Georgia and, though courteous, was short with me. 'Can't talk now,' she said, 'there is a revolution going on outside.'

Nana was referring to the November 2003 bloodless Revolution of Roses, which ousted President Eduard Shevardnadze, who had led Georgia since the Soviet era, in favor of opposition leader Mikheil Saakashvili, a thirty-nine-year-old progressive. In 2018, Salome Zourabichvili became the first woman to be elected as president of Georgia.

Ana Matnadze (photo by David Llada)

The dream of Georgian twenty-first-century gold came true: in 2008 they won the Olympiad in Dresden, Germany. That team combined experience with youthful talent, with Chiburdanidze holding down board one, and younger players on all the other boards.*

In the 2000s and 2010s, more chess stars left Georgia to Spain, France, the Netherlands and to the United States. Among them was Ana Matnadze who was born in Telavi, Georgia and moved to Barcelona, Spain in 2006. Ana learned chess from her mother at the age of six, and was also coached by Nona Gaprindashvili herself, whom Ana called 'her godmother'.[8]

In addition to playing first board for Spain, the fashionable chess champion was featured in a book, called *I am a Vampiress*. The fictional novella, written in Spanish by her best friend Miguel Alvarez Morales, intertwines Ana's chess success with her nightshift as a vampire. As the protagonist explores his own fascination and identification with vampires, he meets Anna, an alluring Georgian-born chess champion. 'I was a crazy young man with two passions in his life: chess and devouring books, articles . . . everything that was related to the vampire order. And as they say, "be careful what you wish for, it can come true."'

Another powerful Georgian International Master, Nazi Paikidze, moved to the United States in 2014. She first came to study at University of Maryland Baltimore County, where she met her boyfriend and now husband. Her name (pronounced Nazee) means delicate in Georgian. Its other associations did not escape mainstream attention when Paikidze won her first US Women's Championship in 2016. Seth Meyers on the *Late*

* The winning 2008 team consisted of Maia Chiburdanidze, Nana Dzagnidze, Lela Javakhishvili, Maia Lomineishvili and Sopiko Khukhashvili.

Show said, 'A woman named Nazi yesterday won the 2016 US Women's Championship. Apparently, she claimed the title when a woman named France just gave up.' I've found Nazi to be wise beyond her years, and we became quick friends, clicking on interests beyond chess, from books and business strategies to exercise to fashion. Despite her diverse interests, Nazi manages to do well in tournaments with players who spend much more time on the game than she does. She credits her edge to discipline. When she plays a game, she almost never gets up from the board, and she is in peak physical condition. Nazi often posts photos on Instagram in the gym at five or six in the morning, when plenty of chess players are winding down a blitz chess session online from the night prior.

Nazi Paikidze on the August 2016 edition of *Chess Life*
(courtesy of US Chess)

Paikidze reflects back to where it all started, 7000 miles from her current home in Las Vegas: 'In Georgia chess has always been a well-respected and admired sport. I believe it is precisely because of that, I felt empowered and encouraged to pursue it as a professional career.'

Nona herself believed that the movement she inspired was attacked at its root in 2020, when the Netflix series *The Queen's Gambit* mentioned her name. The heroine of the series, Beth Harmon, is a fictional chess champion who becomes the best player in the world – man or woman. It has only one reference to a real female chess player. The final episode, End Game, includes the line 'There's Nona Gaprindashvili, but she's the female World Champion and has never faced men.' The book by Walter Tevis, on which the series is based, has a more accurate line, even if barely scraping the surface of Nona's legacy. 'There was Nona Gaprindashvili, not up to the level of this tournament, but a player who had met all these Russian Grandmasters many times before.'

The flubbed line, claiming she never played men, infuriated Nona. When the first ever woman to become a Grandmaster first heard the slight: 'It was like everything I've done has been erased.' She sued Netflix for five million dollars.* The news of the suit was concurrent with the 73rd Emmys, where *The Queen's Gambit* won eleven awards. The story went viral, and the Nona that inspired so many in Georgia is now known to millions more. As Nona explained to the *New York Times*, it is 'part of my legacy that women chess players are accepted and becoming grandmasters . . . It is a fight I began, and it is a fight I am continuing.' The Georgian chess dynasty, which all began with Nona, has now spread within and outside its borders.

---

* At the time of writing, the results of the case are not known.

4

Be Like Judit!

'When I first found out that the J in J. Polgar stood for
Judit, I was so excited. I didn't even know she was a woman,
just that she smashed her opponents like mashed potatoes.
After that, I put her games up on my bedroom wall.'

  Linda Nangwale, chess champion from Zambia

Nona's successes and character influenced the younger
women of Georgia, many of whom cite her as a role
model. 'It all just kept rolling after Nona won the title. She was
the first, and many followed,' says Rusudan Goletiani. Nona's
fame was unprecedented: girls took up chess instead of enrolling
in ballet school; fans would wait to greet Nona at the airport;
people would stop her on the street for her autograph. A statue
of Nona was erected in her hometown, Zugdidi. On her sixtieth
birthday, the Georgian government awarded her two cars. Many
even named their children after her. The movie *Glory to the
Queen* highlights many cases of parents naming their daughters
after Georgian chess champions. In one striking example, the
national women's committee convinced the parents of newborn
triplet girls to change the babies' names to Nona, Maia and
Nana.

Stretching the limits of what was possible for women chess
players, Nona's influence extended outside the game. 'Nona
began an intellectual revolution,' said Rusudan. 'She turned

everything upside down. She was always beating men. If women could be good at chess, they could be good at anything. Nowadays Georgian women are more involved in politics, science, and art. They do not like to sit at home anymore. It used to be more common for women in Georgia to get married as young as seventeen or eighteen, but now they are encouraged to become professionals before getting married and starting a family.'

Rusa's father used to show her newspaper clippings about Nona, Nana and Maia, which she would read hoping 'that one day I would become a great player myself.'

The stars of women's chess in Georgia were particularly powerful role models because they were both accessible and exceptional. Georgian girls could read about them in dailies, meet them at exhibitions, or go to tournaments to watch them play. At the same time Georgian women were international heroes, breaking records and winning championships. Tea Lanchava laments that trying to develop women's chess in the Netherlands is not easy because the girls do not have such national role models to follow.

When Linda Gilbert, a doctor in psychology, surveyed American chess players, she found that the most influential role models were accessible figures such as coaches, teachers, and parents.

I remember my very first female chess teacher, Beatriz Marinello, a Chilean-American chess master who later became the first female president of the US Chess Federation. At a chess camp I went to, Beatriz was one of our regular instructors. I recall her carrying a book from class to her apartment: *Seven Habits of Highly Effective People*. I didn't read the book until much later, but wondered about what might be in it: turns out speculation is not one of the seven effective habits.

Having a strong female fixture at those chess camps was important as I was just starting to realize how sexist the chess world could be.[*]

According to Gilbert's study, when fathers were highly educated, only the sons excelled in chess, but when the mothers were highly educated, both girls and boys excelled. Whether the mothers were chess players made no difference. Successful mothers seemed to transfer their professional ambition to their daughters.

My own experience meshes with Gilbert's findings. My father taught me the rules of the game at an early age, later advising me on the intricacies and most importantly, how to study effectively. My mother's role in my development as a chess player, though less direct, was just as crucial. She was a professor of chemistry (Dr Solomon), an avid games player, a skilled writer, and a gourmet cook. My mom always seemed to be excelling at three or four things at once, all the while having a great time. My mother once claimed that her birth year – 1940 – made her the perfect age to enjoy the sixties to their fullest. Still, she was more serious than many of her peers – despite participating in protests and parties she also wanted a stable career and financial independence.

She never put too much direct pressure on me, but I understood from an early age that, to her, succeeding in male-dominated endeavors, being independent, and generosity were important values. Still, there were things I rejected. The main point of contention between us was my more-relaxed view toward money and a stable future. The tension settled suddenly as my fame in the chess world increased. I appeared on the cover of chess magazines and was profiled in *Smithsonian*

---

[*] Years later, Beatriz completed the circle, speaking to 100 girls at my club about her favorite Vera Menchik games.

magazine. My mother, as well as many friends of the family and relatives, suddenly stopped asking me when I was planning to apply to law school. This delighted me, though I sensed it was based on a misconception that media recognition was lucrative – as if magazine spreads could be endorsed and cashed.

Asking interview subjects about role models is complicated because the concept of a role model is both semantic and deeply personal. When questioned about role models, many of the women I interviewed seemed uncomfortable with the idea and declined to name any. Rebuffed again and again, I began to see that role models to them carried with it a negative or childish connotation, like idol worship. I needed to find a different way to ask my question.

Almira Skripchenko denied having a role model, but when I asked her which women she admired, she had no problem coming up with tennis player Steffi Graf, philosopher Ayn Rand, and Grandmaster Judit Polgar.

The women who were willing to name a role model gave a diversity of answers, often choosing someone they had never met. Some, such as Anna Hahn, cited men; she chose a fellow Latvian player, World Champion Mikhail Tal. Zhu Chen told me her role model was Wu Zetian, the Chinese empress from the seventh century. There was only one person, a chess player, who was named again and again: Judit Polgar.

Hungarian Judit Polgar, the best woman player in history by a wide margin, has had a global impact that extends to girls from six continents. Ecuadorian chess champion Evelyn Moncayo said, 'I have admired Judit since I was nine years old and saw her beating up on all the boys in the World Youth Championships in Wisconsin.' Judit made her realize she could compete against boys.

Irina Krush, like Evelyn, began her chess career at the time that Judit Polgar was cementing her position as one of the world's best players, female or male. I remember a twelve-year-old Irina telling me once, 'What I would give to be Judit Polgar, for just a day.' Recalling this declaration, I was surprised when in response to my question about role models years later, Irina understated Judit's influence on her: 'I admire Judit Polgar, but not in a different way than Karpov.' Irina may have realized that having Judit as her role model would interfere with her own ambition. Irina, on her way to becoming a world-class player, must only want to be Irina. Russian Grandmaster Alexandra Kosteniuk articulated it best: 'I have no heroes in chess. Maybe that's because I want to become a hero myself.'

Judit Polgar at the 1994 Moscow Olympiad in the Open Section
(photo by Bill Hook, courtesy of the World Chess Hall of Fame)

Free-spirited Bulgarian Grandmaster Antoaneta Stefanova cited no role models, although she does describe having a youthful fascination with Bobby Fischer, as did fans all over the world. Fischer's victorious match with Spassky in 1972 caused an enormous increase in the popularity of chess in the United States as the general public – not just chess players – eagerly awaited the results of their every game. Fischer became a symbol for the superiority of individualistic American ingenuity over systematic Soviet training methods. Fischer's skills as well as his good looks and quirkiness were admired, while his poor manners and bizarre demands were accepted as part of the package that made him great. Fischer's awesome feats in chess made it too easy to underestimate his early signs of madness. His descent from American hero into a raving, uncouth anti-Semite was chronicled by journalist Rene Chun in 'Bobby Fischer's Pathetic Endgame', published in 2002 in *The Atlantic Monthly*.

Fischer was shockingly dismissive of female chess talent. In a 1962 interview, he said that women are 'terrible chess players . . . I guess they're not so smart . . . I don't think they should mess into intellectual affairs, they should keep strictly to the home.' [1] An op-ed I wrote for the *Wall Street Journal*, 'Make Way for the Queens of Chess', linked sexism to the demographics of the Fischer chess boom: it included very few women.[2] A letter in response by chess player and professor Marlys Hearst Witte shot back that Fischer personally inspired her in the 1950s New York chess scene. 'He mingled with women chess masters Mary Bain, Gisela Gresser and Mona Karff, who as I, were awed by him. He treated us with respect despite our status as "weakies", his condescending term for chess players inferior to him, male and female.'

As many of the heroines in the book show, individual women can succeed and enjoy the game in spite of sexism. But their examples alone can't fix the skewed gender ratio. They may just have a personality type or support structure that is less

affected by sexism, but we want people of all personalities,
genders, races and backgrounds to enjoy the game. The shockingly low number of women and gender minorities playing is
a better indicator, in my view, that sexist views and statements
in chess do put many off. Those who never felt that they
belonged, but may have been great at chess in a more hospitable environment, are harder to interview or profile. We don't
even know who they are: they never tried to become chess
players.

People who are attracted to men may find having male role
models complicated, since the desire to be like a great man can
easily be confused with the desire to be with a great man. As
a teenager and rising chess player, I remember trying to distin-
guish between the two. At the time I found strong chess players
sexy but wrote in a journal that more than having crushes on
them, I wanted to crush them!

Indian-born American chess player and coach Shernaz
Kennedy was inspired by Bobby at a young age. The first book
she picked up was Fischer's *My 60 Memorable Games*, and she
was immediately intrigued by his clear-cut victories and lucid
writing style. She began to carry a picture of Fischer in her
wallet. (At the time, I coincidentally had a photograph of artist
and master chess player Marcel Duchamp in my wallet.) Later
Shernaz even became a close friend and confidante of Fischer's.
Shernaz played competitively for years, until settling into her
current job as a high-end chess coach. I met Shernaz, her arms
overflowing with shopping bags from ritzy boutiques, at a café
on Park Avenue. As we chatted over iced cappuccinos, Shernaz
joked to me: 'When I was young, I only wanted to date guys
who looked like Fischer!'

Many women chess players find the prospect of dating a
player weaker than themselves unpalatable. 'I would just as

soon date someone from outside the chess world than a weaker player than I,' said Anna Hahn, who likes 'men who are good at what they do.' German Grandmaster Elisabeth Paehtz also told me she is attracted to strong chess players, though she would be reluctant to date anyone too good. 'A player over 2700 is likely to be crazy!' she jokes.

There is nothing unusual about wanting to be with someone who is good at what they do. Elizabeth Vicary, a chess expert and coach from Brooklyn, has always been attracted to strong chess players and is unapologetic about it. 'There must be some reason to be initially attracted to someone, and I admire people who are good at what they do. Liking someone for their chess strength is not as superficial as liking them for their appearance or money.' Elizabeth says chess players are often 'intelligent, imaginative, and hard-working,' and also less likely to be 'entranced by fame and money.' One of my own favorite chess personalities, Marcel Duchamp, echoed Elizabeth's attitude. '[Chess] is purer, socially, than painting, for you can't make money out of chess', he told the *New York Times* in 1956.[3]

As chess rose in popularity and became recognized as an e-sport toward the turn of the decade into 2020, this reality suddenly changed: you could make very serious money from chess, even if you were not the World Champion. Leaked Twitch earnings revealed that some popular chess streamers, such as Levy 'GothamChess' Rozman, five-time US Champion Hikaru Nakamura and the famous Botez sisters, Alexandra and Andrea, were making around $300,000 to $500,000 annually on their Twitch channels alone. These numbers do not account for sponsorships, prize money and other social media revenue sources like YouTube, which could easily drive the earnings for top streamers over one million a year.

The Elo rating system clearly delineates worth in chess, providing its own value system. 1997 World Girls Under 20

Champion Harriet Hunt says that very early she realized that her chess rating was an important part of who she was. Until the millennium the international rating system had assigned ratings that ranged from 2200 to 2800. In 2000 the system was amended, and international ratings, as they do in the United States Federation, go as low as 100. Rating is so vital to a chess player's sense of self that one grandmaster compared losing ten rating points at the top level to losing ten pints of blood. A high chess rating is a status symbol. Many people refer to opponents not by their names but by their ratings: 'I am playing a 2250, or I lost to some 1500,' since the number becomes a more crucial mark of identity than a name. At the highest levels, names are obviously used, and no chess player would say, 'I am paired against some 2700.' After all, there are fewer than forty players rated over 2700,* and part of the deal in becoming that strong is that you do get your name enshrined.

Elizabeth Vicary thinks that her own motivation was squashed, partly because as an attractive woman, she was already a star in the chess world. 'As a young female 1900 in the chess world, I got so much attention – which seemed like respect – from all the best players that my incentives to improve were less. If I were a guy, the only way I could have gotten such attention would be to study all the time.' Proximity to greatness can feel like a substitute for greatness itself. But Elizabeth did become the best in her field: chess coaching. Her teaching style, combining dynamism and preparation with patience, led the Brooklyn school IS 318 to win over fifty National Championships. Remarkably, they became the first junior high school team in history to win the High School Championship. Elizabeth and some of her best students at

---

* There are 38 active players rated 2700 or higher as of 3 November 2021.

IS 318 were featured in the award-winning documentary *Brooklyn Castle* and Elizabeth was recognized as the Chess Educator of the Year in 2019. Elizabeth, who now goes by Ms Spiegel, married a fellow teacher, and they still live in Brooklyn, with their children.

There are countless examples of chess relationships in which a male grandmaster is with a talented, but weaker, partner: from US Women's Champion Mona Karff and International Master Dr Edward Lasker up to many modern day romances. High-rated married couples include Anish Giri (2774) and Sopiko Guramishvili (2383) or Grandmaster Peter Heine Nielsen (2618) and Viktorija Čmiltyė (2538) or the highest rated pairing of all, Katerina Lagno (2550) and Alexander Grischuk (2773). In these high-profile examples, the talent in the relationship is phenomenal and the female players are stars in chess and beyond. Most notably, Viktorija Čmiltyė-Nielsen is a member of the Lithuanian parliament, where she leads the Liberal Movement party.

The tendency for women to choose the top male players is partly because of the skewed female/male ratio at chess tournaments – so few women play chess that they usually have a choice between many suitors. 'Why not pick the strongest?' asked American player Diana Lanni.

Men can also be attracted to the intelligence of a chess player. There are plenty of chess couples in which the strength of the players is equal or where the woman is higher rated. The first Chinese Women's World Champion Xie Jun is married to Wu Shaobin, a grandmaster with a peak rating just under hers. Swedish legend Pia Cramling and five-time Spanish chess champion Juan Manuel Bellon Lopez are both grandmasters, but Pia has a higher peak and current rating. The couple are also now known as the parents of famous Twitch streamer and chess master Anna Cramling.

Pia and Anna Cramling in 2008 (photo by Macauley Peterson)

The generally amiable International Master Almira Skripchenko was clearly annoyed when I asked her whether women had less incentive to get strong for fear of intimidating men. Attractive, charming and confident, Almira has always received attention, but she does not believe that her chess strength detracts from this. 'Guys are impressed by chess skill; it's ridiculous to think they'd be turned off by it.'

Other women players maintain that men are intimidated by smart women. Olga Alexandrova, a Ukrainian-born Spanish chess champion, declared in an interview that the worst thing about being professional women players is that 'men are afraid of us!' When she meets a man, she keeps her profession secret for as long as possible. She finds it unusual for a man 'to appreciate intelligence... there is a common stereotype that if a woman plays chess, she is either abstruse or crazy.'[4] This reminds me of an episode of *Sex and the City* where the powerful law partner Miranda, beautiful but luckless in love, guesses that her power as a law partner is intimidating men. So, she starts lying to guys, telling them that she is a flight attendant. Lo and behold, their interest multiplies. Such anecdotes are supported by research on the links between beauty, intelligence and attractiveness. One study, published by the Warsaw School of Economics in 2014, was based on observations from heterosexual New Yorkers in a speed-dating event.[5] Men found intelligence to be a plus in women that they also found extremely attractive. However, intelligence became a negative when they did not rank the women as beautiful. A beautiful woman's intelligence made her even more beautiful, but if a man considers a woman average-looking, her intelligence did not bump her up to above average.

Alexandrova found a man who was unintimidated by her intelligence: eight-time Spanish chess champion Miguel Illescas. In the 2011 Spanish Championship, Olga had a stellar result, and was paired in the finale with one of the pre-tournament favorites: her husband. Although he out-rated her by over 200 points, the married pair drew quickly. This allowed one of Illescas's rivals to leapfrog his score and claim the Championship title on tiebreak. But it is hard to argue with the final result. Olga and Miguel have been happily married for over fifteen years and have two daughters.

The male fear of smart women is linked to a traditional and heteronormative ideal that men ought to hold the dominant role. Five-time British Women's Chess Champion Susan Arkell (now Lalic), who married an even stronger player, Grandmaster Keith Arkell, was asked by her compatriot Cathy Forbes if she wanted to become a stronger player than her husband. Susan responded, 'How could a man still be a man after being beaten by his wife?' As outrageous as this quote is, in a way, it goes to the heart of how complex it can be for men to accept powerful women as role models or influences. It is common, on the other hand, for women to identify with the accomplishments of men, as the French feminist Simone de Beauvoir pointed out in *The Second Sex*. '[T]he adolescent girl wishes at first to identify with males; when she gives that up, she then seeks to share in their masculinity by having one of them in love with her,' writes de Beauvoir. 'Normally she is looking for a man who represents male superiority.'[6]

My intermingling feelings of envy of and desire for men became clear one Valentine's Day, which I spent in my apartment with my friend Bonnie. Both of us were single at the time* and our intimate conversation eased the holiday's shrill celebration of romance and happy couples. We stayed up late discussing relationships and drinking hot chocolate. We realized that we were both attracted most of all to the men who we might like to be. When encountering such a man, I often am cautious, fearing that my own identity and creativity will unravel, replaced by mere admiration for my lover's brilliance. Realizing all this brought me solace when crushes didn't work out. I know that my desire for some particular man often masks a deeper urge to experience the world in another skin; preferably as a man as I am envious and curious about the more direct way men seem to approach life; ideally a super-talented man, with a high chess rating or fantastic prose style.

'Chess is so heteronormative,'† said my friend Martha, upon learning that it is illegal for two Kings to rest on adjacent squares. Although Martha was joking, the sexual symbolism in chess is a rich topic. Chess is an intellectually intimate game in which two players sit for hours, both gazing at each other as well as at the chessboard. The erotic connotations of chessplay

---

* I am now happily married to a film-maker.
† While this is true in the chess culture itself, as we'll delve more into in later chapters, I don't believe it's related in any way to this rule.

were at a peak in Medieval Europe, where Marilyn Yalom, author of *Birth of the Chess Queen*, points out, 'The Queen sent out vibrations that were responsible for sexualizing the playing field.' In a chapter on 'Chess and the Cult of Love', Yalom describes an engraving of a chess game from a fifteenth-century text: 'The chess match was considered sufficient to tell prospective readers that the poems would be about love.' Yalom also describes a work of fiction from around 1400, called *The Book of Erotic Chess*, in which 'each move on the board represented a decisive moment in the game of love' between the characters.

Yalom despondently concludes that the romantic aspects of chess have mostly faded. There are still plenty of remnants of sexy chess. At a cocktail party I met a woman who told me she shunned chess as a child, but took up the game after she realized that it was a great way to meet guys 'who aren't stupid!' An ironic scene in *Austin Powers II: The Spy Who Shagged Me* depicts chess as erotica. In it, dopey spy comedian Austin Powers sits down to play chess with a buxom, barely clad opponent. The competition quickly turns to foreplay, with chess pieces used as props.

A common charge is that women chess players often win against stronger male opponents, because men are distracted during the play. In one case, a man from Australia who lost to a young woman complained to organizers and journalists that her low-cut shirt had distracted him and caused him to lose.[7] But an attractive opponent can also inspire great play, as one male chess player confided in me: 'Guys play better against women, because they want to impress them.' My own motivation spikes when I play against men I admire or find attractive. I find it fun to play against someone I like, and therefore I work harder at the board.

At one World Girls' Championship, held in the capital of Armenia, Yerevan, I realized that I could also experience heightened concentration against women I admire. I loved my time in Yerevan, a bustling city with ancient history. Irina Krush and I were roommates at the championship, both representing the United States. The conditions at the tournament ranged from shabby to grand. The food at the hotel, often inedible, caused many players to lose ten pounds at the event. Even with heartier fare, it is typical for chessplayers to slim down at events; playing is a physical strain, and nerves contribute to long stretches of fasting. Irina and I subsisted on bread, fresh tomatoes and cucumbers, eschewing the daily mystery meats. We slept on tiny beds with stiff mattresses in rooms with a kind of exotic post-communist charm. Our balconies did open onto Yerevan's central square, an inspirational setting reminiscent of James Bond movies.

The tournament itself began with a dramatic upset on board one, in which Greek player Maria Kouvatsou was paired against top seeded Rusudan Goletiani, then playing for Georgia. After Maria sacrificed two pawns in the opening, Rusudan was unable to shield herself from Maria's onslaught. She resigned, still not castled. Charged by this first-round victory, Maria steamrolled through the rest of the field, beating four players over 2200. Not in the top half of the field, Maria was expected to lose more games than she won. She hadn't planned to play in the tournament, but when she went to the Greek Federation to inform them of her decision to cancel, there was no one at the office. 'I took this as a sign that I should play.'

The movie-like narrative of Maria's charge drew me in; it was hard for me to stop looking at this hip woman from Athens, who wore a nose ring and stylish outfits in bright colors. She had a nearly sublime focus while playing. Her long hair tucked behind her ears, she placed her hands on her temples and stared at the board, immobile for hours.

In the last round, I was paired against Maria. I had no chance of winning the tournament myself, but if I beat her, there was a possibility that my roommate, Irina Krush, would tie for first and earn a medal. I traveled to Yerevan right in the middle of a semester at NYU, and sometimes I found it hard to focus on the chess; while playing, my thoughts would drift to the possibility of drug legalization or existentialist literature. I had no such problems in concentrating against Kouvatsou. I became aware before the game of a certain amount of attraction that I felt toward Maria. I thought she was beautiful and cool, and I wanted to impress her. This new-found clarity allowed me to play my best. I did win, in my best game of the tournament. Maria still won the tournament on tiebreak. In the end, I tied for fifth place, just outside the four-way tie for first, which did include Irina Krush.

Because female players are a minority in a very hetero-normative subculture, top women are constantly being compared to each other. It's hard to ignore. But that doesn't mean jealousy should displace friendship, or even mentorship. A woman, regardless of her sexual orientation, ought to be able to recognize and embrace a wide variety of feelings toward her peers, whether it's admiration, indifference, or even attraction. When I've been bogged down with feelings of jealousy, I reflect on whether I'd really want to have fewer talented friends and colleagues? The immediate answer is, 'Of course I love being surrounded by brilliant people.' Going through that simple mental exercise reminds me that jealousy is often a signal to match my ambition to my work ethic. The negative emotion can be converted into a positive one.

And the complicated admiration that a woman can have for a man is too often displaced by attraction. It should be possible to be attracted to and competitive with your crush – to want to be with him and to beat him. Judith Butler, gender theorist, says, 'Desire and identification can coexist.' I would add that they should, and if we are aware of this peaceful coexistence, sexual relations and friendships will improve.

The first time I saw my childhood idol, Judit Polgar, in person is imprinted on my memory. As a teenager I read voraciously about the Polgars and played through all of Judit's major tournament games. Her style even influenced my choice of openings – I switched from the relatively restrained c3 Sicilian to the riskiest lines of the Open Sicilian, as championed by Judit. Soon thereafter, I gained 100 rating points, pushing me up over the National Master rating.

I was spending a couple of days in the Netherlands, where Judit was playing in an elite grandmaster event. Sightseeing would wait for another trip. I traveled to Tilburg, an hour away from Amsterdam, to the world-class event Judit was playing in, where she was the only woman among twelve men. That day she was playing a strong Dutch Grandmaster, Jeroen Piket, and I studied how she looked at the board with a focused but calm gaze. In the post-mortem, she joked around and assertively waved away a smoker. After the analysis, a friend introduced me to Judit, who was friendly, though she declined to join us for dinner, explaining that she was tired and wanted to study for her game the next day. This disappointed me, but I also admired her decisiveness. In the coming years, I realized how hard it can sometimes be, especially for a woman, to say no when asked to join friends for parties or socializing.

I didn't need to know Judit personally – she was already very powerful to me. Since I didn't know her, my image of her reflected what I wanted to be just as much as it reflected what she was actually like, which is perhaps the essence of a role model.

5

Bringing Up Grandmasters: The Polgar Sisters

'My grandparents fortunately survived the Holocaust. Otherwise my parents and the Polgar sisters would not be here today.'

Susan Polgar, in *Breaking Through*

Whenever Garry Kasparov, the top rated player for fifteen years, plays Judit Polgar, the top-ranked woman of all time, the chess world is transfixed. Garry, with his expressive face and confident swagger, fits naturally into his larger-than-life role as the best chess player ever.[*] Judit stands just over five feet tall, and – aside from her fiery red hair – her appearance is understated; she has a calm presence both on and off the board. The drama of the war of the sexes was heightened by Kasparov's outrageous remarks at the time:[†] 'Chess is a mixture of sport, psychological warfare, science, and art,' he said to the *Times* of London in 2002. He continued, 'When you look at all these components, man dominates. Every single component of chess belongs to the areas of male domination.'

---

[*] Magnus Carlsen, as of 2022, is considered a heavy contender for the 'Greatest of All Time' designation, with pundits generally agreeing that it's either Kasparov or Carlsen.

[†] Kasparov has since become an advocate for women and girls in chess and their talent.

The two stars were paired in Moscow in a 2002 match featuring Russia against the Rest of the World. Judit, as always, opened with her King pawn. Garry chose the Berlin defense, a solid system that usually results in a trade of Queens on move seven. It was a surprising choice for Garry, who prefers complicated positions with the Queens on the board. Moreover, he had recently been defeated by the Berlin system when Vladimir Kramnik used it in their 2000 World Championship match, ending Kasparov's fifteen-year-long world reign. Judit Polgar tends to be even more aggressive than Kasparov, favoring the most violent variations in nearly every opening. 'In analysis, I will sometimes suggest to Judit to trade Queens and she will look at me and chant "no, no, no,"' recalls her trainer, Polish Grandmaster Bartłomiej Macieja. 'She knows she will have more chances to trick her opponent with Queens on the board.'

Talk of Judit's aggressive style can be misleading. She is a world-class player who often wins in long, strategic battles, or in the endgame. Trading queens against the Berlin defense is, according to theory, the most challenging option. So Judit did just that, calmly maintaining her advantage. In a cool performance, she dominated the play throughout the entire game, forcing Kasparov's resignation on move forty-two.

This was Garry's first loss to a woman, and the first time that the strongest woman in the world defeated the strongest man. It was a monumental encounter, moving the once-hypothetical notion that a female could become World Champion one step closer to reality. The milestone, many might argue, could have been reached nearly a decade earlier when Judit played Garry for the first time in a game marred by controversy.

Their first contest was in 1994 in Linares, Spain, where the strongest players in the world met each year for a round-robin tournament. Judit was seventeen at the time. Garry replied energetically to her opening and was able to establish a strong position. Just when he was about to finish off the game, Kasparov picked up his Knight and placed it on c5, a losing square. Noticing that this move would be a grave error, Garry lifted the Knight and put it elsewhere. The question would arise as to whether he had taken his hand off the piece. Judit said nothing at the time, and Kasparov won the game. Afterward Judit said that she believed Kasparov might have let go of the Knight on the fatal square. If so, according to the strictly enforced 'touch-move' rule, he would be forced to leave it there. After examining the videotapes of the match, it was clear that Kasparov did, if only for a fraction of a second, take his hand off the piece. If Garry had realized that he had released the piece, he was morally obliged to abide by the rules. On the other hand, Judit should have reacted when it happened. It is unorthodox to make a claim once a game has been completed and lost. Nevertheless, Judit was furious with Kasparov, accosting him at the end of the tournament, asking, 'How could you do this to me?' For two years Judit and Garry did not speak to each other.

After this loss, Judit dropped eight more games to Kasparov, including a heartbreaking one in which she lost a drawn endgame. She had only a Rook, to Kasparov's Rook and Knight, which theoretically is a dead draw. But Judit was in time pressure, meaning that she had to play several moves in a short time period, sharply increasing the chance that she would make a mistake. Kasparov did trick her, reeling in yet another win.

Judit's victory in Moscow was long overdue. When I asked her about beating Kasparov, she recognized that 'it was a historic moment,' but she was not very enthusiastic about the game, saying 'it didn't feel so special to win, because besides that game, I had a terrible tournament.' Judit's response to her landmark victory was characteristically low-key. Busy studying chess and working on her game, she prefers to leave the discussion of her accomplishments to fans and journalists.

Before the Polgars arrived on the scene, male chauvinism in chess circles was more widespread and virulent. 'The Polgar sisters changed everything,' says master Ivona Jezierska, originally from Poland, who played women's chess both pre- and post-Polgar. 'I am so grateful for what they did.' Judit, along with her two older sisters, Sofia and Susan, was responsible for altering the course of women's progress in chess. The old questions 'Could women ever be grandmasters?' or 'Could women defeat the best players in the world?' were dismissed by Judit Polgar's success. New questions took their place: 'In general, can women be as good as men?' or 'Will a woman ever be World Champion?'

From left to right: Judit, Susan, Sofia and Laszlo Polgar, 1989
(Wikimedia/Fortepan)

Laszlo Polgar was determined to turn his children into geniuses, a project he planned before they were born. In *Bring Up Genius!*, he maintains that with dedication, any parent can raise a genius, writing, 'It is much easier to blame differences in ability on inheritance than to investigate the intricate social roots.' Laszlo was also convinced that girls, if raised shielded from sexist cultural biases, could achieve at the same level as men.

Laszlo was introduced to Klara Alberger through their parents. Their relationship started with letters. After meeting in person for the first time in 1965, Laszlo told her about his plans to start a large family, and nurture them with both love and high standards. Klara, who was also a teacher, was intrigued.[1] They continued to exchange letters, which culminated with a proposal. They married in 1967 and moved to Budapest.

The Polgars' first child, Susan, found a chess set in an old, rusted trunk in 1972 when she was three. The little girl was immediately attracted to the game, mesmerized by the pieces and the stories her father told about them as he taught her the rules. Although he himself was not a skilled player, Laszlo, who had always loved chess, was thrilled by Susan's interest in the game. Just half a year later, at the age of four, she won her first tournament, the Budapest Girls' Under-11 Championship, with an astonishing 10-0 score. 'I was just a little munchkin. I had to sit on pillows to reach the chessboard.'[2] Recognizing her potential, Laszlo began to organize an intensive chess-training program for her. Klara, who saw her daughter's passion for the game, supported the efforts. Laszlo believed that all children who are born healthy are potential geniuses. Chess was a perfect vehicle to test those theories.

Six-year-old Susan devoted time to an alternate intellectual course, advanced math. Laszlo thought she could be a prodigy in either area but wanted her to choose between the two. Having Susan pick was important. Laszlo did not believe a child could be forced to be a genius, but that it was his job to make the children want it. 'It was an easy decision,' she now recalls: 'I hated math.' After abandoning math, she began to devote twice as much time to chess, studying it for six to eight hours a day.

Keeping Susan home from school to focus on chess was controversial. In Susan's book *Breaking Through*, she recalls: 'One time, the authorities came to our house with the police (with machine guns) to warn my father that he was breaking the law by not letting me attend school. Luckily, my parents did not get scared . . . It took about nine months of correspondence until the Ministry of Education finally gave me permission.'

She progressed rapidly and became the strongest girl in Hungary when she was only twelve years old, making her eligible to represent her country in international youth competitions. Susan traveled to the West in 1981 when she played in the World Girls' Under-16 Championship in England. Years later Susan vividly remembers her first impressions of the West: 'It was amazing to be in London. Nowadays you can get anything anywhere, but then, the variety of goods and services was astonishing in comparison to Communist Hungary.' Not that the family could afford to buy much at that time. The Polgars were not well off, so Klara and Susan were traveling on a tight budget.

Susan, who was only twelve, won the gold medal with five wins and two draws. In retrospect, Susan sees this victory as a crucial moment of her career: 'The name Susan Polgar would now be a name to be reckoned with.'[3]

One of Susan's draws in England was against USA player Baraka Shabazz, the first African American to play in the US Women's Championship. Unlike Susan, whose tournament in England was at the start of an illustrious career, this was destined to be Baraka's final international foray.

Baraka Shabazz, the first African American female to become a chess expert (photo courtesy of the World Chess Hall of Fame)

Baraka's stepfather also pushed her to study chess for long hours, sometimes from seven in the morning until late at night. Baraka became the sixth ranked female player in the United States at just fifteen years old. The Shabazz family moved from Alaska to San Francisco so that Baraka could train with the best coaches. Her stepfather's control over his daughter was troubling, especially in retrospect.

The *San Francisco Chronicle* reported that her stepfather hovered protectively over Baraka, 'hardly allowing her to speak for herself.'[4] He was banking on Baraka's abilities to provide financial success. 'We are poor people . . . Now we have discovered our daughter can be an asset.' Baraka got a lot of media attention for her successes. Her stepfather predicted that exhibitions, books and tournament prizes would make their whole family rich – he even envisioned a Baraka doll. He spent a lot on those dreams, using their savings, and pawning the same computers they bought to help her with chess. Baraka did become an expert – the category just before master, the first African American woman to do so. But she stopped playing the game in 1983, at the age of eighteen and just before becoming a master. In a brutally candid article in the *Washington Post*, 'Ex-Queen's Gambit', Baraka revealed that the mounting pressure made the game she once loved unpleasant.[5] She said that she couldn't be a normal kid, and felt 'I represented Blacks, children of all creeds, females, everyone.' She also said chess destroyed her home life. 'Ever since chess was brought into my family's life, it's been in disarray, messed up, totally ruined . . . When I see a chessboard now, I just smile and look away.'

In contrast to the inspirational chronicle of the Polgars, the short-lived career of Baraka Shabazz is a cautionary tale. Excessively pushy parents may guide their children to greatness but they could also lead them into early retirement. There are many such cases, often under-reported because the children quit before they reach outstanding goal posts.

Why wasn't this so with the Polgars? There are so many possible reasons, from proximity to a strong chess culture and great coaches, to the girls' quick successes and strong sibling bonds as well as deep passion and talent for the game.

By July of 1984 the name Susan Polgar appeared at the top of the ratings list for women. Susan at fifteen was already higher ranked than the world champion, Maia Chiburdanidze. Susan was ready to play stronger opposition and made it clear that she wanted to compete against the best men. In the fall of 1984, she was awarded the prestigious international master title, becoming the youngest woman ever to receive it. 'At this time in my career, it felt as though the sky was the limit,' said Susan.

Susan's appearance fees, prize money and endorsements signif-icantly improved the economic status of the family. They moved out of their one-room flat in Budapest into a much larger apartment. Laszlo and Klara quit their teaching jobs to concentrate on training Susan and her sisters, Sofia and Judit, who were born in 1974 and 1976. From their experiences with Susan, Laszlo and Klara had gained invaluable knowledge. While Laszlo taught Susan and Sofia the basics, Klara taught Judit the rules of the game. They also started Judit out much later, at the age of five. Susan wrote, 'My father felt that five is the ideal age to start. While one can possibly teach a four-, or even three-year-old, the time and effort invested would not be in proportion to the speed of progress. Children that young have a shorter attention span, and it is difficult to keep them focused.'

Although his daughters were able to beat him quite quickly, Laszlo's role in their training was integral. Laszlo could now afford to hire trainers to coach the girls. He made sure that the girls had access to all the best books and latest periodicals. He laboriously collected and organized games from all over the world – a task that today would take minutes with an Internet connection.

The Polgar routine was rigorous and structured. They awoke at six and started the day with three hours of table tennis. The sisters were home-schooled by Laszlo and Klara, who were using their savings to support the girls' full-time education. Laszlo warns that school is 'very dangerous for talented children because leveling out happens at a low standard.'[6] Glad to have escaped the daily grind of the classroom, middle sister Sofia says, 'To go to school is a major waste of time. You could study a textbook for a year that it is possible to read and absorb in a week or two.' The parents made sure to cover subjects outside chess including many languages: English, Russian, Spanish and Esperanto. In a fitting chess coincidence, Esperanto became the 64th language added to Google Translate, in 2012.

The Polgars had very full daily schedules, including up to

eight hours of chess, as well as intense table tennis sessions (all the sisters were excellent players). There was even a designated block of time for telling jokes. Defending himself against the many critics who have accused Laszlo of robbing his daughters of normal lives, he says, 'They did have a real childhood, because they are not building sandcastles, but real castles, castles of knowledge.'[7] When questioned about her structured upbringing, Susan answers with a balanced view. 'My sisters and I traveled to forty countries and had the chance to see things that most children could only read about in *National Geographic*. On the other hand, we missed out on doing some of the typical things that young people do, like going to the movies or hanging out with friends.' When I ask Susan what she regrets missing in particular, she seems at first to have trouble finding the words, then simply replies, 'Goofing off!'

Susan's battles were not with her parents. From a very young age she had disagreements with the Hungarian Chess Federation, which thought that she should play in the Hungarian Women's Championship in order to prove herself as a top woman player. Susan refused, worried that playing against weaker opposition would be a waste of time and an impediment to her progress. She thought that the only way to earn her own grandmaster title was a steady diet of male grandmaster opponents. As punishment, she was barred from playing in tournaments in the West for the three years between 1982–85. Susan complained that this 'crippled my career at a time when I had peak interest.'

When the ban on traveling was finally lifted, Susan and Sofia went to the United States with their mother, Klara, to play in the 1985 New York Open. From the start Susan fell in love with the city: 'I used to sit on the subway and marvel that each person was a different color. That kind of diversity was unheard of in Communist Hungary. I knew I really wanted to live in New York City.' Susan's wanderlust, evident from her first trips to London and New York, combined with her rocky history with the Hungarian authorities, foreshadowed the move that would come a decade later.

The Polgar sisters on the November 1992 edition of *Chess Life*
(courtesy of US Chess)

Even more painful for Susan than the ban on traveling was the ratings fiasco of 1986. FIDE made a controversial decision to increase the ratings of all female players by 100 points. The thinking behind this strange move was that the ratings of women were kept artificially low since they played only amongst themselves. Adding the rating points was thought to be an appropriate countermeasure. Since Susan, at this point, played exclusively against men, FIDE refused to add the points to her rating, making her the only woman who did not reap the benefits of the bonus points. As a result, Susan lost her first-place ranking among women: Maia Chiburdanidze leap-frogged over her. Susan told me, 'I was heartbroken. My parents always taught me that, in chess, if I study and work harder than my opponents, I will beat them. It felt like good results were not enough anymore. I got really depressed.'

While Susan was fighting the chess bureaucracy, younger sisters Sofia and Judit were being intensively trained to follow in her footsteps. In 1986 when Susan returned to play in the New York Open, her younger sisters accompanied her.

Their results were incredible. Ten-year-old Judit won the unrated section with 7.5/8, while Sofia tied for first in a reserve section. In the following year they returned to New York, where both Sofia and Judit defeated their first grandmasters. Judit's strength was particularly impressive, drawing glowing praise from the British daily the *Guardian*: 'She is the best eleven-year-old of either sex in the entire history of chess.'

The trio was a sensation. Here were three sisters who were possibly the strongest women players in the world. The Hungarian public and the chess world wanted the Polgars to prove themselves against the mighty Soviets, who until then had been resting on their laurels, unchallenged as the top women players. The Polgars abandoned their usual refusal to compete in women's events by accepting an invitation to play in the 1988 Olympiad in Thessaloniki, an old port city in Greece, enclosed on one side by the sea and on the other by mountains. American Grandmaster Larry Christiansen describes rough conditions in Thessaloniki: 'The traffic noise outside our hotel extended to the early hours. The playing hall was utterly smoke-filled, and the restrooms were primitive. Pollution was bad.'

Still, Larry says the players had a great time, at after-game parties concentrated in a bustling hotel in the downtown. The Polgars did not socialize at all, devoting their free days and evenings to preparation. I asked Susan if her father forbade his daughters from going to the Bermuda party, the big dance held before a free day. 'It was not recommended,' she said.

The Hungarian team was composed of Susan, nineteen; Judit, twelve; Sofia, fourteen; and Ildikó Madl, eighteen, another promising junior player. The Olympiad competition is structured according to the Swiss system, in which teams are paired in the first round based on ratings. If there are ten players, the first-ranked would play the sixth-ranked, the second would play the seventh-ranked, and so on. Starting from the second round, teams with the same scores play one another. Top teams such as the Soviets and the Hungarians tend to be paired near the middle of the tournament. This time they were paired together in the fifth round, dubbed by the tournament bulletins as 'The Clash of the Amazons.' In the three games of the round, Judit and Susan both drew and Madl won (Sofia sat out), giving Hungary a crucial 2-1 victory over the Soviets. But it wasn't over. Teams can only play each other one time, meaning that the winner of the entire event hinged on which team routed their opposition more harshly in the final rounds.

Twelve-year-old Judit finished with 12.5 points out of 13, the half coming from her draw in the Soviet match. The way she won her games was just as memorable as her awesome score. Her quick seventeen-move victory against the Bulgarian player Pavlina Angelova introduced the world to Judit's inspired style, which featured graceful development, a subtle Bishop sacrifice, followed by a Queen sacrifice that forced her opponent's King into an inescapable trap. The game was over: it was checkmate. Judit's style was already becoming legendary.

Just winning was not enough for her – she tore her opponents to pieces.

It was this tournament in which Elena Akhmilovskaya made her sudden unannounced departure to marry John Donaldson, paving the way for a Hungarian triumph. The young squad composed of teenagers and preteens broke Soviet dominance of women's Olympiads, which dated back to the inception of the events in 1957. 'We were euphoric,' says Susan.

The chess world was impressed, while the Hungarian press hailed the Polgars as national heroines. Susan recalls how 'the victory changed our lives completely.' Judit said, 'Everybody now wants to help us who before were against us.' Judit sarcastically mocks these fair-weather friends. 'Oh, yes, you are very nice.'[8]

Two years later the Polgars attended the 1990 Olympiad in Novi Sad, Yugoslavia, hoping to repeat their gold-medal performances. This time the three Polgars played on the top three boards: Susan, first; Judit, second; and Sofia, third; with Ildikó Madl as the reserve player. The Polgars had improved in the past two years, but so had the Soviet squad. Women's World Champion Chiburdanidze was joined by former champion Nona Gaprindashvili along with two younger players, Russian Alisa Galliamova and Georgian Ketevan Arakhamia. The crucial match between Hungary and the Soviets did not go well for the Polgars – Judit and Sofia both lost, while Susan managed to narrow the margin to 2-1 by defeating Chiburdanidze on the first board.

The final rounds decided the contest, just as they had in Thessaloniki. This time the Soviet and Hungarian teams had accumulated the same number of points. The gold medals would have to be determined by the first tiebreak: the final scores of all the teams the USSR and Hungary had played throughout the event. Judit recalls, 'It was during that endless wait that I took the decision not to play in any more women's tournaments. Achieving a close to perfect result and not being sure it was enough to win was unpleasant.'[9]

The Polgars won by a hair. The medal for the top performance rating in the Olympiad went to Georgian Ketevan Arakhamia, whose spectacular score of 12-0 exceeded Judit Polgar's 10-2 – not a bad result for anyone, but with Judit's astronomical FIDE rating of 2555 her fans expected even more.

After the Novi Sad Olympiad, the three girls never again played together as a team. Judit never played in another women's tournament. The paths of sisters Sofia, Susan and Judit were about to diverge, both geographically and professionally.

Her sisters overshadowed middle child Sofia, sandwiched between pioneer Susan and prodigy Judit. She became less focused on the game, and more interested in exploring life outside of chess. Although Sofia generally had the lowest rating in the family, she had no shortage of talent. One of their trainers wrote, 'I believe Sofia had a comparable talent [to Judit] and with some luck in the mid-eighties she might have had a similarly astonishing career.'[10] Susan herself wrote that 'I think (and my parents agree) that Sofia is probably the most talented of the three sisters.'

When she was fourteen years old, Sofia had the result of a lifetime in an open tournament in Rome. Out of the nine rounds, Sofia won eight games and drew the last. Five of her opponents were grandmasters, and seven had higher ratings than Sofia, whose rating was 2295 at the time. This was one of the best performances of all time, enough not only for her to win the tournament ahead of top grandmasters, but strong enough to earn her the first of three norms required for the title of grandmaster. Her success caught the attention of the chess press – one headline screamed, 'Super Sofia! Third Polgar sister lashes out in Rome.'

Sofia Polgar (photo by Bill Hook, courtesy of the
World Chess Hall of Fame)

Over a decade later I asked Sofia about Rome. 'It was a great
performance on the heels of our victory of Thessaloniki, and
my interest in chess was then at its peak,' Sofia recalled. 'At
the same time, my result in Rome was difficult to live up to,
and it may have been too much, too soon.' Sofia's triumph in
Rome was to be her one and only great result. She never came
closer to becoming a grandmaster. She grew out of her status
as a child prodigy and was uninterested in continuing her career
by playing in women's tournaments. Her level was not quite
high enough to compete with the top male players.

At a chess tournament, Sofia met her future husband, Yona

Kosashvili, a grandmaster and an orthopedic surgeon. They married and moved to Tel Aviv, Israel, where they have two children. Sofia was interested in so many things outside the game, so her marriage to 'someone involved with chess at all' was a surprise to her sister Susan. Living so far from both of her sisters and her beloved hometown was difficult for Sofia. 'I miss Budapest, the architecture, and my own language. And most of all, I miss being together with my family.'

Sofia has never felt resentful or unhappy about her chess position in her family. Her other interests are important to her; she studies interior design, paints and draws, and is passionate about art and literature. Her favorites include Vincent van Gogh and Czech writer Milan Kundera. 'In other fields, just like in chess,' says Sofia, 'women have not been allowed to rise to the top because of cultural constraints.' There is one woman she admires most of all: 'I don't really have any female role models besides Judit. When growing up, our parents taught us to believe in ourselves.' When I ask her if she is a feminist, she replies, 'I am just an average woman of the twentieth-first century. I have my feminist ideas, but I also want to stay at home with my children as much as possible.'

The intensity and talent with which Judit approaches the game has made her unquestionably the greatest female chess player in history, so far ahead of any other woman in chess that she almost never played women in competition. 'My attitude toward the game, especially in my youth,' Judit tells me, 'could be called obsessive.' Her childhood was decorated with unprecedented achievements. In the same year that she scorched Thessaloniki, Judit became the youngest player of either gender to gain an international master norm. Also, in 1988 Judit became the first girl to win a mixed world competition, the so-called Boys' Under-12 Championship in Romania. And 1988 was only a typical year.

As a preteen Judit began her quest for the highest title in chess, grandmaster. She was racing to break Fischer's record in acquiring the grandmaster title at fifteen years and eight months. It seemed as if Judit was on track. A twelve-year-old Judit scored her first GM norm at the start of 1989, in Amsterdam, causing a sensation in the chess-crazed nation: 'Polgaritis conquers Holland,' wrote Hans Kottman, a reporter for *New In Chess*, going on to describe Judit's conduct at the board: 'She smilingly rattled off deeply calculated variations, leaving her male opponents quite embarrassed with the situation.' Almost two years later, after many near misses, Judit scored her second norm in a round-robin tournament in Vienna. Judit had only one major tournament in which to score her last norm and break Bobby's record: the 1991 Hungarian championship.

Judit Polgar age eleven at the New York Open, 1988
(photo by Gwen Feldman)

Both Judit and Susan played in the nine-round all-play-all national competition. Judit began the event with three draws: the first against her sister Susan – who performed well in the event, placing third – and the second and third against two veteran grandmasters of Hungarian chess – Lajos Portisch and Andras Adorjan. Portisch's irritating remark that 'a woman world champion would be against nature' may have provided the additional and necessary motivation for Judit.[11] Portisch realized that he was old-fashioned, pointing out that people once thought that no man would ever walk on the moon. However, a female chess champion, he said, would be an even less-likely circumstance.

In the second half of the tournament, Judit was unstoppable. At her level, having the first move was an enormous advantage, and in rounds four and six, she used the white pieces to devastating effect. Her opponents helped her by choosing very tactical opening variations, turning the games into the mad melees in which Judit was brilliant. By the last round, Judit had five points out of eight and was in a fantastic position.

A draw would clinch her the grandmaster title, but a win would earn her the title of Hungarian Champion. Would Judit play a quiet line in order to secure the draw, or would she go for the tournament victory as well? She played the most uncompromising line imaginable. Navigating through the thicket of variations, Judit emerged from the scramble into a winning endgame. Her opponent, International Master Tibor Tolnai, was twice her age. He resigned on move forty-eight: Bobby Fischer's record was shattered. Judit became the first woman to win a national championship, and only the fourth woman to gain the GM title.

Judit's list of accomplishments started to read like a laundry list, as British master and chess journalist Cathy Forbes points out: 'Reports of the Polgar sisters' successes, at first astonishing, began in time to sound like a litany – repetitive and predictable

. . . the repetitive refrain, symbolized by stark numeric scores, was only success.'[12]

After gaining the grandmaster title, Judit improved even more and advanced into the elite group of players rated over 2600. Chess was a lucrative profession for Judit where she battled the top men in the world in well-sponsored round-robin tournaments and rapid events in glamorous locations such as Aruba, Monte Carlo and Buenos Aires. Judit is always in demand – as the only woman in the world able to hold her own against the world elite. Judit's presence ensured peak media interest, and her single appearance fee was about $10,000, back in the 90s.

Judit's first success in a high-profile 'super' tournament was in Madrid in 1994. She placed first in a strong field that included Latvian Alexei Shirov and Russians Evgeny Bareev and Sergei Tiviakov, all world-class players. *New In Chess* described her victims as 'lamentable figures reminiscent of the gloomiest Goya pictures,' to which Judit added, 'I am now eighteen and they behave as though they lost to a little girl.'[13]

When I congratulated Judit on a surge in the world rankings, she, like a true champion, reacted with customary dissatisfaction: 'True, my rating has gone up, but it's been ages since I won a tournament!'

Judit is picky about squeezing interviews into her schedule, so I was pleased that she had time to meet me for a one-hour interview. I took a cab to the green and posh neighborhood in Budapest and walked up two flights to Judit's immaculately decorated apartment, which she shares with her tall, dark and handsome veterinarian husband, Dr Gusztav Font. She met her husband when she took her dog to his office; he recognized her and asked her out for a game of tennis. Among the decorations in Judit's apartment are a fine collection of chess sets and a tiger-pattern rug. I inquired about her veterinarian husband's feelings about the rug, and Judit replied with a laugh, saying, 'Oh, this is not his work. Don't worry.' The two got married in Budapest in August 2000. Soon after, Judit achieved some of her career milestones, beating Kasparov and breaking the 2700 rating for the first time. Judit, at the start of 2004, was ranked eighth in the world – a new height for her.

Judit credited those epic achievements to a happy marriage. 'My husband supports me and works part-time so that he can travel with me to tournaments. You can even see that my playing style has changed. My life is more stable, and my play is more solid. Before, I would sacrifice and lose a point, where now I would relax and make a draw.' Judit, especially in her youth, was famous for her ruthless, verging on the reckless, attacks. But for her to compete with the world elite, it is neces- sary that she have a more universal style. 'When I was younger, people would say my style was too aggressive, and I just didn't understand what they were talking about!' That her victory over Kasparov was an endgame, where technique takes prec- edence over attack, is symbolic of her more balanced style.

When I asked Judit, back in 2003, if she's a feminist she quickly replied, 'I'm not a feminist!' However, my definition of the word may have been lost in translation: 'In America I hear stories about women getting angry at men for holding the door for them or buying them dinner. I think women have the same mental capabilities as men, but I still like it when a man treats a woman as a man should treat a woman.'

When I ask her about future plans, Judit is also traditional in her framing. 'Right now, I care more about family than career.' Drinking tea with her on that Tuesday morning, it struck me that Judit might resent the idea of being a symbol for feminism, or any other cause. Her cool manner and traditional opinions surprised me – I was hoping that Judit would be more bombastic about her own accomplishments. She says, 'I've been playing chess since I was a little girl and I have achieved so much. There is nothing new for me in the chess world. Being in a serious relationship is new and excites me more. I will continue playing chess, but I am not putting any timeframe on when I will have a child, regardless of how it affects my career.'

The ordinary and the extraordinary flipped for Judit, who had been trained from infancy to aspire to dazzling heights in the chess world. Judit's work ethic, supportive family and immense talent made for a fast, smooth road to the top. Starting a family, on the other hand, wasn't always easy for Judit. In an interview with Dominic Lawson for the *Independent*, she bravely revealed that she had suffered a miscarriage in 2002, at thirteen weeks pregnant.[14] Miscarriages are quite common, with about 20% of pregnancies ending in one.* I've had one too. And yet, the topic is still widely misunderstood and taboo, so the emotional and physical cost often ends up invisible. In the final part of her autobiographical trilogy, Judit writes, 'The road to becoming a mother was not smooth at all', calling her miscarriage, 'a tough experience, but I had to learn to live with it, as so many other women do.'[15]

Soon after the miscarriage, Judit had her best tournament ever, and her highest ranking ever. 'It was a terrible time personally but a great time professionally,' she told the *Independent*. 'It was then that I decided to stop playing. I thought, perhaps if I stop playing then I will be able to get pregnant again.' And Judit would succeed in starting a beautiful family, as Oliver arrived in the summer of 2004 and Hanna followed in 2006.

Throughout our interview Judit asked me questions about my thoughts on feminism and my experiences in Budapest. Even after years of being interviewed, she is still uncomfortable with the format, and would prefer just to have a conversation.

---

* Thirteen weeks is unusually late and thus particularly painful. The large majority of miscarriages occur before twelve weeks.

As soon as the interview is over, Judit's guarded posture and diction morph into those of a friendlier person.

Judit has been hounded by the press for as long as she can remember. When I asked her about the plusses and minuses of celebrity, she disregarded the first half of the question: 'When I was younger, it was particularly unpleasant. I would walk around, and people would be pointing at me and whispering, but they wouldn't even approach me and introduce themselves – just point.' The Polgar family was known for maximizing financial opportunities, even billing for interviews, from which I was happily exempt.

The custom of charging journalists for interviews was Laszlo's idea – and certainly one that made many people less sympathetic to the girls. Reputable magazines and newspapers rarely pay subjects, since it would create an atmosphere for auctioning off celebrity interviews to the highest bidder. Laszlo probably did this to shield his daughters from an onslaught from the media. After all, if Judit accepted every interview and TV spot she was offered, she would have little time to work on her game.

Susan has mixed feelings about fame. She reveled in the international recognition she and her sisters received after winning gold in Thessaloniki. Highlights included a trip to the White House and a spot in a commercial for OPT, the biggest bank in Hungary. When the press threatened to swallow up too much of their time, Susan says, 'Laszlo was very good at pulling us away.'

The Polgars have always been sensitive about their public image, and the entire family was disturbed by an unauthorized biography, *The Polgar Sisters: Training or Genius* (1992), written by Cathy Forbes. Laszlo said, 'The book strives to portray us in a negative light,' a summary that, in my opinion, is untrue. The ethical standards, however, are fair to critique – Cathy often quotes anonymously or from unreliable sources. (She describes an incident in which Judit and Susan are chatting in the bathroom – as heard from a woman eavesdropping in a stall.) She did not attempt to contact the Polgars themselves. In her own defense, Cathy says, 'Any book which tries to be interesting and truthful is bound to offend a lot of people.'

I met Cathy at a café in Selfridges, the historic department store in London, to discuss her views on women in chess and the criticism of her book. Selfridges was the same place where, in 1926, handsome Cuban World Champion Jose Capablanca gave a simultaneous exhibition to thirty-six women. The exhibition came about when a princess, Tatiana Wiasemsky, was asked what she wanted for her birthday and said: 'to play Capablanca.'[16]

Capablanca playing a simultaneous exhibition in 1929
(Selfridges Archive, courtesy of Olimpiu G. Urcan collection)

Despite its historical import, Selfridges is an inconvenient meeting spot, since there are several cafés in the department store, and when I finally did find Cathy I was more than half an hour late and frazzled. She calmed me immediately with friendly greetings. Cathy was extremely well put together, with neat red hair and small features. I marveled as she consumed cappuccino after cappuccino while explaining her views. Cathy quotes intellectuals in casual conversation, a habit that might seem pretentious if it weren't for her passion. Such writers as Germaine Greer, Naomi Wolf and Oscar Wilde all came up as we chatted. 'I always memorize a few quotes from the books I love.' Cathy has been removed from the chess world for some years. The controversy over *The Polgar Sisters* wounded her and she prefers to talk about other subjects, such as literature, politics and London.

When I do get her to speak about her book, Cathy intimates that she took the criticism of her book to heart and is nearly in tears when she tells me that she 'regrets deeply not trying to contact the girls,' adding that she 'didn't have a thick enough skin to accept the harsh reviews.' She says, 'I was twenty-two when I wrote it. Such a young biography is bound to tell more about the writer than the subjects, and upon reading my own work today I see myself more than I see the Polgars.' Indeed, on the last page of the book, Cathy, a competitive player herself, writes, 'I respect and envy – yes, envy – their achievements . . . and have sometimes wondered whether I could have . . . been brought up in the same disciplined way.' Cathy concludes that her 'lazy freedom has always been so dear to me!'[17]

Cathy's thoughts have become even clearer in retrospect. After our interview, Cathy wrote me a letter:

My book rather clumsily attempts to express the tension between a positive feminist response to the sisters' achievements on the one hand and unease on the other at the personal and ethical price of those achievements. The Polgars seemed to me to belong to the type of people who are interesting primarily in what they do rather than in terms of who they are. Oscar Wilde, my hero of creative individualism, was the opposite type; he put 'all [his] genius into [his] life, and only [his] talent into [his] works.' His friends felt that his conversation was more brilliant than his writing, and the dramatic tragedy and pathos of his life is more moving and fascinating than his fiction or his plays. The genius of the Polgars, however, is to be found in their chess, not in their personalities. I instinctively felt profoundly disappointed by the apparent completeness of their compliance with the parental project. Ideally, a female chess grandmaster, to have a more lasting feminist role-model value, should be more self-invented.

Cathy, who still believes that the Polgars have had a positive impact inside and outside the chess world, says her expectations going into her research and writing were quite high, confessing, 'I wrote the book because I wanted to be them.'

I have a soft spot for Forbes' book. I devoured it over and over as a teenager. In those days, it wasn't easy to find Polgar games online, and I was ravenous for more inspiration from the groundbreaking trio. I always dreamed of having a sister (sorry Greg and Francois!) and so the book was like a fantasy novel to me: all rook sacrifices and globetrotting with my sister champions.

But I disagree with Forbes' conclusion that the Polgars' achievements are less significant because of their upbringing and support. To me it shows the systemic hurdles that often prevent girls and children from lower-income families from fulfilling their potential. To conquer the patriarchal and classist chess world, extreme measures were called for, especially in the 80s and 90s when the Polgars rose to prominence.

At the start of 1986 Susan Polgar was the highest-ranked woman in the world, her name at the top of the list published by FIDE. She had won the women's grandmaster title and the girls' junior competitions. Eager to compete with men, seventeen-year-old Susan tried to enter the Boys' Under-20 Championship. The Hungarian Federation refused to send her. They argued that since boys were not permitted to play in the girls' sections, girls ought not to play in boys' sections. At the time, all of the most prestigious tournaments on the chess calendar were strictly divided by gender into separate sections – women against women and men against men. Included in these was the most prestigious of them all, the World Championship, for which Susan should have qualified when she tied for second in the 1986 Hungarian Championship. Once again, the Hungarian Federation refused to send her. She was bitterly disappointed – devastated. 'How would you feel if you were invited to the big dance and never got to go?'

Susan went to war with FIDE and her federation, battling for the right to play against men. She won on paper during the 1986 FIDE Congress, when the name of the World Men's Championship was changed to the Absolute Championship. Women could play in either the traditional women's event or, if – like Susan – they were qualified to play against the stronger competition, in the absolute championship. The problem was that the national federation of each country decided who would go, and the president of the Hungarian Chess Federation had a bad relationship with the Polgars, and did not want Susan to play against men.

Finally, in 1988, the FIDE president at the time, Florencio Campomanes, intervened. He demanded that the Hungarian Federation begin to nominate Susan and her sisters for absolute titles. That year in Adelaide, Australia, Susan was finally permitted to play among her young male peers. She placed a respectable eighth in a strong field of fifty-two players.

Susan was the first woman to challenge the gender divisions in international chess tournaments. She set the precedent. Women's tournaments still exist, but it is now commonplace to see a handful of women playing in the 'men's Olympiad', or in the boys' sections at the World Junior Championships. Susan and her followers, who compete and succeed in tournaments once comprised solely of men, threaten the fundamental assumption upon which the segregated structure was based – the one that implies that men are stronger than women.

Susan was the first woman to become a grandmaster in the customary way. (Nona Gaprindashvili and Maia Chiburdanidze, the first two female grandmasters, were awarded the title on the basis of their World Championship titles and high standard of play.) After years of near misses, Susan's third and final norm came in 1990 in Salamanca, Spain. She told me that 'it was a joy to finally win the grandmaster title.' Then, as if to dispel any notion that she might have been worried about winning it, she added, 'There was no doubt in my mind I would achieve it.'

Susan made history as a teenaged chess prodigy. She led the women's rating list and fought to give women the right to compete with men. All her accomplishments, though, were eclipsed by her younger sister's meteoric rise to the top. When Susan was just nineteen, her twelve-year-old sister Judit had a rating that exceeded hers, which must have been painful for Susan. We were talking about Judit's play in a recent tournament in Budapest when I detected a hint of resentment: 'I am proud to have paved the way for my sister Judit. By the time she came onto the international chess scene, I had already fought and won many battles.' After I remarked that Judit must be very grateful for this, Susan pauses before saying, 'Yes. You would think she'd be grateful.' In an interview for *New in Chess*, Judit acknowledged what her sister went through: 'I was the lucky one. Whenever someone was against my father's ideas, she [Susan] would be the first to hurt.'

In 1992, Susan decided to make a comeback by going all out to win the Women's World Championship. Laszlo was dead set against this, believing that the separation of women and men in chess was unnecessary and insulting. Daughter Sofia echoed her father's strong opinion: 'I have always hated the idea of separate women's tournaments. It is like admitting that we are weaker than men.' Judit, for whom women's tournaments were never very important, was somewhat less critical. She said, 'I have only played in three women's tournaments in my life,' adding wryly, 'I'm not a big fan of them.'

Susan, however, had much to gain from playing in the Women's World Championship. Changing her mind dramatically on separate women's tournaments, she now saw them as a way to encourage more girls and women to play and improve. 'I came to realize that for an average girl, who did not have the support I had, there is much more resistance from both society in general and the male-dominated chess world. My father always believed that I should shoot for the ultimate and not play for women's titles. But I was determined to play because I knew that the title would give me the respect from the press I needed in order to promote chess fully.'

Susan had to undergo a grueling qualifying cycle to determine who would challenge the Women's World Champion at the time, Xie Jun from China. After the final qualifier the two women left standing were Susan Polgar and Georgian Nana Ioseliani. Nana, often overshadowed by her countrywomen Nona and Maia, is a great player, and like Susan has a composed, commanding presence. The two would meet in Monte Carlo for the right to play the champion.

Rated 100 points higher than Nana, Susan was the heavy favorite in the match. Living up to her ranking, Susan got off to an early lead (3.5-1.5), scoring three wins and a draw in the first five games. Unfazed, Ioseliani began to climb back into the match.

She won the sixth game, and Susan's lead narrowed to a single point. By the final game, Nana could tie the match with a win. She traded Queens early, hoping to squeeze a full point out of a slight endgame advantage. Susan's nerves got the better of her, while Nana, calmly and coolly, managed to exploit her advantage and eke out a win.

The match was tied, the winner to be decided by a series of tiebreaks. After three mini-matches, Susan and Nana were still deadlocked. At that point a bizarre FIDE rule came into play: if, after twelve games, a tie has not been broken, the match can be decided by the drawing of lots. To no one's surprise, Susan was opposed to the unorthodox tiebreak. FIDE also agreed that the rule was unfair. If Susan and Nana both consented, the tie could be broken by more usual methods. However, Nana, who must have understood that she was the weaker player, took the logical position that she preferred a fifty percent chance by drawing lots.

An absurdly complicated ceremony was staged to determine the winner. First, Mrs Van Oosterom, wife of the organizer, picked between two envelopes, pulled out the one that read 'Nana Ioseliani'. Then, Ioseliani chose between two more envelopes. The paper inside that one read 'Susan Polgar'. Then Susan was asked to pick between two boxes offered by the arbiter. If she selected the gold coin, she would be the new champion. When she opened her box, Susan's heart dropped. Inside was a silver coin. 'My eyesight was blackened for a few seconds, I thought I was fainting. The meaning was clear: you are second.'[18] In her entire career, Susan could recall no more disappointing moment. Ioseliani went on to lose to Xie Jun in the Women's World Championship match.

While all of this was taking place, Susan was reeling from another type of heartache. Her grandmaster boyfriend, who was in Monaco to accompany and assist her, had made up his mind to break up with her. He had not yet told Susan, but she guessed that something was amiss by his uncharacteristically cold behavior. A grandmaster lover can be beneficial for multiple reasons. According to trusted wisdom on the chess circuit, women perform even better when having sex at tournaments, while men are more easily drained and fornicate at their own risk. Only a rigorous scientific experiment could test the theory. But without question, emotional drama does not mix well with a World Championship match.

After the fiasco in Monaco, Susan was more determined than ever to compete at the next Women's World Championship in two years. Once again, she made it to the semi-finals, where she would face an even more formidable Georgian opponent, former World Champion Maia Chiburdanidze, who was hoping to avenge her 1991 loss to Xie Jun. This time Susan had the support of her sister Judit, who trained her especially for the cycle. After seeing how disappointed Susan had been to lose to Nana, Judit 'was determined to do anything I could to help Susan.' In the match against Chiburdanidze, Susan was victorious, taking her one step closer to the championship.

The match against Xie Jun was held in Jaen, a small town in the mountains of northern Spain. The first game was a comedy of errors for Susan. With the white pieces she overextended her position, squandered her opening advantage, and later miscalculated, giving Xie Jun a winning endgame. Susan regained her composure with draws in the next two games, followed by a win with the black pieces in the fourth. The match was tied at 2-2. At this point Susan was ready to unleash her secret weapon. Throughout her chess-playing career she had almost always started her game with white by moving her Queen pawn two squares (d4), one of the two leading ways to open the game.[19] Beginning with d4 tends to lead to slower, more strategic battles, while the slightly more popular alternative, e4 (moving the King's pawn), results in more tactical games. Judit and Sofia have always been e4 players, while Susan was loyal to d4. Most professional players stick to one or the other, because there are dozens of ways to respond to either, all of which must be studied in detail and require experience to master.

For the first time in her career in this crucial game, Susan opened with e4, a radical switch for a professional player in any game, let alone a game of such importance. Xie Jun was shocked. She could have had no inkling that Susan would do such a thing, and probably spent little or no time preparing for King pawn openings. Xie lost the game in just twenty-five moves. Susan's brave opening strategy delivered a psychological blow to her opponent. Xie Jun was never able to regain her ground and Susan won the match easily, with a lopsided score of 8.5-4.5.

Susan was accompanied in Spain by two people who loved and supported her: her sister Judit and her new husband, Jacob Shutzman. In 1994 in New York, Susan had been introduced to Jacob by his brother, a chess fan. The couple had such a good time in New York that Jacob went to Hungary to visit her, where they fell in love. Susan was thrilled to start a new life in New York City, where Jacob had moved from Israel to work as a computer consultant. 'I think one of the reasons I loved New York so much more than my sisters,' she explained, 'is because I subconsciously wanted to get out of Europe, having bad memories from my past relationships with FIDE and the Hungarian Chess Federation.'

Jacob and Susan worked together on various projects, including starting a chess school in Queens, the Polgar Chess Center, and co-writing *Queen of the Kings Game*. Susan and Jacob divorced soon after 11 September 2001, an emotional and tumultuous year for many New Yorkers. Susan was left briefly disillusioned with romance itself. 'Well, I'm still happy to live in New York, although I'm no longer thrilled about my reason for moving here.' When

I asked Susan whether it is better to date within or outside the chess world, she responded cynically, 'Either way leaves very low chances for success.'

When she started the Women's US Olympic training program in 2004, Susan had not played in a serious competition since her victory against Xie Jun in 1996. An invitation to defend her title was issued to Susan in 1999 only months in advance of the scheduled match. At the time, Susan was pregnant. 'FIDE refused my request for a reasonable and proper delay,' writes Susan. 'I was illegally stripped of my title.'

Motherhood, like menstruation, is often cited as an explanation for the less-frequent participation, and decreased enthusiasm, of women in competitive chess. In one US Championship, three-time champion Anjelina Belakovskaia dropped out unexpectedly. She needed to rush home and breastfeed her baby. Another US Championship participant, Shernaz Kennedy, dealt with her problem in a more imaginative manner – she express-mailed her breast milk home from a tournament in California to New York.

The 1989 US Women's Champion, Alexey Root, wanted to play the 1993 US Women's Championship while nursing her four-month-old baby. Alexey, now a professor and author of many chess books, accepted the invitation to the one-week event in Bloomington, Illinois, determined to do both. She wrote about the joys and challenges in an article for La Leche League, an organization that advocates for breastfeeding rights:

> My baby and husband had settled into a comfortable makeshift nursery, out of earshot of the players, but only 25 yards from my chess games. I had learned that on average, I needed to save a half hour per game to tend to Clarissa . . . things were falling into place and that round I drew a terrific chess game that will be published in three different chess magazines.[20]

I've had plenty of encounters in which motherhood was cited as an obstacle to my future success. In negotiating a possible book, I was told, 'I'm not sure if you plan to continue with your writing and chess careers or if you intend to just pop out a couple of babies.' When I did have a child, in 2017, people were surprised when I quickly resumed my poker and chess travels, often hitting the road with my baby and husband.

Not all agree that motherhood is an impediment to chess results. Lithuanian Grandmaster Viktorija Čmilytė-Nielsen was asked in a press conference, 'What do you think of the Russian saying that each baby takes off fifty points from your rating?' Čmilytė-Nielsen responded, 'I think each baby adds fifty points to a woman's rating! Motherhood is such a stimulating experience for a woman.' Later, she explained that being a mother was so demanding, that it instilled discipline. In comparison, preparing and playing chess was easy.

Despite the upbeat comments of women like Čmilytė, the reality is that motherhood in many societies leaves women with the bulk of the childcare responsibilities, often interfering with any leisure time – especially interfering with the time needed for highly focused and demanding activities such as chess. Some chess couples with young children take turns playing in tournaments. A practical solution to encourage the participation of parents would be to make childcare available at tournaments, either with group childcare or a stipend for a babysitter or nanny. Susan believes that the schedule for Women's World Championships should be announced and set at least a year in advance, so women can make plans based on this.

As a mother of two, Susan expressed to me that her interest in chess will never be as intense as it was when she was in her twenties. Susan, who competed in the 2004 Olympiad in Mallorca, told me that the main reason for her comeback was not to reach new chess heights, but to promote chess in America. Indeed, despite going out of her way to organize the training sessions, Susan did not often compete herself. In a rare outing, Susan played in a tournament in Oklahoma in which the whole Olympic team played against local players. Since the members of the team did not play each other, Susan's rating was far higher than any of her opponents'. From her posture one would have thought that she was competing for the World Championship. She was deadly serious, rarely getting up from the board. Susan won her first six games, as expected, but in the seventh she drew a player with a rating 500 points lower than hers. Susan, playing with the black pieces, used her prepared double King pawn opening, but was frustrated by her opponent's unambitious opening strategy – he took few risks, and she had few chances to win. Afterward, Susan was clearly upset about the draw, wondering if she should have chosen a more double-edged opening strategy.

Our Dream Team training sessions gave me the opportunity to spend time with Susan. Despite her formal demeanor, her love for chess is evident: she always comments on the beauty of surprising finishes or subtle finesses. During meals and breaks, Susan is a gracious conversationalist. Choosing her words carefully, she would ask questions of all of us about our favorite cities and our current projects. Her reactions are so consistent and composed that it is difficult to tell whether she is enjoying herself.

A relentlessly hard worker, Susan bounced back quickly from her disappointments in chess and in love. Susan started a college chess dynasty, as the head coach of Texas Tech University, and then at Webster University in Saint Louis. At Webster she was particularly successful: her team won seven straight college championships. In 2006, she married her business partner, FIDE Master and coach Paul Truong, who also worked at Texas Tech and Webster. Paul's hyper laugh and personality are in sharp contrast to Susan. Paul said he 'never sleeps more than three hours a night.'

Sometimes I wonder if Susan would like to break out of her conservative persona. 'I rarely drink,' she once told me. 'Sometimes I have a glass of wine, but I never finish it.' The one time I did see Susan lose control was on lunch break at a Dream Team training session. We were treated to a sumptuous buffet. Its crowning glory was a magnificent dessert spread – flan, triple chocolate mousse, and a selection of fancy Italian pastries. We all started out by choosing and eating one. It was obvious that we all wanted to sample more, but no one wanted to go first. 'Let's repeat moves,' someone said, then, furthering the play on chess lingo, said, 'how about three-move repetition?' Finding this absolutely hilarious, Susan began to laugh so hard she doubled over. She went on laughing for several minutes, which was totally unexpected from this otherwise perfectly composed woman.

A devoted ambassador of chess, Susan promotes the game all year long, giving simultaneous exhibitions and book signings at National Scholastic tournaments, working on writing and media projects, and organizing coaching sessions. Her new attitude toward separate girls' tournaments has led to the founding of a 'Susan Polgar Tournament for Girls' – a yearly invitation-only event, the first edition of which was held in Fort Lauderdale, Florida, in the summer of 2004. The winner, Roza Eynullayeva, was from Massachusetts. The response to the event was overwhelmingly positive. Ohio representative Emily Nicholas called it 'the best tournament I have ever been to' and said 'meeting Susan Polgar made me feel important. She really made us feel like she cared about us and that she wanted us to keep playing chess.' Stephanie Heung from Florida called it a 'a flawless blend of chess and girls.' The Virginia representative, Ettie Nikolova, said the Polgar tournament was 'the first time in my life where girls were not only excited about chess, but also advanced enough to play good games.' The most famous graduate of the Susan Polgar tournament is superstar streamer and Stanford graduate

Alexandra Botez.* Now a member of Susan's board of directors, the chess champion built a mainstream social media chess brand along with her younger sister, Andrea Botez, attracting millions of followers and fans.

Judit Polgar surprised her legions of fans in 2014 when she announced her retirement from chess at the age of thirty-eight. Since then, Judit has worked tirelessly, founding a global chess festival, writing an award-winning trilogy of books, and becoming an ambassador for Play Magnus, a global chess media and educational brand. Through this work, she spoke to hundreds of girls at a workshop I organized for US Chess Women. Several of the girls asked about confidence. Bianca, a sixteen-year-old filmmaker from New Mexico, wondered if Judit ever suffered from imposter syndrome. Madison, an eleven-year-old chess champion from Indiana asked how Polgar kept up her motivation through loss and doubt.

Judit said that she rarely suffered from self-doubt, because she was so strong at such a young age and grew up in such a supportive environment and family. I was struck by her frank answer. The students were caught slightly off guard. They expected Judit, like many of our other guests, to tell a story about a time when she lacked confidence or worried that she wasn't good enough. She just didn't have many stories like that. Though she did recall cheering herself up during a bad tournament by playing over some of her attacking masterpieces to remind herself of how she could play at her best. Her win against Alexei Shirov in Buenos Aires would give any chess player a boost.

I was struck by the tension between the girls who wanted to hear about Judit Polgar overcoming imposter syndrome, and her actual boundless confidence. It reminded me that we need

* Botez and I have also hosted many empowering events together for women, including Isolated Queens, a series of online women's blitz tournaments.

to be cautious about festishizing bounceback stories, especially tales of bouncing from agonizing self-doubt to extreme confidence. It's great to learn from failure, but you can learn a lot from winning too. In my view women are encouraged to lean into their insecurities too often. Sometimes it's better to run away from the painful moments, and into the arms of your most memorable attacking victories.

After the sisters retired from active competition, many were curious as to how seriously the Polgars' own children would take up chess, or if they would choose another subject to immerse their children in. While Susan, Sofia and Judit all introduced their children to chess, none have raised prodigies. On the Canadian television program *The Fifth Estate,* Laszlo Polgar predicted the girls would regret their choice. 'My grandchildren are now university students and I have a feeling that during these years and after they've graduated, my daughters will realize that their children should have gone through the same path that they did. Because achieving outstanding results requires a lot of effort.' Susan replied that, 'Me and my sisters made our choices, good or bad, and we have to live with it.'

To me, the Polgars are the most significant players in the history of chess. They opened up half the world to the possibilities of what one might accomplish in chess and beyond if not for the pressure of being told you can't.

When Polgar beat Kasparov, one woman wrote Judit a personal note[21]:

> [Judit Polgar] has redrawn the map of our brains with her talent and bravery. Thank you Judit! Thank you in the name of the present and future women of the world!
>
> I Love You,
> Yoko Ono

6

Women Only!

'Winning feels good. Winning feels to me like catching a
one 100-pound fish feels to a fisherman.'

   Chess-in-the-Schools student, after winning a huge
trophy in the All-Girls' Nationals

Chess tournaments are social occasions for kids, especially
when they get to stay in hotels. After their rounds, they
stay up late watching movies, playing blitz and pranks.
Elevators, ice machines and sneakers are all fertile ground for
mischief. If a child is one of the only girls, she can be left
out of the fun. For instance, at a summer chess camp, one
girl, due to a strict policy pre-empting romance, was barred
from hanging out at the after-lesson pizza and blitz sessions
held in the boys' dorm. There were not enough girls for her
to form similar chess parties, so she had little fun at the event,
and learned less chess too.

   I went as a coach with ten students to the first ever All-Girls
Nationals in 2004. The event was held in Chicago, in the Adler
Planetarium right beside Lake Michigan. Between rounds, girls
could race along the shore of the lake, photograph the Chicago
skyline, or look through solar telescopes. The event was organized on short notice, but there was great support for it, from
coaches, organizers, and the players. One of my students, Laura
Edgard, was excited to participate, despite being a tomboy used
to playing boys. Laura is one of the most determined students

I have encountered. Before the first round of a crucial tournament, I had asked Laura how she felt about her chances, and she looked me straight in the eye and declared, 'I'll bring back their heads.' In Chicago, Laura told me it was 'fun for a change' to hang out and play against girls. My students all had a great time at the event – they appreciated the beautiful tournament site, the games, and a side trip to the top of the Sears Tower. But what made these girls the happiest was that we had to take an extra taxi to the airport to carry all the trophies they had won.

The event is now the Kasparov Chess All-Girls Nationals, attracting hundreds of girls each year.* In a video I made with director Jenny Schweitzer and producer Richard Schiffrin, participants spoke about the power of girls' chess tournaments.[1] 'In my grade, I am the only girl who plays chess,' said one. 'A lot of girls are intimidated.' Another said that in the mixed competitions she usually plays she hears boys whispering, '"I'm going to beat her" but then when I beat them, they say, "How did I lose? How did I lose to a girl"?' But in events like the All-Girls Nationals, 'There's no whispering that you're going to lose because you're a girl, because we're all girls.'

The social aspect can't be underestimated, especially for elementary school girls. As one said, 'I get to play girls that I didn't know, and I get to make new friends with them.' One junior high school girl summed it up: 'You know that you're not alone. Or you know that there's way more than just you.'

Susan Polgar helped organize that first Chicago tournament and was in attendance throughout. She played a simultaneous exhibition, signed books, had photographs taken with each prize-winner, and even played casual games between rounds.

* The event, generally held in the spring in Chicago, is presented by the Kasparov Chess Foundation, in association with Renaissance Knights Chess and US Chess.

This was all from a woman who grew up with a world view that rejected women-only events.

The divergent opinions in the Polgar family mirror those in the chess world about separate women's tournaments, titles, training, and prizes. One side argues that incentives are necessary to increase the paltry percentage of female participants, and the other contends that these incentives are condescending and will ultimately stunt the development of female players.

Those outside chess often get confused because they hear about one women's or girls' tournament and assume that all events are gender-restricted. The truth is most chess tournaments are mixed gender, but those occasional women and girls' events have been inciting controversy for over 100 years.

Chess champion Jessica Hyatt at All-Girls Nationals
(photo by Betsy Zacate)

The first-ever international women's tournament was held in 1897 in London. At the time, critics of the event worried that 'the players would collapse with nervous strain at having to play two rounds a day for ten days.'[2] Thirty years later, also in London, the first Women's World Championship was won by Vera Menchik.

Once thought of as progressive, women's tournaments are now controversial for the opposite reason. Separating women and men is antiquated, said British master and writer Cathy Forbes, who thinks that many women are ashamed to play in gender-restricted events. 'A feminist chessplayer is faced with a dilemma. Her belief in the equality between men and women does not mesh with her decision to participate in separate tournaments.' Ultimately, Cathy believes that women's tournaments are detrimental to women's progress in chess. This, according to Cathy, is because men are motivated to work harder, since they do not have the 'soft options' of playing in weaker tournaments and winning qualified championships and prizes.

Almira Skripchenko, the seven-time French women's champion, also told me that 'separate tournaments hold women back, because in order to play at the level of a strong man, it is necessary to play strong grandmasters. The best method,' Almira says, 'is to have prizes and titles that serve as incentives for strong women to improve and keep playing, but to hold the tournaments co-ed.' Almira believes that in order for women's chess to progress, women ought to get the best of both worlds – the money for being top female players as well as the toughest competition against all.

My own occasional participation in women's tournaments used to make me feel uncomfortable, even embarrassed. I enjoyed the competitions, the traveling, and the prize money, yet I could not reconcile playing in women's events with my feminist views. The more I thought about it, and the more I coached girls and women, the more my views changed. I have stopped thinking about such events as less than Open events and started to think of them as a way to meet and compete with female colleagues. I reframed the question that I am often confronted with: 'If women are as strong as men, why would they ever play separately?' to 'Why might women and non-binary folk enjoy playing separately from men?'

Separate tournaments offer women space to compete in a positive way – opportunity for intellectual competition and camaraderie among women that can be lacking in our society and media portrayals. I watched so many inspiring movies as a kid, from *Rocky* (boxing) and *Hoosiers* (high-school basketball) to *Searching for Bobby Fischer* (chess) that address complex relationships created by competition among men, but *A League of Their Own* (about a women's baseball league during World War II) was one of the few I watched featuring women.

As I studied gender theory in college, I read a number of books that explored women and competition, including Rosalind Wiseman's *Queen Bees and Wannabees*, Leora Tanenbaum's *Catfight: Women and Competition*, and Rachel Simmons' *Odd Girl Out: The Hidden Culture of Aggression in Girls*. *Mean Girls*, a movie and Broadway musical, was directed by Tina Fey, based partly on material from *Queen Bees and Wannabees*. The common theme in all four works is that competition between women is catty and covert, taking its most vicious forms in bathrooms and cliques rather than in sports arenas or classrooms. As Tanenbaum writes in the introduction to *Catfight*, 'I concentrate on the negative aspects of competition because that is what we need to fix.' It is not self-evident to me that revealing the details of cruel behavior has anything to do with eliminating or even reducing it. I believe that we need, instead, more positive – but equally complex and enticing – portrayals of females in competition with one another. Chess is an ideal battleground to form such relationships.

I read the novel by Walter Tevis, *The Queen's Gambit*, as a teenager, but was more interested in playing over Polgar games at the time than reading about the brilliant orphan girl who drank, popped pills and preferred to play 1.d4. When the hit Netflix series first dropped in October 2020, I was immediately struck by two themes that I had never seen so perfectly portrayed on screen before. The show revealed the beauty of thinking, and the beauty of a woman in deep thought. Anya Taylor-Joy, in playing Beth Harmon, put her head in her hands, and in her head was the whole world. 'Chess is not just about winning,' she said, 'it can also be beautiful.'

The Queen's Gambit also showcased something I'd been trying to convey via my work with children and writing for many years. Chess is not just a game, it's a culture and a lifestyle. For the top players in the world, it's not just studying the Sicilian, it's grabbing a drink in Paris with a good friend you didn't even expect to see and talking chess and life for hours. It's a world that moves from city to city, and that now also lives online, that connects people of all genders, backgrounds and ages. Beth Harmon was almost always helped by the men she competed with, showing how your fiercest rivals in competition can often become your biggest allies later in life.

But Beth had no female chess friends or rivals. Grandmaster Harmon was a singular woman who defied the odds. In contrast, most girls had no interest in chess. The show was written by a man, based on a book by a man and produced and directed by men. Even the beautifully crafted games played onscreen were all based on games by male players, selected by male consultants.* A masterpiece in spite of the fixed male gaze, not because of it.

The Queen's Gambit vision of female genius was not intersectional. Though Beth grew up in poverty, her beauty, sexuality and whiteness were pivotal to her ultimate acceptance. Almost every man in the series fell in love with her, and she flew around the world with ease. There were few Black characters in the series, with the notable exception of Beth's best friend Jolene DeWitt. Jolene was kind, frank and funny, as memorably portrayed by Moses Ingram in the TV series. Jolene did not play chess but was always there when Beth needed emotional or even financial support. Jolene's character is a variation on the mammy trope, here a magically supportive Black friend, whose own desires and conflicts aren't explored. As Dr Chanda Prescod-Weinstein, author of *The Disordered Cosmos* and an avid chess player, wrote, '*The Queen's Gambit* gives us a vision of what we can accomplish when people are helpful instead of being patriarchal monsters [and] foot soldiers. It is incomplete in its whiteness but even so: What a start for a vision. We long for the world where Beth and Jolene rise, unimpeded.'

During my last two years in high school and throughout college, Irina Krush was my main chess rival, and she inspired me to become a stronger player. Whenever I played against her, the stakes were raised, even if it was just in a casual weekend event, such as our 1997 encounter in Allentown, Pennsylvania. It was a large open tournament split up into different sections based on ratings. In total, there were about two hundred players, and less than ten percent of those were women. Irina and I were

* The consultants were former World Champion Garry Kasparov and writer and renowned coach Bruce Pandolfini. In my view, their contributions led to the most accurate depictions of chess on screen in history, albeit with missing female moves.

the only women in the top section, but coincidentally, we were paired in the last round. Irina attacked me mercilessly. I defended well until I made one careless move. As soon as I took my hand off the piece, I nearly gasped. It was a terrible move to which Irina had a brilliant win. I am very expressive and was sure that my face would show her I made a mistake. This was long before I took up poker: at that time, I had no prayer of hiding my emotions. So I got up from the board and paced, preparing myself to resign. Then I saw that my clock was ticking, but she had played a different move. She didn't see it! I jumped right back into my chair, stymied her attack, and proceeded to win.

My next game against Irina was at the 1998 US Women's Championship, where Irina and I were among the favorites. We both won our first two games, and were to play in round three. I was nervous. I knew this game would likely decide the tournament winner. Irina was well prepared, choosing a variation I had never seen before. Once again, she attacked me with verve. This time she was successful, sacrificing a Bishop to break open my King's protection. I was forced to resign on move twenty-three. This was the beginning of a brilliant tournament streak for the fourteen-year-old Irina. She won eight games, drawing one and losing none. Anna Hahn and I, who were the second- and third-place finishers, went shopping together afterwards, a slim consolation for me. For months, I had been training daily for the event, and was dreaming of winning. Anna must have felt the same way: 'I'm happy at least,' she said, 'that I scored the one draw against her.' After such an amazing result, I imagined that Irina would be flooded with interview requests, invitations to strong tournaments, as well as lucrative sponsorships. I was jealous and worried that everyone would write off my own potential. I realized that I would have to work harder in order to get attention.

Irina Krush vs Jennifer Shahade in the US Championship
(Jennifer Shahade collection)

Irina and I first became friends as roommates in a junior competition in 1999 in Yerevan, the capital of Armenia, where we stayed up late, giving each other romantic as well as chess advice. However, I didn't consider her a close friend till 2002 in Bled, Slovenia, when we played together on the American Women's Olympic team. Through the three weeks of intense chess matches and parties with players from all over the world, Irina and I supported each other in the mornings before the game, and gossiped at night. When we came back to New York, Irina posed for me in all pink, on my roof, for a photo series I was compiling. Later I hung the photos of her and other friends and family members – including my mother, father, and brother – along with pink Christmas lights for a pink party at my place. For the occasion, my friend Mikey, a game designer and expert chess player, spray-painted me a chess set with pale pink representing white, and fuchsia representing black. Irina, who doesn't like large crowds, did not come. Irina and I did hang out regularly, trading books and playing basketball or blitz. While our friendship started in the chess ranks, our relationship off the board eventually eclipsed our chess rivalry, and I root for Irina in every game except those she plays against me.

In high school, I liked playing boys, and liked even more to score upset wins against experienced male players. On day trips to New York City, I would play, and usually win, against the macho men at Washington Square Park. I knew I would win most games, but they usually didn't. A crowd would gather to watch me defeat the hustlers. They would often squirm, curse, or refuse to pay me. I was used to playing against men, had no female rivals in my school or in Philadelphia, and had never played in an all-women's tournament.

Then I was invited to be one of two female representatives in the World Youth Festival in Guarapuava, a small landlocked city in southern Brazil. It was 1995 and I was about to turn fifteen. My father and brother accompanied me on this, my first international trip where teenagers from five continents were gathering to crown World Youth Champions: Girls' Under 16; Girls' Under 18; Boys' Under 16; and Boys' Under 18.

Right away I understood that this trip was going to be about more than chess. My brother and I visited a local school, where the students crowded around us to get our addresses and to practice English. They invited us to their gym class, where they outclassed us in soccer and we got them back in basketball. After the rounds, players went to the Frog, a club where samba and salsa played all night. Till then, my experiences in dancing had been limited to awkward school parties and bar mitzvahs. After an initial few days of being shy, I began to open up. Beautiful Brazilian men flirted with me – apparently they found my freckled skin and blue eyes exotic. One player joked to me, 'Latin men love gringas.' I was very inexperienced at the time. In an elaborate matchmaking game on the dance floor I was paired with a Brazilian guy so gorgeous I froze. I was too confused to understand that I was supposed to go over and dance with him, and ended up inadvertently rejecting him. For months afterward, my friends back home teased me for tastes I picked up in Brazil, such as collecting samba music and developing crushes on Latino boys.

In spite of the good times, I was intensely nervous. I had never before competed in such a prestigious competition. Before the first match, I lay on my bed and read *200 Brilliant Endgames*.[3] It was filled with 'studies', brilliant positions not from real games, but composed from scratch to show off the artistic elements of chess. The aesthetic, often paradoxical, solutions inspired me and calmed my nerves. It became my pre-game routine for the tournament.

In the first round, I won a complicated attacking game, then won the second game as well, against a girl from Estonia, a country I'd never heard of before then. My most memorable game was with Martha Fierro, a charismatic Ecuadorian master whom I had admired since we met two years before at a tournament in Washington, DC. Facing Martha now in Brazil, I surprised myself with my own strength, sacrificing with confidence – first a pawn, later a Bishop, and finally a Rook in order to force checkmate. It was my best game to date and my first victory over a master. For the first time I saw how winning could be an end in itself.

In the second half of the tournament, I faltered, losing several games in a row. It was hard for me to understand why, because I wasn't playing badly: my opponents were just outplaying me as well as choosing openings that they thought would make me uncomfortable. Probably they had studied my games from the first half of the event. In one particularly frustrating game against the German participant, I lost without even realizing where I had gone wrong. The string of losses deflated my ego, which had ballooned after my great start.

In the United States, many tournaments are held in hotel ballrooms, where the fluorescent lighting and frigid air-conditioning create a sterile atmosphere. The ratio of males to females at such events is usually about ten to one. Now I had something to compare with that – an exciting trip with interesting teenagers from all over the world, including excellent female competition. After that tournament my dad predicted that I would become a master within a year. And I did.

In retrospect, I can see that my time in Brazil was formative, deepening my passion both for chess and for living. Ever since, I have taken chess seriously and played in dozens of two-week tournaments in locales ranging from Istanbul, Budapest, Curaçao and Honolulu to drabber sites in the suburbs of Boston or Denver. The expenses for most international events are covered by the host city or the United States Federation, while many American tournaments are paid for by the players. Though most of the tournaments I played in were mixed gender, the women's events I played were significant to my development as a player.

Women's tournaments, which are inclusive to transgender players, have proliferated in the United States in recent years. There are now multiple girls' and women's regional events, a US Women's Open, a US Junior Girls' Invitational, and the Ruth Haring Girls Tournament of State Champions.*

---

* This US Chess event is named after Ruth Haring (1955–2018), a former US Chess President, Women's International Master, and lifelong advocate for women in chess.

International women's events and tours have also flourished, including blitz and rapid series. What was once a novelty is now a fixture, creating lifelong networks and motivations. 'I have a friend in every state,' said Veronika Zilajeva, winner of the 2018 National Girls Tournament of Champions.

Anna Hahn, former US Women's Champion, also has positive feelings: 'I consider myself incredibly lucky to have gotten the opportunity to play in women's tournaments.' In Anna's case, playing in women's events had little to do with prize money. After graduating with a degree in computer science from the University of Pennsylvania, Anna moved to New York, where she worked in lucrative jobs such as programming at Goldman Sachs and trading on Asian markets. Anna thinks that she would be a weaker player without having played in separate women's events such as Olympiads or World Championships. 'I don't consider these experiences degrading or detrimental to my chess in the least,' she says. 'You have to judge results based on the quality of your play and your performance. It doesn't matter whether you are playing against women or men.'

And still, some chess players prefer to channel Judit Polgar or Beth Harmon, a player who revels in the open arena. As much as it annoys me to answer for the 1001st time, 'Why are there even women's events?', we do crave women who ask those questions, if not with their words, with their moves.*

In preparation for the 2004 Olympiad, Susan Polgar, Rusudan Goletiani, Anna Zatonskih, Irina Krush and I met eight times for week-long training sessions. At one of these sessions, held in midtown Manhattan at the New York Athletic Club, we all raced to solve two-dozen deceptively simple-looking positions

---

* In the 2020s, one woman smashing barriers is Aleksandra Goryachkina. At twenty-two, she became the sixth woman ever to break 2600, and the fourth-highest-rated woman in history in 2021.

involving only a few pieces: Rooks, pawns and Kings. We had only a few minutes to solve each, after which our trainer for the day, Michael Khodarkovsky, would set up a different problem and reset the clocks. The stress of wondering if I was getting the answers right heightened when I saw my teammate Anna quickly and confidently filling her paper with variations. As it turned out, I got a decent number right, though not as many as Zatonskih.

Anna Zatonskih playing a blindfold exhibition at the
Contemporary Art Museum in St Louis, Missouri
(photo courtesy of St Louis Chess Club/Spectrum Studios)

Hungry after this intense mental workout, the team went out for Greek food, when Michael announced something so astonishing that I assumed it was a joke or an empty promise: the great champion Garry Kasparov (whom Michael had worked with in the past) had agreed to work with the women's Olympic team starting with a session a few months later, in the summer of 2003. As it turned out, Michael was serious. It would be Garry's first outing as a coach. Garry wanted to help boost the stature of chess in America, and thought that the Dream Team members were good candidates to help instigate such a change.

When I arrived in West Orange, New Jersey, a ritzy suburb of New York, it seemed surreal that I would be analyzing with Kasparov in a couple of hours. Excited anticipation mixed with nervous apprehension. Garry was known to make sexist comments when interviewed. Would he be condescending about the level of my play? Would I be offended by any of his sexist remarks? All of us, even Susan Polgar, were nervous. Garry entered the conference room, dressed in jeans and a cotton shirt – I had only before seen him in a suit. When he asked who was going to demonstrate her games first, I avoided eye contact with anyone who might latch onto a glance and cajole me to the front. It was Irina Krush who bravely stepped up to show him a game, an exciting Sicilian. Kasparov's eyes lit up when the position became complicated, and rattled off variations at high speed. He slowed down whenever he felt we weren't following – typical of his behavior at the training session, which was attentive and charming. 'You see the position clearly many moves ahead,' was his compliment to Anna Zatonskih, adding, 'I know many top male grandmasters who can't do that.' The focus of the session was our games, and Garry seemed genuinely interested in our repertoires, especially our response to Queen pawn openings: 'What is there to do against d4?' he asked.

During breaks, we became acquainted with Garry Kasparov, who was perceptive in conversation. In one instance, some of the members at the table were making sexist, unfunny jokes about men with several wives. I did not put on a poker face and was grimacing – Garry came to my defense: 'I don't think Jennifer likes that!' He noted that 'women are starting to reach the highest level in chess, a reflection of their entrance in other fields.' When I asked Kasparov his opinion of women's tournaments, he thought they could actually accelerate the progress of women and thus increase the chance 'to create ten Judit Polgars.' I asked Kasparov why his comments were so different from the often-sexist remarks I had read in the press. He claimed that journalists tend to distort what he says. It could also be that Kasparov is sensitive enough not to insult women at a women's chess training session. Or he could have changed his mind, in view of the recent crop of young women talents, and his first-ever loss to Judit Polgar, which he simply described to me as 'a loss to one of the strongest players in the world.'

Since then, Garry's foundation adopted the popular All-Girls Nationals, and he has admitted the errors of his past comments in dozens of interviews. As he told the *New Yorker Magazine*, 'I just got older and wiser, and can only apologize that it took as long as it did!'[4]

The ratings needed to become a grandmaster or an international master are about 200 points higher than those for the corresponding women's titles. British author Cathy Forbes, an outspoken feminist who once held the title of master herself, objects violently to these special titles, convinced that 'in the title "women's grandmaster", women is just a euphemism for "inferior".' The justification for women's titles have been undermined in recent years because of the increasing number of women who are meeting the requirements for regular titles. There are now forty women with the grandmaster title, a constantly growing figure.* I used to agree with Cathy and really hate women's titles, but my opinion is now split.

* This figure is from February 2023.

Chess is a global game. In many countries, women face even more cultural and logistical obstacles to becoming a serious chess player, and the WGM title may help them on that road. For instance, tournament organizers can offer room, board and pocket money for women GMs and IMs thus enabling female participation. I now find it rude to critique an award for a high standard of play in a culture as misogynistic as chess.

When the title 'WGM', an acronym for 'women's grandmaster', is listed next to a female player or commentator in a livestream on Twitch or YouTube, the chat is usually totally dominated by the discussion of 'W' meaning 'weak'. In many cases, people already know all about women's titles, but are just keen to bring up the topic of female inferiority. This specific type of trolling has a name: sea-lioning, an incessant and bad-faith attempt to engage in debate. The WGM title represents a rating of about 2350: an extremely strong player in the top 1% of rated players. Most of the haters couldn't dream of such a high rating. I hate to let the trolls who are obsessed by women's titles win.

But I remain troubled that the title confuses and offends laypeople and media who are approaching the topic in good faith. In a debate on women's events in my US Chess girls club, several of my students agreed that they are OK with women's events but find women's titles offensive. They have an intensely negative reaction to the phrase 'women's grandmaster'.

So I suggest merging the WGM with the international master title, a gender-neutral title that is a step below grandmaster. WGMs would become WGM/IM and they could decide which they prefer to display, with the WGM title possibly fading out over the years.

Irina Krush, who became a regular international master at sixteen and a grandmaster in her twenties, does not like gender-based titles. She has no problem with separate women's tournaments, but as for the WGM title – awarded to her without her knowledge – she told me, 'I have no interest in this title.'* Cathy Forbes concedes that stripping proud recipients of their titles would be unfair, so she proposes, 'Women grandmasters should take matters into their own hands, and revoke their titles.'

Jennifer Shahade teaching a group of girls at After Schools Activities Partnerships in Philadelphia (photo by Rachel Utain-Evans)

Though I only occasionally participate in women's events, I have often been disappointed by my results in them. Since I was fifteen years old, I dreamed of winning the US Championship, where ten of the country's top women meet in a round-robin tournament. In my first attempt, as a sixteen-year-old, I played

---

* This is an important distinction, since many female players I've spoken to share Irina's opinion in disapproving of women's titles, but approving of women's events. Women's tournaments can be supported with many arguments like camaraderie that don't necessarily follow for women's titles. Women's titles are also far more confusing.

well, tying for fourth place. Three times after that, in 1998 (third place), 1999 (second place), and 2000 (third place), I came within reach of the title. Each time I either choked or another player would start to win game after game, leaving me behind.

In one game, played in the 2000 tournament, I played well in the opening (my favorite Dragon variation) and middlegame against National Master Olga Sagalchik. Transposing into a winning endgame, I realized that this win with black would put me back in the running for first place. I played quickly and confidently despite having more than a half hour to finish the game. Then my heart dropped. One of my rapidly played moves was an enormous error, allowing Olga to achieve a draw. I was inconsolable after this disaster.

I tried commiserating with family and friends, but it only made me feel worse. Stronger than sadness was a feeling of incompetence – my brain felt like a machine doomed to malfunction at just the crucial moment. I struggled to accept the pain of losing, but I had no choice. Sometimes, hanging out with non-chess players is a helpful distraction. Trying to deny the importance of the result by staring at the mirror and shouting that it's just a game, or drinking a bottle of wine, just delays or even exacerbates the inevitable pain.

In the summer of 2001, I was informed that the next US Championship was to be held in Seattle. The prize fund had doubled, and for the first time men and women were to play in the same field. The top-scoring woman would win a large prize and the title of US Women's Champion. The new format had been designed by American Foundation for Chess, a Seattle non-profit. I was determined to train harder than ever for the tournament during my summer break from university. I had just moved to a new apartment in Brooklyn. The room was so small, my final decision to move in hinged on whether I could fit my queen-size mattress into the widest side of the room.

On the other side of the bed was my chess table. A huge back-yard, a rarity in New York, compensated for the lack of space. I studied chess intensively, often outside, working for at least four hours a day, and also got into good physical shape, playing basketball and lifting weights. I was feeling good and on top of my game. In August, I had a disappointing finish at a tournament in Boston. After playing well, I blundered my Queen in the final game. I decided to take a week off from training.

My fall semester at NYU had just started on 11 September 2001. I was in Brooklyn at the time, and had a devastating view of the crash. Like many Americans, I felt compelled to examine my life in larger terms. I was questioning my devotion to chess, which had seemed much more important just a week before. A few days after 9/11, classes resumed and I began a challenging schedule, including courses in Spanish literature and journalism. I was further distracted by the process of moving. I moved into a larger space just two blocks away. The one-week hiatus in August turned into months of half-hearted attempts to reopen my chess books.

Nevertheless, come 2002 I was in better spirits. I had just celebrated my twenty-first birthday on New Year's Eve in my new loft apartment in Brooklyn, my semester had ended, and I was able to refocus on chess. I arrived in Seattle a day early to relax, explore and look over some of my openings. I liked the vibe of Seattle, which reminded me of my hometown, Philadelphia, but I was less used to how new and spacious everything was. I had never seen such a clean city. A man dressed up enough for a business lunch asked me for a spare dollar. I soon found evidence of Seattle's less-glossy side. Capitol Hill, a hip, commercial neighborhood, was filled with tattoo parlors and second-hand clothing and music shops, in which I pined over a pricey red leather jacket, and bought *This Is Hardcore*, an album by a Britpop band, Pulp. The songs soon became some of my favorites; they are forever entwined with my experiences in Seattle.

Before the first round, I had mixed feelings about the men's and women's championships being combined. I was excited about playing with the best players in the country, but wondered how the new format would affect my chances. Players ranked higher than me often intimidated me.

In the first round I played against Gennady Sagalchik, a grandmaster and the husband of Olga, whom I had blundered against in the previous championship. I had spent the morning searching through the two million games in my computer database. First I looked at Gennady's games (of which there were 250), and then I studied the opening positions that I thought I might get. I worked till thirty minutes before the game. Then I left my gleaming white Westin hotel room, which would slowly become littered with coffee cups and newspapers. I walked the mile to the tournament hall in the convention center, just adjacent to Seattle's signature Space Needle. My preparation was successful, and I achieved a great position in the middlegame. At a critical moment, I made a mistake and gave away most of my advantage, but Gennady had become rattled, used up all his time, and lost. It was my first victory over a GM in a national event.

Midway through the event, I lost to Grandmaster Alexander Fishbein. I needed to get my mind off of chess, so I went to the Crocodile Cafe, a bar and concert venue. Upon entering, I was surprised to see another chess player, Grandmaster Larry Christiansen, with a beer and a steak, also unwinding from the tournament stress. I ordered a glass of wine and later went next door, where there was live music from local punk-rock bands.

The break was refreshing. Apparently Larry was also relaxed by his break. He went on to win the tournament. In the rest of the event I played with unprecedented confidence, earning draws against players I had previously been in awe of, such as Grandmasters Yasser Seirawan and John Fedorowicz. In the penultimate round, I played against a master originally from Armenia. After twenty moves, the position was equal, but I saw a chance to set a trap. I made a move that seemed like a blunder – he could win my Rook. He followed this variation, but missed the zinger I had at the end. A few moves later, he resigned. I couldn't get up for a few minutes after the game. I was sitting on my legs throughout the game, and now they were numb.

I felt dizzy with happiness – I had clinched the US Women's title with a round to go. In the final round, I played against a grandmaster. If I won this game, I would place third and win a norm toward my grandmaster title. I ended up losing that game, playing very badly. One of my most brutally honest friends wondered if the reason I played so poorly was because, having already clinched the women's title, I had relaxed. Perhaps if I were a guy, he suggested, I would have played harder, knowing that the only way to get attention at a US Championship would be to prevail against the entire field. This sharp comment reminded me of the reasons that the Polgars questioned women's prizes and events. But I'm sure I would not have been on that high board in the last round if it hadn't been for the women's tournaments and prizes that encouraged me in my teens to stay with the game, starting with the fateful trip to Brazil. I needed to access the motivation for the women's title, but then release it totally when a loftier goal was in sight. It's a tricky calculus that I hope more female champions will master in the future, with the help of both technical and performance coaching.

Despite that last-round loss, the tournament was a big success for me. In interviews I was asked if I liked the new format. I had won. Of course I liked it.

I celebrated a lot. On the Saturday after the tournament, I

went to an all-night warehouse party back in Brooklyn with Gabi, a dancer and artist whom I've been close friends with since high school. Proud of my victory, she was wearing a shirt that was meant to say 'Jennifer Shahade is a man-eater' in gold marker, but the pen ran out of ink midway through, so it only read 'Jennifer Shahade'. I was flattered nonetheless. At this party, no one played chess, but word spread through a few circles that I had just won the US Women's title – news that was greeted with congratulations combined with disbelief: first that chess was a professional sport, and second, that the happy, blue-wigged girl was its new champion.

Often I am eager to promote the game and tell non-players all about my career, but other times I keep my status secret. I fear that the conversational dynamic will change into one of surprise, sometimes disbelief, followed by a litany of questions that can turn an equal exchange into an interrogation. To avoid this I either say, 'I'm a teacher/writer' – which is of course true – or I make an outrageous claim, like circus performer. Just don't ask me to walk on a wire.

On the other hand, I can also be annoyed when I get no recognition as a specialist. One time when I was at a bar with Gabi, we met a charming man with lots to say about film and politics. When the bar closed at four, the conversation retired to my apartment. The topic of chess had not yet come up. Glancing around the room, the man noticed chess magazines and sets scattered around, and he began quizzing my roommate Eric on the game, assuming that the male of the house had to be the player. Eric, who is a strong amateur, noted my annoyance and tried to divert the questions to me, but the guy was not getting it. By this time the sun was coming up, and I was ready to call it a Saturday night. This man, despite ignoring me on chess matters, was interested in me and wanted my phone number. I must have been bitter or just too tired to respond, so he left dejected, numberless. Gabi described the incident as painful to watch, while Eric said, 'I felt so bad – I gave him my business card!'

Until Seattle, I had not realized how important the title was to me. The money was also important. Moving, books for college, and New York prices had strained my budget. I needed the $9,500 check, along with the pay increases, invitations and exhibitions that followed the title. I was particularly excited about the US–China chess summit, scheduled for Shanghai, China, in the summer of 2002. The Chinese women's chess team was the best in the world, and I hoped that in Shanghai I might be able to understand why and how they were the best.

Chinese Style

'Women hold up half the sky.'

Chinese proverb

A long the back streets of today's Beijing, hidden from the hustle and bustle of bicycles and cars, dozens of men crowd around dusty chessboards, playing xiangqi, or Chinese chess, in the open air. Exploring Beijing on foot, I rarely encountered a girl or woman playing these casual games. A lay observer would have no way of knowing that it is young women who are the stars of board games in China. Chinese women captured six team Olympiad gold medals – 1998, 2000, 2002, 2004, 2016 and 2018. They have hailed seven Women's World Champions, more than any other country since the title's inception. The Chinese government has supported the promotion of chess, a trend that was accelerated by the success of Xie Jun, the trailblazer of women's chess in China. Young players, many of whom were adept at xiangqi, were encouraged to switch to chess and enroll in the training center in Beijing, where they were able to develop their talents under the tutelage of experienced masters and coaches.

Xie Jun was born in 1970 in an army base outside Beijing, where her father was posted. Jun means soldier in Chinese, a reference to her father's occupation, but the choice of Xie Jun's name has a larger significance.[1] 'The name Jun is more often given to boys, but the year of my birth was in the midst of the

Cultural Revolution. During this turbulent period in modern Chinese history, it was common to minimize the differences between men and women, and this was also reflected in the names given to newborns.' During the Cultural Revolution, launched in 1966 by Mao Zedong, Chinese culture was meant to be purged of the 'Four Olds': old ideas, habits, customs and culture. At this time, traditional Chinese games such as Go, Mahjong and xiangqi were banned. Books were burned, historical temples and sites were destroyed, and traditional gender roles eroded.

The Cultural Revolution ended with Mao's death in 1976 just before Xie Jun turned six, and the ban on board games was lifted. Jun learned xiangqi at six years old and took to it immediately. Her father accompanied her to the streets, where she competed against middle-aged and older men. At eleven, Jun won Beijing's girls' championship in xiangqi. She was spotted by chess trainers, who taught her international chess and entered her in the Beijing team. Her passion for xiangqi transferred easily to Western chess. The skills required for excellence at both games are similar. Jun's progress in chess was rapid. She became, at fourteen in 1984, the youngest Chinese national master. In 1988 her local team found a sponsor, which permitted her to travel to the World Junior Championships in Adelaide, Australia. She became more serious about chess after she tied for second place.

Xie Jun's spectacular breakthrough came two years later, in the candidate cycles – a two-year series of tournaments to determine the challenger to Women's World Champion Maia Chiburdanidze. In 1990 Xie Jun won a preliminary tournament in Malaysia, qualifying to participate in the candidates' finals in Georgia. In the second round, Xie Jun won against local heroine Nona Gaprindashvili. Xie Jun's compassionate nature is evident in her description of the encounter:

Xie Jun (photo by Bill Hook, courtesy of the World Chess
Hall of Fame)

I felt overcome by a feeling of sadness at this moment, when
Nona realized that she had no more chances and I was about
to mate her, I could see the tears in her eyes. Every time when
Georgian players won a game, the three to five hundred spectators applauded enthusiastically. But now there was a dead
silence in the hall. I could not feel as happy as one would
normally expect. The whole situation had touched me and I felt
too much sympathy for my opponent.

Xie Jun won her last round game against Nana Ioseliani, cata-
pulting her into a tie for first with Yugoslavian Alisa Maric. The
two would play a match to determine who would face
Chiburdanidze later that year. Xie Jun won the match, held in

former Yugoslavia, by two whole points. The chess world and the Chinese press were astonished: Xie Jun was the first Asian to compete for a World Championship in chess. She was just twenty years old.

To Chinese head coach Liu Wenzhe, Xie Jun's qualification for the finals was a triumph of historical proportions. In *The Chinese School of Chess*, Wenzhe promises, 'The Chinese school will be pre-eminent in the chess world. This is the necessary logic of chess history.' But such an upheaval would take time, and Xie Jun's victory caught even the optimistic Wenzhe by surprise. In assessing Xie's chances, Liu was reserved: 'Taking into consideration Chiburdanidze's skills and experience, as well as those of the Soviet coaches, the overall strength of the Soviet team is greater than ours. It will therefore be very difficult to win the match. Xie Jun has to undertake thorough preparation.'

All of China's chess resources were poured into the upcoming match against Maia. Wenzhe summoned every grandmaster in China, all men at the time, to provide support for Xie Jun. Ye Jiangchuan, first board for the Chinese national team and a coach of Xie Jun, told me that the Chinese women play so well 'because the men help them.' When I reminded him that men had also helped the women in the Soviet Union, he laughed and said, 'Here, the men really help the women.' Each grandmaster was assigned a different set of openings to work on at home. They were to convey to Xie Jun their deep understanding of the positions along with detailed and original analysis. During this period Xie Jun's days were tightly scheduled. Eight hours were devoted to chess, along with blocks of time set aside for light exercise and meals. (The transcripts of the training program are published in Wenzhe's *Chinese School of Chess*.)

The chess confrontation between the Soviet Union and communist China coincided with a turbulent time in the USSR, which was crumbling as the match was played. Midway through,

Xie Jun realized: 'Maia was not at her best throughout the match. The timing coincided with huge changes in the former Soviet Union. In Georgia, civil war had broken out and I cannot imagine that Maia ever had a peaceful mind.' Indeed, Maia confirmed in interviews that, at the time, she was distracted by politics.[2]

Because Xie Jun had played in few international tournaments, she was something of a mystery. It was clear that she was young and talented, but her legendary Georgian opponent was higher rated and a big favorite. The match was held in Manila, Philippines, the first time a Women's World Championship was held in Asia, and the crowd was rooting for Xie Jun. In the first game Maia achieved a better position with black, but Xie Jun played resourcefully, finding a Knight sacrifice that led to a draw after a ten-move variation. The eventual triumph of youth over experience was underway. The second game was a quick draw. Maia made a mistake in the third game, and Xie Jun pounced, drawing the first blood of the match. Maia then came back to win two games in a row. A series of draws followed, until Xie leveled the match with the black pieces in round eight.

Xie Jun gained momentum after her eighth-round victory and she won her next two games with white. Maia was unable to catch up, so Xie Jun won the match, a final score of 8.5-6.5.

Her upset victory created a stir in China, where Xie Jun became a major celebrity. 'I was not sure where I was or who I was. Chaos had set in,' wrote Xie Jun. 'It was impossible for me to plan anything – my life had become a whirl of excitement.' She was even elected as a member of the parliament in 1993. Though the post was mostly ceremonial, Xie Jun rejoiced in her new role as politician, which she 'considered a great honor. It was a tremendous experience for me . . . and a nice break from chess.' Xie Jun also took some time off from chess to pursue her university degree in politics.

Xie's political career was short-lived. Toward the end of 1993, she resumed her training regimen, preparing for her match in Monaco, where she would defend the title she had won two years before. Xie Jun considered being a world champion an enormous responsibility, so she worked hard to improve her chess understanding after her unexpected victory. She gained the grandmaster title and raised her rating to over 2500. Her opponent was Georgian Nana Ioseliani, who had won the right to challenge Xie Jun after winning in the controversial tiebreak against Susan Polgar. Ioseliani was mercilessly defeated by Xie Jun, in an overwhelming 8.5-2.5 victory. Her improved skills were evident as she defended her title. Describing the one-sided match, Xie Jun's remarks were once again gracious and compassionate: 'Luck was on my side in the first game . . . I felt in great shape and winning four out of the first five games was beyond my wildest dreams . . . for Nana it must have been horrible.'

Xie Jun's third title defense in 1995 was unsuccessful. She faced a determined Susan Polgar, who duly crushed her, forcing Xie to confront the first major setback of her chess career. The kind and sympathetic words Xie had once had for both Maia and Nana were gone, replaced by an angry diatribe. She complained about the poor conditions in Jaen, Spain: the food did not suit her and there were no decent translators for the Chinese delegation. A chief gripe was the unprofessional conduct of organizer Luis Rentero. Rentero sent both Susan and Xie Jun letters, which harshly scolded them for making quick draws, imposing unprecedented fines. Rentero wanted every game to be exciting, but the rules had already been established and Xie and Polgar both found the fines disrespectful and distracting. Xie Jun claims she was unable to calm down afterward. She gave Polgar nominal credit for her play: 'I cannot say that her victory was undeserved.' She continued, though, 'The incident with the letter was unforgivable. All I can hope for is that one day I will have the opportunity to play another match against Zsuzsa [Susan], under different conditions.' These candid remarks reveal Xie's fiercely competitive streak.

Xie Jun was determined to reclaim her title. During Christmas 1997, she played in a nine-player qualifying tournament held in the Netherlands. The two top finishers would play a match to determine the challenger to Susan Polgar. Russian Alisa Galliamova won first place, and Xie Jun came in second. So that neither player gains an unfair advantage, most title matches are held in a neutral location or split between both home sites. Half of Xie–Galliamova was set for Jun's native China, in the large city Shenyang, and half in Kazan, Alisa's hometown. At the last minute, Kazan backed out and the entire match was switched to China. Galliamova did not accept these conditions, didn't show up for the match, and Xie Jun won by forfeit. Susan Polgar, who was starting a family in New York, protested the rushed proceedings of the Polgar–Xie rematch, and refused to play. Galliamova was chosen as a replacement, and invited to play Xie Jun once again. This time the match was conducted as anticipated, half in Kazan and half in Shenyang. The games were interesting and hard-fought, in my opinion some of the most interesting chess of any World Women's Championship match ever. Xie Jun prevailed in the end, winning five games to Alisa's three. Jun's victories ranged from a 29-move checkmating attack to a 94-move win in an endgame.

The event was the last Women's Chess Championship held with the classical match format until 2011.* Kirsan Ilyumzhinov,

---

* From 2010–2018, the format alternated between knockout and matches. Starting in 2019, it switched back to a biennial match format, with Ju Wenjun

the president of FIDE at the time, decided upon an entirely new system, which he thought would help to popularize chess. First of all, the time control (a preset time limit for a player to complete her moves; if exceeded she will lose the game) was changed, so that the average game lasted about three or four hours instead of the standard five or six. The tournament format shifted to that of a knockout, in which sixty-four players play two-game elimination matches. Ties of 1-1 are broken by rapid matches. The field is whittled down, round by round, into 32, 16, 8, 4, 2 until there is a four-game final, at the end of which a champion is crowned. The grand prize was over $50,000. The new idea was certainly more exciting, and the large starting field gave young players a chance for the first time. Detractors argued that the knockout format and quickened pace resulted in games of much lower quality than those played in classical format. A player who would have few chances in a regular candidate cycle could have a few good games and emerge as World Champion. Elisabeth Paehtz described the new knockout as 'more like gambling in a casino than world championship chess.'

Xie Jun, the highest-rated and most experienced player in the first edition of the event, held in New Delhi in 2000, was able to win handily, even in the more random format. She outplayed her first five opponents calmly, meeting her young compatriot, Qin Kanying, in the final round. Xie Jun outplayed her with a win in the second game, and drew the others.

The all-Chinese final was indicative of the dominant position of China in women's chess at the start of the twenty-first century. In the two decades after 1981, when Xie Jun first

(China) winning against Aleksandra Goryachkina (Russia) in a January 2020 duel.

turned her attention from xiangqi to chess, the number of casual chess players in China soared from a few thousand to five million.³ From all over the vast country, talented young players were recruited to train at the National Chess Center in Beijing. China's future female team was coming together.

Zhu Chen was only seven when she began to play chess in a local club. Just four years later, in 1988, she traveled to Romania to play in the World Girls' Under-12 Championship. She won first place, becoming the first Chinese chess player to win a gold medal in an international event. After this victory, Zhu Chen was summoned to the capital to train. Zhu Chen desperately missed her family and yearned to return home, but her parents implored her to suffer through the homesickness by throwing herself into her chess. She did just that. She describes being so tired after grueling eight-hour sessions that she would collapse into bed at night, going on to dream of chess variations.⁴

Zhu Chen with young fan (photo by Jennifer Shahade)

Unlike Xie Jun, whose ascent to World Champion was swift, Zhu suffered a number of setbacks on her way to the top. At the 2000 World Championship, held in New Delhi, India, she failed to survive the first round of the knockout. She was upset by American teenager Irina Krush who, after drawing the first game, dispatched Zhu in an unbalanced game that could have gone either way. 'I was so excited after this game,' Irina told me 'that I threw up afterward.' Early in the following year Zhu Chen was awarded the grandmaster title, becoming the seventh woman to be so honored, and the second Asian woman.

A year later Zhu Chen had another chance to capture the ultimate title at the 2001 World Women's Championship. She arrived in frigid Moscow with high hopes for the tournament that was to be held in a majestic hall in the Kremlin. Zhu was the highest-rated Chinese woman there, since Xie Jun chose not to defend her title. I had also qualified and was paired against a young Russian, Alexandra Kosteniuk, in the first round. I lost the match, 0-2. My sole consolation after this disappointing loss was in watching Alexandra handily dispose of all her opponents that followed me. Among Alexandra's victims were Almira Skripchenko, the reigning European champion; Hoang Trang, an international master from Vietnam; and Xu Yuhua, another of the new wave of Chinese stars.

Meanwhile, Chen was tearing through her half of the field, defeating two Georgians in back-to-back rounds – first Nino Khurtsidze and then the legendary Maia Chiburdanidze. The final match between Kosteniuk and Zhu was dramatic and entertaining. Seventeen-year-old Kosteniuk, a native Muscovite and crowd favorite, has been featured in dozens of fashion magazines, and was nicknamed 'the Anna Kournikova of chess.' The two striking young women exchanged blows while the chess world followed the event online and in Moscow. To the satisfaction of chess fans there were no short draws that so often detract from the entertainment value of World Championship matches. For the first eight games the women exchanged victories – first one, then the other – until Chen finally broke through with consecutive wins. The title was hers. Seventeen years after Zhu Chen first learned to play chess, her dream of ultimate glory was realized. Another Chinese woman was champion of the world.

I met Zhu Chen at the closing ceremony of a friendly match between the American and Chinese teams in Shanghai. Held in a ballroom on the top floor of our luxury hotel, we had a spectacular view of Shanghai's recently developed Pudong skyline, with buildings designed in futuristic shapes such as rockets and cylinders. We were feasting on an eight-course meal of crispy duck, shark-fin soup, and peeled shrimp. As is the custom in high-end dining in China, no rice was served so that diners have room for the rich meats and sauces. As I was musing upon this, Zhu Chen commented, 'Sometimes you have to wonder why we are eating this fabulous meal while other people are starving. I hope to use my position as Women's World Champion to help less fortunate people in my country and around the world.' As our conversation continued, Chen frequently expressed her devotion to helping the less fortunate and bridging cultures through her power as a champion. Zhu Chen also showed her playful side when she sang a lively rendition of 'que será, será', to the delight of her proud mother, who was sitting with us. Chen's mother could hardly have seen that her daughter's future would be as the Women's World Champion of chess.

Thoughtful and playful, Zhu is at turns controlled and wildly impulsive. She has demonstrated how disciplined she can be by enduring the rigors of the Chinese chess school. Her chess control contrasts with her lifestyle, in which she frequently defies convention. Once she shaved off all her hair. In FIDE's official yearbook, the photos of the women's world champions throughout history include a black-and-white shot of a bald Zhu. An outraged woman remarked to me, 'She looks like a concentration-camp victim!' I disagreed with this perception. Many women shave their heads to make a statement, including Indian feminist Arundhati Roy, writer of the bestselling novel *The God of Small Things*. She shaved her head after being elected one of *People* magazine's '50 Most Beautiful People in the World' because she didn't want to be seen as 'some pretty girl who wrote a book.'[5] American chess coach and expert Elizabeth Vicary has shaved her head twice. The first time she was a senior at Columbia University, and was shocked at how differently people addressed and treated her. 'Before people would listen to me just because I was pretty – after shaving my head, I learned to be a better conversationalist.' Roy and Vicary both chose to abandon the conventional standards of feminine beauty, even though they would benefit from these standards. Wondering about Zhu's motives for her impulsive act, I asked if she were taking some kind of feminist stand, but she assured me that she 'wasn't trying to make any statement' and 'just got bored of the same haircut.' A little later, after thinking it over silently, she told me, 'Shaving off all my hair is an expression of my individuality, and you can also see this in my chess career.'

Zhu Chen's patriotism sometimes conflicts with her free-spirited nature. Zhu Chen believes in the future of chess in China: 'Chess history always follows the great nations. China is destined to become the next great chess dynasty.' However, she repatriated after marrying a grandmaster from Qatar, Mohammed Al-Modiahki, whom she first met at an Asian youth tournament in Malaysia in 1994. Although she and Al-Modiahki shared no common language, according to Chen, they were able to communicate over the chessboard. 'There are many

combinations with the King and Queen that are quite beautiful.'[6] Since then, Zhu Chen has gained a good command of
English, a language in which Al-Modiahki is also fluent. Chen's
mother did not approve of the marriage and tried to convince
her daughter to find a nice Chinese man, but her efforts were
in vain. 'Nothing,' said Chen, 'could have stopped our marriage.'
Like Zhu's mother, Al-Modiahki's parents also believed that
the many cultural, racial and geographical differences were
insurmountable, and Zhu refers to the familial disapproval as
a 'cold war'. There were certainly no financial restrictions to
stop their relationship. Like many citizens of Qatar, Al-
Modiahki is heir to a great oil fortune.

Zhu's relationship with Al-Modiahki is featured prominently
in her first book, published in May 2003, an autobiography,
the title of which translates, *Lay [the] Piece Without Regrets:
Waits and Dreams of a Mermaid*.[7] Zhu Chen is as optimistic
about love as she is about chess. 'Chess is a good way to
bridge different cultures in a peaceful way, and my relationship with Modiahki is a great example of this. Love can defeat
any resistance.'

As impressive as the individual personal triumphs of Zhu Chen
and Xie Jun were, even more striking was the proliferation of
Chinese women chess players, many of whom were playing at
the level of international masters or even grandmasters. By the
late 1980s their performances in the Olympiads were already
beginning to attract worldwide attention.

In the 1988 Olympiad in Thessaloniki, it was the Polgars and
the Soviets who grabbed all the headlines. Quietly, though, the
Chinese women were gaining ground, finishing a respectable
fourth. Two years later in Novi Sad they had climbed to third,
bringing the first Olympic chess medal home to China.

The 1992 Olympiad in Manila was held just after the

break-up of the Soviet Union. For the first time the fourteen newly created republics could field their own teams. World-class players from Georgia and Ukraine and Russia, who had been left out of the powerful Soviet teams, could now participate. As a result, the tournament fielded more top-flight teams than ever, despite the absence of the Polgars. The Chinese team got off to an excellent start, in first place after ten rounds. However, the team faltered in the closing rounds, having to settle for the bronze medal once again. Hoping for gold or silver, a disappointed Xie Jun consoled herself by remembering that this was probably the strongest field ever assembled for an Olympiad. 'Viewed in that light,' she concluded, 'bronze was not bad at all.' In the 1996 Olympiad in Yerevan, the capital of Armenia, China came ever so close, narrowly missing the gold medal, which went to Georgia.

In 1998, the Olympiad was held in Russia. With great performances by Xie on first-board and Zhu on second, China finally won gold ahead of Georgia (silver) and Russia (bronze). In the 2000 Istanbul Olympiad, they easily won again, clinching first place before the last two rounds were even played. The stars of the Istanbul team were Xie Jun, who held down board one, and Zhu Chen, who posted a performance rating of 2700, gaining the top individual performance of the women's Olympiad. As the twenty-first century arrived, the dominance of China's women's team was clearly established.

In the 2002 Bled Olympiad in Slovenia, Xie Jun did not participate. She had just had a baby with fellow Grandmaster Wu Shaobin.* Because of China's deep and strong women's chess tradition, a pool of seven Chinese women who played at or above the international master level (around 2400 Elo) was

---

* Wu Shaobin, the eighth Chinese player to earn the grandmaster title, now represents Singapore.

available to provide Xie's replacement. The Chinese team was still top-seed. If the size of the women's teams were increased to five or six players, the Chinese women's team would have been an even bigger favorite. Nevertheless, without the experienced Jun on the Bled team, the road to a 'three-peat' was not going to be easy.

The Russian, Georgian and Polish teams all presented serious challenges to the Chinese. Even the United States, ranked eleventh going into the tournament, delivered a shocking blow to the Chinese squad. It was round five, and our usually optimistic coach, Ilya Gurevich, having studied our positions on the board after the first two hours, was convinced that we were destined to lose the match, 0-3. On first board, Irina Krush was playing against Xu Yuhua, the fourteenth woman ever to earn the grandmaster title. Yuhua is free-spirited, which once got her temporarily kicked off the Chinese team, and stylish, wearing clothes such as a red blouse with the word 'Only' stitched in silver sequins. Yuhua had recently earned her share of the limelight by twice winning the prestigious Women's World Cup championships. In each victory, she won $16,000, prevailing over her compatriots as well as the best European women players. In her game against Irina, Yuhua chose a tame but solid system, leaving Irina few chances for counterplay. It looked as though Yuhua would slowly squeeze her way to a victory. Then the nearly unthinkable happened. Yuhua gave up an exchange for free, trading her Rook for a Bishop with no compensation, an error that most coffee-shop players would be stunned to commit. A few moves later, Xu resigned.

Meanwhile, on board two, I was mounting an attack against Wang Pin that she could thwart with her best play. The correct move for Wang was to neglect her own development and play a rash-looking Queen move. To my delight, she played the incorrect move, allowing my attack to crash through.

Xu Yuhua (photo by Jennifer Shahade)

Both Wang Pin and Xu Yuhua had blundered, allowing us to win the match 2-1, to the surprise of everyone in attendance. In spite of this stumble, the Chinese women were once again triumphant, winning their third consecutive Olympic gold.

Our small victory in Bled provided sweet revenge for what had happened to us earlier in the summer of 2002, a few months before the Olympiad. We'd been invited to Shanghai to play in a friendly summit match between the men's and women's Chinese teams. Irina Krush, Elena Donaldson and I represented the American women.

Our Chinese hosts could not have been more hospitable. We stayed in a beautiful hotel, were treated to lavish banquets and parties, and ate dumplings on a cruise down the Yangtze River.

The generosity of the Chinese Federation appeared to be boundless – that is until the competition was underway and they posted the wrong pairings. The United States players thought they were playing different opponents. As a result, members of our team were studying the wrong games for their upcoming matches, putting us at a serious disadvantage. The visiting US officials were flexible and cooperative in their efforts to set things right, but the Chinese wouldn't budge until they finally had no choice but to admit their error. One of the officials had been especially friendly and cheerful until then, graciously insisting that we call her Abigail, because her Chinese name might be too difficult to pronounce. I can still see the anger on her no-longer-smiling face as she glared at the e-mail that forced her to admit that the US team had been misled.

The chess did not go as hoped for the American women. Xie Jun played with the Chinese men, so we would not have to face her. But we did not fare well against the others. I lost both of my games with Wang Pin, and was promptly benched. Elena Donaldson managed one draw and half a point from her two games against Wang Pin. Irina Krush scored 1 out of 4 against Zhu Chen. This gave the women a grand total of 1.5 points to the 6.5 points for our opponents.

The American men did better, but once again a Chinese woman undid us. Xie Jun scored a crucial win against Grandmaster Alexander Shabalov in the last round. She played the most aggressive defense against 1.d4, the King's Indian. Shabalov achieved a good position, but committed an error, which Xie Jun pounced on, going on to sacrifice all her pieces while stripping his King of all defenses. This victory clinched the match for the Chinese. Joking about Xie Jun's participation in the match, one player complained, 'It's not fair. Two players against one!' Xie Jun, at the time, was eight months pregnant.

The skills of Chinese women chess players can be mystifying. 'What are they doing to those girls?' asked Woman International Master Anna Hahn. 'Everything about them is different,' notes another top female player, 'from the way they shake hands to the tiger balm.' Before games, Xu Yuhua and Wang Pin like to rub tiger balm on their temples, releasing an intense odor. Before one of our games I asked Wang Pin for a dip. She laughed, then handed over the container of transparent balm.

Westerners are often unaccustomed to or even intimidated by what they view as exotic Chinese culture. The feeling can be mutual. In her book, Xie Jun reveals how foreign her first Western opponent, Jorg Hickl, an international master from Germany, appeared to her. 'I felt very nervous . . . there he sat, a foreigner with a different coloring of the eyes and hair, with a high nose of a type I had rarely seen before. Maybe I was the first Asian girl he had ever played.' After the game, which finished in an exciting draw, Xie really wanted to discuss the game with Jorg, but they had no language in common. Xie was determined to learn English, so that she could communicate with her opponents. It is unfortunate that verbal communication between Chinese and Western teams is often limited, but at least there is chess to help transcend language barriers. Once at the 1999 World Youth Championship in Yerevan, Armenia, I played against a Chinese girl, Kuang Yinghui. Our game, which ended in a draw, was interesting and long, lasting for six hours. Although we couldn't talk to each other, our communication over the chessboard connected us without words. We walked home together amidst tanks on the dark boulevards of Yerevan on that day in autumn, the season of Armenia's independence day. After a few minutes Yinghui grabbed my arm and began to sing in Chinese. We skipped together arm-in-arm the whole way back to our hotel.

There is a controversy about whether cultural differences

extend to styles of playing chess. Many trainers and players have insisted that 'the Chinese play more like computers.' I myself used to be under the vague impression that Chinese players blundered less frequently than most, that is, until Bled, when both Wang Pin and Xu Yuhua made huge errors that turned winning positions into losses. One trainer even told me that the Chinese school won't reach the level of the Russian school because 'despite having the same intense training and fighting spirit, they lack creativity.' Such spurious claims, in my opinion, are rooted in the same kind of racism that assumes that 'all Asians are good at math.' Some Westerners even claim that Asians look so much alike to them that it is difficult to recognize individuals. One American grandmaster joked that when facing a Chinese opponent, he could actually be playing against several opponents – his opponent could get up from the table every few moves and switch with another teammate. 'I would never be able to notice.'

The idea that the Chinese fight hard and long without blundering while Western players fill their games with blunders and brilliancies appears to be based on little more than prejudice and anecdotal evidence. I decided to take a serious look at the games of Chinese women to see if any playing-style patterns would emerge. After examining dozens of games involving Chinese women, it became clear to me that their styles varied widely. Xu Yuhua plays deep positional chess. Zhu Chen has a minimalist style, is a tough fighter, and often pulls out wins in even positions. Xie Jun is an aggressive tactician and the most well-rounded – and, ultimately, the strongest Chinese woman player. I also compared the games of the two teenage stars of the 2002 Bled Olympiad, one from China, the other, Russia. With an amazing score of 10/11, seventeen-year-old Zhao Xue wore a Mickey Mouse sweatshirt and a sly smile to her games. She ruthlessly scored point after point. 'My only regret in my first Olympiad is losing one game.'[8]

Tatiana Kosintseva, a sixteen-year-old Russian, who wore her long, light-brown hair in a ponytail and played with a poker face, finished with a score of 10.5/12. These fantastic results earned Xue and Tatiana the gold and silver medals for the best performance ratings of the entire Olympiad. In looking at their games I noticed that one of the women played with a fierce attitude and a fearless attacking style, crushing her opponents. In an equal position she lost a drawn position with a rash exchange sacrifice. The other player's games had fewer fireworks, but showed off her fighting spirit by often picking up points when her opponents faltered in equal positions. Throughout the tournament, she made nary a blunder. The blunder-free games were those of Kosintseva. The more creative games were Zhao Xue's. In this case, stereotypes would have incorrectly predicted from the national origin of the player.

In his book *The Chinese School of Chess*, Liu Wenzhe, however, argues that the Chinese do have a different style of play from Westerners. Liu Wenzhe explains that the Chinese tend to have a shallow knowledge of the opening, making up for this with a deep understanding of the middlegame and relentless fighting spirit. He points out that many of the Chinese players who were recruited by the government to learn to play international chess were brought up playing Chinese chess, xiangqi, and so there are some remnants of that game in their play. In chess, players often set up pawn structures early in the game. Pawn structures are locked formations which rarely unravel, since pawns cannot move backwards nor capture forwards. In such closed positions, pieces are hemmed in by pawns, limiting tactical contact between the pieces and favoring long-term strategic ideas. Although the pawn is the weakest piece, they often determine the pace and nature of the game, causing Philidor, the great French player from the eighteenth century, to declare, 'Pawns are the soul of chess.' In Chinese chess, on the other hand, pawn structures are less stable, resulting in more open positions, which require constant tactical vigilance. Wenzhe thinks that, as a result, Chinese players tend to be very comfortable in open games.

Zhao Xue (photo by Jennifer Shahade)

The Chinese women I asked were less sure that Chinese women play differently from other women. Xu Yuanyuan, a twenty-one-year-old woman grandmaster, said, 'It's all the same game.' If the Chinese do play differently, the differences are subtle, especially in the highest circles in contemporary chess, where finding the right move tends to override individual style. Zhao Xue, the star of Bled, claims to have no preference for a particular type of game: 'I like an easy position.' Professional chess players worldwide access the same chess databases, computer programs, and expert annotations, furthering the standardization of chess expertise.

In the eighties and nineties, beginning with Xie Jun, Chinese chess trainers began to successfully train the women to play at the grandmaster level. Liu Wenzhe, the head coach of the women's team since 1986, knew he had to replace the former leading players of China in favor of very young players who could be trained intensively from scratch. Raw talent was not that important, as he writes: 'Systematically training players is more important than selecting them.' His program focused on middlegame study and careful scrutiny of a player's own games. He criticizes programs that emphasize games of world champions above all: 'It is a fallacy reflecting the obsession with celebrities.' By the twenty-first century, Liu Wenzhe was confident that he had achieved his goal, declaring: 'The battle between the Russian and Chinese schools in the field of women's chess ended in a Chinese victory.'

Almira Skripchenko offered her opinion as to why the Chinese women of the early 2000s was stronger than the Soviet women of the 80s: 'The Chinese team, supported by the Chinese government, has a goal to become the strongest women's team in the world. They will do what they need to do to reach this goal, just like the Soviets did what they needed to do to reach the pinnacle of women's chess.' In order to win Olympiads, the Chinese had to have a team of girls strong enough to compete against the Polgars and the Georgian champions. The bar was raised, and the Chinese women climbed over it.

And one player would climb even higher. Hou Yifan was born in Xinghua, China and discovered chess at the age of five.[9] Unlike many of her predecessors, she did not start with Chinese chess. She was attracted to the shapes of the pieces in international chess, and picked up that game directly.[10] She rapidly ascended to the national team, which brought her family to Beijing. According to Louisa Thomas in the *New Yorker* magazine, 'Her parents told her she could "go back to normal life" whenever she wanted, but she was not a normal talent.'

Yifan's accolades were numerous. She earned the Grandmaster title at fourteen-years-old, a year younger than Judit Polgar. She became the youngest women's World Champion ever at the age of sixteen, and reached a rating of 2686 in 2015, the highest achieved by a woman outside Judit Polgar. She seemed poised, after Judit's retirement, to carry the mantle of the only woman who could compete in elite open events. And she could have, defeating some of the top players in the World, like number two rated player Fabiano Caruana, and former World Champion Vladimir Kramnik. In 2012, she even became the first woman to defeat Judit Polgar in over a decade.

Hou Yifan vs Judit Polgar in Gibraltar, 2012
(photo by Macauley Peterson)

Despite her extraordinary success, she had more diverse plans for her career. In 2012, Hou Yifan enrolled in Peking University, full time. In December of 2017, she continued her studies at Oxford University on a Rhodes Scholarship. She takes her academic career as seriously as her chess, which eliminates the chances, for now, that we'll see her playing for the overall World Championship.

Although many fans would love to see her march up to the top ten, Hou Yifan's path is also powerful. She is a role model for transferring chess success to academic success. That connection is important for advocates of chess for children – it convinces parents to sign their daughters up for chess class, from Philadelphia to Shanghai.

The success of so many Georgian women initially planted the idea that women could be great chess players if they had role models and training. The Polgars proved that it is possible for women to play at the highest level of chess, even though critics called them 'exceptions to the rule.' The Chinese, in addition to the Polgars, are adding weight to the idea that women, in general, have equal chess potential to that of men.

The success of the Chinese women suggests that female chess players do not have different cognitive abilities from men, but rather that they are lacking a thorough and equally intense training program.

In explaining the development of a great player, one has to confront the controversy over just how important genius is. Overestimating the importance of genius understates the role of training and motivation. If genius were all-important, then the lack of opportunities for women in chess would hardly be relevant. After all, isn't genius likely to override all circumstances?

Juno and Genius

'The mind of the man and the mind of the woman is the same, but this business of living makes women use their minds in ways that men don't even have to think about.'

Patricia Hill Collins

At the age of seventeen I believed that men and women had equal intellectual potential. However, when discussions about gender differences arose, I lacked the experience and theory to back up my ideas. I recall how frustrating it felt trying to hold my own in arguments like the one I had with a twenty-one-year-old grandmaster at the 1998 US Open in Hawaii.

He'd just lost an important game to Judit Polgar, who was twenty-two at the time, ultimately giving her first place in the tournament, which made her the first woman to win the title. Analyzing after the game, Judit joked around and tossed her hair while she zipped through one variation after another. The young grandmaster could barely keep up with her. Later he told me, 'I lost because she is very well-trained,' adding bitterly, 'she is no genius. Name for me one female genius; I can name hundreds of male geniuses.' I was pressed for the right words as he continued to goad me: 'If women are as smart as men, why aren't there any great female chess players?' I tried as best as I could to rebuff his claims, but failed.

Years later, after reading art critic and feminist Linda Nochlin's essay 'Why Are There No Great Women Artists?' in an art history class at college, I looked back on that argument and saw how I could have responded. Nochlin criticizes feminist thinkers who respond to the question of why there aren't more female artists or geniuses by trying to name counter examples. She challenges the concept of genius that assumes 'art is a free, autonomous activity of a super-endowed individual.' According to Nochlin, the greatness of artists develops when they are given proper training and financial and psychological backing.

The word genius derives from the Roman genius, a guardian spirit who watched over the birth of men and their works. The female counterpart, Juno, who attended the women, would have been the alternate choice for genius. Later genius came to signify a person born with extraordinary intellectual gifts. The word genius is applied to either gender, but men still far outnumber women. In *Genius*, a tome by conservative cultural critic Harold Bloom, only thirteen women are included in a survey of one hundred brilliant writers. In the 2020s, you can find similar, or even worse, male to female ratios in countless popular books and podcasts.

In *Why Men Rule: A Theory of Male Dominance* (1993) scholar Steven Goldberg is overt in his attempt to demonstrate the intellectual superiority of men. Goldberg, also the author of *The Inevitability of Patriarchy* (1973), was a professor and the sociology department chairman at the City College, City University of New York. 'I suppose that those who explain the greater incidence of male genius in environmental terms have never had the fortune to be exposed to a mind of genius for long,' he writes. 'Anyone who has will know that it is inconceivable that genius could be held back by social factors.' Goldberg suggests that anyone who disagrees doesn't know any real geniuses. Nochlin, on the other hand, disregards first-hand experience (such as conversing with brilliant people) as relevant evidence, explaining that genius may 'appear to be innate to the unsophisticated observer.' Goldberg goes on to assert that no woman could ever reach the level of a strong grandmaster, a prediction that would soon be shot down by Judit Polgar.

Goldberg compares intelligence to height:

Only males possess the extraordinary aptitude for abstraction that is a necessary condition for genius in mathematics and related fields [chess], and the fact that far more males than females possess the high aptitude for abstraction that is a necessary condition for near-genius in those fields virtually precludes the possibility of female genius in those areas and guarantees a preponderance of males in the genius group and at the near-genius level. This is perfectly analogous to height, a quality whose etiology is overwhelmingly physiological – all people over eight feet tall, nearly all people over seven feet tall, and the vast majority of people over six feet tall are men.

Goldberg's 'perfect' analogy is dubious at best. Height is measured by a standard scale. There can be no debate that a seven-foot man is seven feet tall. Intelligence and genius are far more difficult to measure, and the criteria for geniuses are a tricky mix of objective achievement as well as subjective values.

I think passion can be mistaken for talent, or even genius. When I was a young girl, I was convinced that I had little talent for the game, because my father and brother Greg were both much better than me. I was paranoid that people wondered why Greg was already a master and I could barely break even in lower sections. There were many reasons for my lack of progress. My motivation was less intense since I was intimidated by the skills of my brother and my father. Besides, I wasn't having fun playing chess. When I reached middle school, the few girls I had hung out with at tournaments, eating Doritos and watching cartoons, dropped out of the game. I still played in tournaments, but I was not enjoying them nor was I improving. I began to shift my energies into theater and writing, figuring I would be the non-gamer in the family.

My parents supported this move and encouraged me to go to theater camps and bought me books on Shakespeare. So one summer, as Greg played his usual schedule of tournaments, my mother drove me to upstate New York for a one-month intensive theater program. I didn't like most of the classes, which were based on improvisational games that I disliked because they demanded that I be clever on cue. Despite being pricey and studded with the children of celebrities, the camp was overcrowded and I had trouble making friends. I felt left out of the clique of four girls with whom I shared a room. They talked about boys and shaved their legs sitting on the carpet. During my unhappy downtime at drama camp, I often lay on my stuffed mattress, obsessively writing lists of words in my journal – not difficult or provocative words, just adjective, verbs, prepositions, and nouns. It was as if I were suddenly overwhelmed by the vastness of language and wanted to encapsulate a chunk of it in a yellow spiral-bound notebook. My obsessive streak would soon find another outlet, in the study of chess openings. One evening my roommates confronted me for not including words such as love or kindness in any of the lists. Only a few hours later did it sink in that they had no business attacking me for not including certain words – I should have been angry at them for going through my stuff. But I avoided their eyes and shrugged, waiting for them to find something better to do. Perhaps if theater camp had been the creative and social experience I expected, I never would have gone back to the chess world, which I did soon after returning from camp.

My father wasn't too much help at first. He thought the pressure of living up to Greg's chess results would be too much for me. In one ugly incident when we were analyzing chess positions, he told me that I was improving quite slowly. I got so angry that

I cursed at him and fled. At the door, I was still clutching *Your Move*, a chess book[1] filled with the chess problems we were looking at. With hatred welling up for that book I tore its cover off. It felt so great that I continued, ripping out page after page, leaving a black and white mess of chess diagrams and variations on the gray carpet by the doorway. Recalling that incident years later, my dad laughed and said, 'After that afternoon, she got good really fast.'

Many years later, well into adulthood, my dad revealed to me that Greg had scored the highest IQ in the history of my public elementary school. Apparently, I also scored above average, but nowhere stratospheric. My reaction to this news was gratitude. My parents never let on to me this family secret as they realized it may have a negative effect on my self-esteem, fragile in adolescence. As an adult, I found it amusing. I'm not that tied to the concept of IQ. It also helps explain some things

Jennifer as a preteen with a chess trophy
(Shahade family collection)

about Greg: why he gets good at every game so quickly from Scrabble to poker to Codenames.

In the summer of 1994, a year after the theater camp, I went with my brother and father to Chicago to play in a two-week chess tournament. I was now thirteen, and hanging out with boys had become more fun for me. For the first time, I played blitz all night long and threw myself into my daily matches. My results and play improved immediately. Variations began to click and pieces danced into place. Sacrifices revealed themselves to me. Suddenly chess coaches and peers began to notice my talent. My dad also was stunned and impressed, taking me to tournaments, and arranging lessons for me. Obviously, I still had the same brain and the same neurons, but now I was motivated.

After Chicago I began to study the game seriously, on my own as well as with my schoolmates and my family. I would scrutinize my past games, looking for places that I played badly and searching for the reasons why I faltered. In this form, chess could measure my mind, which would sometimes expand to a size I wouldn't have imagined possible, but at other times would contract, resulting in lazy play.

Post-game analysis has a rich tradition in the chess culture, and most tournaments have skittles rooms where players discuss their games freely. Moves that were discarded during the game for being too risky or just wrong are tried out in analysis, where pieces can be sacrificed at whim. If the combination doesn't work out, the pieces are reset and another sacrifice is tried. Jokes and animated input from kibitzers replace the strict silence and head-to-head format of a tournament game. In the best cases, such post-mortem sessions become more satisfying than the game being analyzed, much like a Sunday brunch, where yesterday's party breaks down over Eggs Florentine.

In the room I had lived in until college, I have copies of

notes to my old games. 'Not patient enough,' I scribbled about one rash move. 'I need to be more comfortable in waiting for something to happen.' I was hard pressed to resolve one inexplicable blunder: 'I threw myself right into the rocks.' I did give myself credit for nice wins, though. In the notes to one win I wrote, 'I was able to find the hammer blow right away.' This rigorous introspection has carried over into my life outside of chess, where I often dissect my own behavior in conversations and encounters.

I often wonder how different my life would be without chess. Many of the other selves might have been happier, more politically active, and more likely to land in stable relationships and jobs. But without chess, I would be less confident and cosmopolitan, with fewer varied experiences and international friendships.

In China, a great chess tradition for women is greatly assisted by the government, which sponsors training and provides salaries for top players. The Georgian women of the former Soviet Union were offered similar resources. Recognition and support for chess players is becoming more typical in the United States, where, until recently, chess was seen as an eccentric or nerdy hobby more than a serious intellectual pursuit. Unless parents can pay for training or a child goes to a school with a chess program, American chess players (both males and females) are left to fend for themselves at the start of their careers. Stipends and sponsorships are beginning to increase for chess players all over the world, but it is still unprecedented for the entire chess resources of a country to come together for a top female player, like China did for Xie Jun's monumental 1991 match against Chiburdanidze.

A player has to be very motivated to pursue chess in a country without systemic support. There are so many career options for an intelligent person to pursue that to play chess seriously requires a very passionate attraction – an attraction that could be called obsession.

Grandmaster Aleksandra Goryachkina often plays in top mixed gender events (photo by Eric Rosen)

While it is viewed as normal for girls to obsess over clothes, weight, or men, it is not perceived as normal for them to obsess over chess. As American Grandmaster William Lombardy pointed out, 'Women are not as good at chess as men because they are more interested in men than chess.' A woman who does spend all her time on chess is often seen as bizarre, particularly in places where a woman is expected to marry at a young age. Linda Nangwale from Zambia told me that women in her country are expected to be married by their early twenties. She wonders, 'What kind of man is going to understand that I'd rather play blitz all night or study the Sicilian than hang out with him?'

The two greatest American players have reinforced or, to a certain extent, created, the image of a chess player as an obsessive genius. The first American chess legend, Paul Morphy, traveled to Europe in 1858, where he stomped on his opponents in brilliant style. He quit chess soon after returning to his hometown, New Orleans, where his madness bloomed. Wandering around the French quarter, talking to imaginary people, Morphy had already gone mad when he was found dead in his bathtub in 1884. He was forty-seven years old.

Bobby Fischer, the ultimate symbol of individualism in chess, spent even more time on chess than a Russian schoolboy does, but he did it alone in his room in Brooklyn or in the hotels at tournament sites, surrounded by his stacks of chess books. Unlike the more glamorous, free-spirited eccentricity of a musician or an artist, the image of chess players like Morphy and Fischer is more often one of narrow, introverted weirdness that descended into madness with age.

Fiction reinforces the stereotypes. Chess fanatic Aleksandr Ivanovich Luzhin in Nabokov's novel *The Defense* was unable to disentangle the events of the real world from the events on the chessboard. He became a great player, but his life ended in disaster when he threw himself out of a window. Even Beth Harmon in *The Queen's Gambit* is portrayed as an obsessive outlier.

Obsession may not be required for phenomenal success in chess, but it certainly helps. As a result, chess fever is romanticized, and young players yearn to be more obsessed than they actually are. Harriet Hunt of Britain compared herself unfavorably to an ex-boyfriend, a grandmaster who was far more focused on chess than she was. 'He would spend hours studying esoteric pawn endgames, and this really made me feel inferior and jealous that I was not as obsessed as he was. Women have this problem in chess, that we are not as obsessive as men.'

At tournaments, women may find it more difficult than men to completely lose themselves in the game and reach a Zen-like state of total focus. That women are trained from a very early age to be constantly aware of how they appear may explain this.

John Berger, author of *Ways of Seeing*, coined the term the 'male gaze' – the feeling that many women have that they are being watched, even when alone. He writes, 'A woman is almost continually accompanied by her own image of herself. Whilst she is walking across a room or whilst she is weeping at the death of her father, she can scarcely avoid envisaging herself walking or weeping. From earliest childhood she has been taught and persuaded to survey herself continually.'[2] Such an extra layer of self-consciousness makes it hard to experience life directly or to feel pure freedom. As Leonore Gallet, a prodigy violinist and amateur chess player, once said, 'When [a woman] thinks of a beautiful move, she is liable to think also about how beautiful she looks in making it.'[3]

In chess, expert player Elizabeth Vicary thinks that women are also often watched in a very literal sense. As one of the few women in American open tournaments, Elizabeth and her games often attracted a lot of attention. Although this can be embarrassing and annoying, it can also have positive side effects, according to Elizabeth. She feels that being mindful of their audiences makes women play more exciting chess.

A former Olympic women's team coach, Grandmaster Ilya Gurevich, also believes that women are particularly conscious about what other people think about their games. 'Women players are mostly worried about what their coaches will say after the game – usually men are just upset to lose.'

In the view of my coach, Victor Frias, putting in fewer hours is the main reason the best female players are not at the level of the best males. He praised Judit Polgar as the first woman to break into the world's top-ten list, because she was 'the only woman in chess who eats, sleeps, and breathes chess, just like her male counterparts.' Some feminists and writers agree that women do spend less time on chess, but think that the problem is not with women, but with the hyper-competitive structure of the chess culture. Alexander Cockburn wrote in *Idle Passion*, 'It can be taken as a creditable sign that women have largely not become involved in chess or as expert as men in its execution, because they are happily without the psychological formations or drives that promote an expertise in the game in the first place.'

Anti-chess feminism, a way of thinking that I encountered time after time in my interviews and research, accepts the premise that women spend less time on chess, but questions whether the problem is with women – or with chess. As Margaret Mead said, 'Women could be just as good at chess, but why would they want to be?' Nine-time American women's champion Gisela Gresser considered men obsessed with chess bizarre. She said, 'You know women are too reasonable to spend all their time on chess.'

Such rhetoric is not limited to the chess world. In the 23 October 2003 edition of *The New York Times Magazine*, the cover featured a woman sitting with her baby next to a ladder. The article by Lisa Belkin was titled 'The Opt-Out Revolution'. The so-called revolution was about women leaving the work force to pursue more old-fashioned feminine roles. Sally Sears, a lawyer-turned-homemaker, said that women were leaving 'the rat race' because 'we're smarter.'

That women might be too intelligent to waste their time on chess is usually said in a flippant way. We reward excellence in most areas with money and respect, so to inquire casually if women are too smart to be obsessive requires a total upending of our values.

Surprisingly, some radical feminists would agree with conservatives that women and chess don't mix well. Sexists might say that women aren't playing chess because women are stupid, while 'anti-chess feminists' could say that women aren't playing chess because chess is stupid. Le Tigre, a radically feminist pop-rock band, wrote a song called 'Mediocrity Rules', with a CD cover that reads: 'Behind the hysteria of male expertise lies the magic of our unmade art.' In this view, the existence of superstar figures such as grandmasters or rock stars are based on a pyramid structure of power. The accomplishments and ideas of a few are celebrated, while the majority is overlooked. To replace 'the hysteria of male expertise' it would not be sufficient to simply add a few women to the top of the pyramid, but to tear down the whole structure in favor of something more egalitarian and inclusive.

Chess players are categorized in a pyramid structure, determined by their chess ratings. But this is not only a function of chess, but also the way the chess culture is set up, which could change in a way that valued participation, creativity and enjoyment in the game along with masterful play. I support ideas and organizations that broaden the appeal of chess. I'd love to see more prizes for beautiful moves rather than the current situation where – with the rare exception of brilliancy prizes (in which a panel determines the most artistic games of the tournament) – all awards go to the winners. There could be more experimental matches in which the performative aspects of the game are highlighted, such as Marcel Duchamp's match against musician John Cage, held in 1968 in Toronto. The artists designed a board on which each square was wired to respond to a move with an eruption of sounds and images.

The online chess boom of 2020 allowed us to see a chess world based on personality, style and popularity, as well as chess skill. Chess.com organized one of the most viewed chess events of all time, Pogchamps, a tournament with celebrity streamers and YouTubers with little or no chess knowledge. Many of the participants were gamers and they got good quickly. The second Pogchamps winner Rumay Wang, known online as Hafu, is a Hearthstone champion and streamer with over one million Twitch followers. Hafu took the competition so seriously, she played hundreds of games and solved thousands of puzzles on an anonymous burner account. After her win she said, 'I think if you added everyone's practice it still would be less than what I played. It's sickening.'

The success of the Pogchamps led into many similar events and promotions. The efforts gave unprecedented attention to chess. But hierarchy seems unavoidable nonetheless. Instead of rating, the important metric for becoming good enough to be a player or commentator on Pogchamps is also a raw number: your follower count.

It's a fun thought experiment to wonder what chess would look like, and if it would even be sustainable, without hierarchies. I'm entranced by the idea of multiple ways to be the best, creating an inclusive chess world that embraces more types of great minds.

As much as I embrace the brave new chess world that makes space for everyone, I profile great champions like Judit, Zhu Chen and Nona because I believe that the focus and passion required to excel at chess is a beautiful thing. Some of my fondest memories are of those periods when I was most engrossed in chess. Hours would go without my being aware of their passing as I played or studied intricacies. Losing track of time while immersed in chess fills me with a satisfaction so profound – for me the way being alive is supposed to feel.

European Divas

'Sexy, self-confident, sociable . . . can we be talking about
a professional chessplayer?'

Journalist Sarah Hurst on Grandmaster Stefanova

Nineteen-year-old Antoaneta was wearing a black wool
jacket over her waifish frame on our way to a nightclub
in a cab. The next day, Christmas 1998, was an off day from
the tournament in Groningen, a Dutch college town. I was
seventeen at the time and intimidated by Antoaneta, but after
a couple of drinks I was loosening up and we began to talk.
With her enchanting Bulgarian accent, dimpled smile and quick
wit, Antoaneta Stefanova has such charm that it is hard to meet
her without wondering, 'How cool can you get?' Already among
the top ten women players in the world, Antoaneta – before
hitting the dance floor – told me, 'I prefer to beat men.'

Antoaneta (pronounced Antwaneta, and shortened by friends
to 'Ety') was born in 1979 in Sofia, the capital of Bulgaria,
where, at the age of four, she learned to play chess from her
father. Her remarkable talent for the game was clearly demonstrated when she swept the 1989 World Girls' Under-10
Championship in Puerto Rico with a perfect score of 11-0. 'I
was winning all my games and very happy!'

Antoaneta extracts pure pleasure from winning, which I
observed after playing her in a tournament in Spain a few years
ago. Though an underdog, I was holding on to my position

until she took a risk in mutual time pressure, sacrificing a pawn to gain control of the dark squares surrounding my King. This threw the game into a mad scramble. Under tremendous pressure, I eventually blundered. After the game, Antoaneta and I went to a restaurant with some Israeli friends. Glowing with the pleasure of victory, Antoaneta lingered over her tiramisu, luxuriating in what she calls 'my fifteen minutes of feeling good about myself.'

Later in that tournament, I was introduced to Antoaneta's sharp sense of humor. Waiting for a taxi outside a disco at around 5:00 a.m., Antoaneta impatiently complained: 'When will this stupid fricking taxi get here?' causing one friend to tease her. 'Ety – you're so negative . . .' 'Oh, sorry,' she quipped, 'where is the very nice and highly intelligent taxi?'

At her peak, Antoaneta Stefanova was one of the most active professional female chess players in the world. A typical yearly travel schedule for Ety included trips to Argentina, Turkey, Russia, India, Israel, Indonesia, Curaçao, and nearly every country in Western Europe. Although Antoaneta usually prefers hot climates, she has added Iceland to her list of favorite countries. In the spring of 2002 Antoaneta and I were both there for the biennial Reykjavik Open, a strong international tournament. The Icelandic Chess Federation went to great lengths to support women players, inviting women from around the world and paying all expenses.

This was not my first trip to Iceland. In high school, I played in a friendly Iceland vs. US chess match. I turned fifteen in the midst of the spectacular Icelandic celebration of New Year's Eve. I was hanging out with teenaged Icelandic chess players, who were drinking beer while I sipped Coca-Cola. All over the country, families and friends gathered early in the evening to light roaring bonfires. By midnight the skies were lit up with fireworks. Iceland, a depressing place in the winter when days can remain black for as long as twenty-four hours, has one of the highest alcoholism and suicide rates in the world. One Icelandic master explained darkly, 'In Icelandic winters, we don't drink to have fun.'

Antoaneta Stefanova (photo by David Llada)

This time, it's March, and Iceland was on the cusp of spring. The event was held at the city hall in the center of Reykjavik. An hour early for my first game, I ordered an expresso in the café adjacent to the playing hall, where wide windows looked out on the icy landscape, and I could see school children skating on a pond. By the time of my last game the ice had melted.

Antoaneta had a below-par result in Reykjavik, but still managed to enjoy the virtues and vices of Iceland. The healthy lifestyle of fresh food included the finest salmon in the world. Clean, crisp Arctic air contrasted with the vibrant nightlife of smoky discotheques. We stayed at a mega disco till early in the morning, relieving the stress of six days of chess. Just before departing from Iceland, Antoaneta and I visited the famous Blue Lagoon Geothermal Pools, where tourists and locals bathed in the open air in all seasons. As the end of her stay in Iceland drew near, Antoaneta wasn't sure she was ready to leave: 'Iceland is one of the most interesting places I've been in a while and I would like to see more of it. But,' she added, 'when I am in the same country for more than a week and a half, it feels strange, like it's time to go.' At tournament's end, she was off.

Antoaneta is unusual in the highest echelons of women's chess in that she generally travels alone. I asked her why she rarely brings a coach, and she says that it is often prohibitively expensive. She also feels freer when traveling alone, explaining, 'When I bring a coach I often feel more responsible for my results. I can easily become nervous and play badly.' Many coaches would also have problems with her free-spirited behavior. 'I travel to chess tournaments ten months out of the year,' Antoaneta told me. 'Wouldn't it be a shame if I didn't enjoy myself?'

If there is a discotheque near the tournament site, Ety is likely to be there, dancing to the pounding music and flashing lights. She smokes Cartiers and drinks Bacardi. Time permitting between moves, Antoaneta heads for the hallway, where she can puff on a cigarette while contemplating her position. When she was a teenager, Johnnie Walker sponsored her tournament expenses. Antoaneta has recently toned down a little. 'When I was younger I used to be able to go out every night and still play well, but now if I go out more than two nights in a row it will show in my results.'

A major milestone for Antoaneta was to achieve the grandmaster title. She made her first norm during a trip to the United States by tying for second at the 1997 Hawaii International. The

US chess circuit was impressed by the young Bulgarian, who celebrated her eighteenth birthday during that tournament. In the weeks before Hawaii, Antoaneta had played in open tournaments in New York and Las Vegas on her first trip to mainland America, where she did not enjoy herself at all. She did not plan to return until she turned twenty-one, when she could legally enter bars and clubs.

Antoaneta struggled for a few years before earning her second norm in a round-robin tournament held in Salou, Spain. Her third norm came soon after in the 2001 Andorra Open, where she tied for first. She was awarded the title in 2002. At twenty-three, Antoaneta Stefanova became the eighth woman to gain the grandmaster title.

The twenty-first century found Antoaneta Stefanova among the highest ranked Bulgarian players, male or female. For the 2000 Olympiad in Istanbul, rather than agree to play first board on the three-board women's team, Antoaneta accepted an invitation as a reserve on the mixed team. In Bulgaria, where the popularity of chess is similar to that of Olympic figure skating in the United States, an angry press attacked her decision. She could not think straight in Istanbul, Ety tells me, because of critics who wanted her to play on the women's squad, where they thought she would contribute more points. Despite winning only three out of seven points in Istanbul, Antoaneta was able to play against tougher competition and was convinced she had made the right decision. 'If I had to do it over again, I would do the same thing.'

Despite Antoaneta's high ranking, she didn't win many major women's titles in her early career. That began to change at the 2002 European Women's Championship in Varna, Bulgaria, a seaside resort lying on the shore of Varna Bay on the Black Sea, once a favorite spot of Bobby Fischer. The first prize of $12,000 attracted most of the top women players in Europe. Onlookers were rooting for Antoaneta, the hometown favorite. She would not disappoint. Antoaneta was in fine form, scoring 6.5 points from the first seven games. She eased into first place with draws in the last three rounds. The championship was the jewel in a crown of excellent results throughout 2002 and 2003. Her FIDE rating peaked at 2560, and when the April 2003 rating list was published, Antoaneta Stefanova had become the second-ranked woman in the world.

Antoaneta discussed those successes with me, speaking with characteristic candor: 'I made some good decisions in my life, for instance, moving my home base back to Sofia, where my friends and family are, instead of living in some stupid place in Spain.' That place was Salou, a resort town near Barcelona. Salou's spectacular beaches and discos provided good times as well as convenient access to strong European tournaments. But Antoaneta missed too many elements of her own culture and decided that she had to go back to her roots.

The adventurous spirit that sparks Antoaneta's behavior also appears in her style over the chessboard, especially in her early years, when she liked to play off-beat openings. The lines were not theoretically challenging, but were likely to catch unprepared opponents off-guard and leave them frustrated. 'How could you live with yourself playing chess like this?' one opponent wondered out loud during a blitz game. Antoaneta was playing one of her favorite systems, the London, an extremely solid opening that is difficult for many players to fight against. 'Oh believe me, I can live with myself,' she said and then proceeded to crush him. Antoaneta now plays more conventional lines, and writes off her earlier opening strategies to laziness. 'At some point I just realized I didn't have the discipline to study the main lines in depth,' she said. She believed her natural skill would give her an edge and that she would score more points with sidelines.

Antoaneta's strength, both over the chessboard and in her personal life, has allowed her not only to survive in the male-dominated arena of European Open tournaments, but also to thrive there. She told me, 'I'd rather do feminist things than talk about feminism.' Antoaneta is not afraid to confront tournament organizers and journalists, as I discovered when interviewing her. At the time, a question I'd used in other interviews seemed entirely reasonable to me and so I asked her, 'What is your favorite [chess] piece?' Even though Antoaneta and I have been friends since we met at a tournament in 1998 in the Netherlands, she gave me a withering look as though I'd gone mad, then said, 'I can't believe that you – as a chess player – asked me that.' She added, 'When journalists in Bulgaria ask me questions like that, I tell them to learn something about chess and then come back for an interview.'

At least I didn't make the mistake of trying to interview her too early in the day. Antoaneta, who usually prepares at night and sleeps until just before a game, was outraged when an organizer once tried to schedule an interview for her in the morning. 'What – they want me to get no sleep and lose my game?' The interview was rescheduled.

She does not tolerate disrespect. At one tournament, I ran into an angry Antoaneta, who had just spoken with a Lebanese organizer. He wanted her to come to Lebanon for a month to give exhibitions and play in a tournament. She was offered a paltry sum for her services and, to make matters worse, she would have to play in a tournament with opponents far below her level. When Antoaneta explained that her Elo rating was 2550, and she deserved better pay and better competition, the organizer challenged her: 'But that's 2550 Elo for women, right?' There has never been a separate Elo rating system for women. After this insult, Antoaneta walked off without further negotiations.

In Europe, playing chess professionally is a viable occupation. All year long there are tournaments where prize money, free room and board, and sometimes sizeable appearance fees are offered to top female chess players. To hone their skills, the top players must endure demanding playing schedules that often require sleeping in several different countries each month, a lifestyle that is not for everyone. Judit Polgar commands a large enough appearance fee to make her living by playing in just five or six tournaments a year, but still thinks that 'traveling is the worst part about being a professional chessplayer.' To those who long to see the world, this may seem hard to believe, but 'the dream-life gets old,' says Grandmaster Artur Kogan, a globetrotting professional.

Antoaneta adapts well to a schedule that is at once grueling and glamorous, and even sets herself a yearly goal to visit two countries she has never seen before. Still, the traveling and focused activity wears on her, and she often talks about switching to another field. Her main academic interest is in psychology, but recently she has completed a course in business and gotten involved in Bulgarian real estate. She tells me that she will move away from chess when it feels right, not after she accomplishes any particular goal. But she is certain that her lifestyle will not last forever. 'Come on,' she says, 'I am not going to be playing and traveling to tournaments like this when I'm seventy.'

Antoaneta's charm and intelligence led her to a twist in her career path. In 2021, she became a member of the Bulgarian Parliament. 'In politics as in chess it is very important to have a clear plan and see at least two moves forward. Winning the election is a capital you can easily scatter if you don't use it.'

The relationships formed on the professional chess circuit tend to be both sporadic and intense. At tournaments, old friends pick up where they left off, even when years have separated their last meeting. The friendships are further complicated since players are often competing against one another for prizes and invitations. Almira Skripchenko is one of the most popular top players, so knows a lot about playing friends.

Almira was born in 1976 in Moldova, a country once part of the USSR, separated from Romania on the west by the Prut River and surrounded on the north, east and south by Ukraine. She is the daughter of a chess family. Her mother is a woman grandmaster and her father was a chess politician.

Almira Skripchenko and Hou Yifan
(photo by David Llada)

In 1994 at the Moscow Olympiad she began a romance with Joel Lautier, the top grandmaster from France. When they married in October 1997, Almira moved from her native Moldova to Paris. By then she was one of the top female players in the world. Besides chess, the couple shared an interest in the cinema, literature and philosophy. Both approached life with an intensity bordering on hedonistic. In explaining to me why he took up smoking for a few months, Joel described it as 'another pleasure' to add to an apparently already lengthy list. To Almira, who is interested in art and fashion, Paris is a cultural playground where, she says, 'I could spend most of my days in museums.' Both are adept at languages. Joel speaks fluent Russian, and Almira was quick to learn French. They have long since separated, but they remain friends.

Almira does not have the fierceness of Antoaneta, admitting that she suffered from a tendency to accept draws against players who were higher-ranked than she, even when her position was better. When she played against one of her many friends, the game often ended in a quick draw. It was difficult, she said 'to be comfortable with my aggression.' Almira's big breakthrough came at a tournament in 2000, in Italy, where she gained her first norm toward the grandmaster title. 'Instrumental to my improvement,' said Almira, 'was developing an aggression and being able to separate my conduct off the board from my conduct on the board.' She attributes the change in her attitude to the influence of philosopher Ayn Rand, whose fictional bestsellers *The Fountainhead* and *Atlas Shrugged* are built around the theme that individual development and creativity are primary over empathy. 'For instance, in the past I was sometimes peaceful, and would even feel pity for my opponent. Ayn Rand's books and her philosophy helped me to respect myself as an individual.' In Italy she refused every draw offer. Soon afterward in Macedonia, Almira won the 2001 European Women's Championship.

Almira Skripchenko and Antoaneta Stefanova were among more than one hundred female chess stars from thirty-one different European countries to arrive in Turkey for the 2003

European Women's Championship. The variety of individual personalities on the European women's chess circuit makes the annual European championships a much-anticipated contest. The competition was held in Kumburgaz, a suburb west of Istanbul. The players stayed in the Princess Marine, a four-star hotel housed in a luxurious pink high-rise, which looked entirely out of place on the desolate stretch of unmanicured highway. Among the favorites were the champions from the previous two years, Almira and Antoaneta, along with established players Alisa Galliamova from Russia and Pia Cramling from Sweden. The field was rounded out with a bevy of young stars, including Viktorija Čmilytė from Lithuania, Elisabeth Paehtz from Germany, and Tatiana and Nadezhda Kosintseva from Russia.

Alisa Galliamova had a spectacular start, winning 6.5 games out of her first seven against some of the strongest players in the tournament: Pia Cramling; Corina Peptan; and the Georgians, Ketevan Arakhamia and Nino Khurtsidze. Thirty-one-years old at the time, Galliamova is modest and devout, covering her head with a scarf while she plays. By the time I arrived to watch the ninth of thirteen scheduled rounds, Alisa was leading the event by two full points. According to the Swiss format, players with similar scores play one another. Galliamova was so far ahead that she could lock up the gold medal with a few draws against her final opponents. In round nine, she was able to draw with the black pieces against a frustrated Stefanova, moving her closer to the championship. But in the next rounds, she faltered. She played a quiet system with white against Viktorija Čmilytė, who responded with a violent attack and a victory. Tatiana Kosintseva, whose solid play and steady nerves had earned her the nickname 'The Rock,' ended Alisa's chances in the eleventh round with an elegant Queen sacrifice in an already dominant position. What appeared a few rounds before to be a clear-cut victory for Alisa Galliamova had turned into a complicated free-for-all with as many as four women contending for the title.

Going into the final round, Viktorija Čmiltyė and the teenager Tatiana Kosintseva were tied for first place. Since they had already faced each other earlier in the tournament (a draw), they had to be paired against different opponents. Čmiltyė drew her game against young Marie Sebag from France. Meanwhile, Kosintseva lost to Swedish Grandmaster Pia Cramling. This left Viktorija Čmiltyė tied with Pia Cramling. A sudden-death playoff would decide the winner of the prestigious title and the $12,000 purse. The first game ended in a draw, but Cramling won the second. It was over. Pia Cramling prevailed over all the young stars to become the 2003 European women's champ. The chess world, so used to victories by teen players, was stirred up by the success of Cramling, who two months before had turned forty. It was another example of baby luck. A year prior, Pia had a daughter. That toddler was Anna Cramling, now a chess player and star streamer.

Pia is a mild-mannered, slight woman with ash-blond hair. She began her chess career in the 1980s, playing mostly in mixed events. Winning a chess clock in a school tournament at the age of thirteen convinced her that she was destined to master the game. Pia's goal was to become a respected player among men and women, not to become a women's champion. In fact, there is no women's championship in Sweden. She earned the grandmaster title in 1992, a monumental achievement that received little attention in light of the even more impressive feats of the Polgar sisters. Pia started to play in more women's tournaments as more women earned the grandmaster title, explaining, 'I used to play in very few women's tournaments, but now the level has increased and it is much more interesting.' It took time for Pia to find her top form. 'I used to have a lot of problems playing against women. I got so tense, like I had to prove something.'

Pia does not think of herself as a celebrity. As a teenager, she became annoyed when reporting results was not enough for the Swedish newspapers, who also expected to interview her regularly. 'I wanted to be left alone to play chess.' Many of the top women chess players share this distaste for publicity. Romanian champion Corina Peptan says, 'Fame takes away from freedom. Suddenly you are not a person anymore but a brand, like McDonald's. It is very hard to feel free if people are looking and pointing at you all the time.'

Antoaneta believes that 'chess needs promoting,' and she wants to do her part, but has mixed feelings on the personal consequences of fame. Antoaneta was a guest on the most popular talk show in Bulgaria, which has an audience of two million viewers. After the show aired, she encountered a lot of attention from strangers on the street, which she thought was 'funny at first, but then it started to get annoying. I couldn't walk down the street without someone stopping me. Luckily, people in Bulgaria have very short memories, so the attention only lasted a short while.'

The tendency of the media to dwell on the accomplishments of young people is exaggerated in the world of women's chess, where young and attractive women have been so successful. Cathy Forbes remarks, 'To put it humorously, women need the right to get old.' When I asked Antoaneta about the way the press tends to concentrate on beautiful female chess players, she replied, 'What do you expect from the press? If you're going to beat Kasparov, then you can be anyone, but if you want attention and you can't beat Kasparov, you'd better be young and beautiful.'

Notably absent at that particular European Women's Championship was Russian star Alexandra Kosteniuk, who was finishing her high-school exams in Moscow. Kosteniuk, the tenth woman ever to become a grandmaster, has been a fixture in the top female players in the world since her teens. She was also way ahead of her time in her promotional activities, predicting social media trends over a decade before Instagram and Twitch were born.

I first met Alexandra at the 1996 World Youth Festival in Menorca, Spain, when she was twelve years old. Alexandra often came around to visit our mutual friend, Irina Krush, who was also playing for the US in the Under-14 section. Alexandra struck me as a tomboy when I saw her playing blitz with spunk against boys. I remember watching one game where she slammed down her Rook, in a quiet – yet powerful – move, played so instinctively that it could only have come from intense positional training. Alexandra learned the rules of chess at five, when her parents gifted her a chess set for her birthday. Her father, Konstantin, a professional chess coach, trained her methodically. Alexandra loved the training so much that during a vacation to the country all she wanted was 'to go home and study chess with my dad!' The family had little money so Alexandra, and her younger sister Oxana, gambled on casual chess games to fund chess trips.[1] Oxana would recruit opponents and Alexandra would beat them. 'Since that time, I have been very careful with money, because I knew what it was worth.'

Alexandra's competitive streak and talent, combined with intensive training, quickly paid off. In Spain, she won her second World Youth Championship. At fourteen, Kosteniuk earned the woman grandmaster title. At fifteen, she became an international master among all genders. The most shocking success came in the 2001 World Championships, held in Moscow at the Kremlin. She nearly snagged the Women's World Championship crown, making it to the final, only losing against Chinese player Zhu Chen. I played Kosteniuk in the first round of that knockout. Both of the games in our mini-match were in wild, wide open variations of my favorite opening, the Sicilian. But Kosteniuk was ruthless, and beat me twice in my own game.

Alexandra was precocious beyond chess. At just sixteen, she posed in heavy make-up and a tight black dress with black-and-white checkered belt and choker for a photo series sponsored by FIDE. She was wearing the new so-called 'chess uniform'. (Such a costume was never used in official tournament play, and there was no men's uniform.) Alexandra jumped at the opportunity to model. As a preteen, she told me how she used to mail her photos to model-of-the-year competitions, but never received a response. Those early FIDE photos are overtly sexy as Alexandra looks at the camera with pouty stares. Alexandra later said, 'They're not my favorites . . . I was wearing too much make-up.'

Alexandra's style developed along with her chess level. In 2002, in her hometown of Moscow, a photo of her wearing a pale blue evening gown while playing chess on her laptop was plastered all over city billboards in advertisements for the electronics company LG. 'It was a strange thing,' she later recalled, 'to be walking through Moscow and see the trolley rolling by with my own smiling face on them.' Kosteniuk appeared in Russian *Vogue*, *Newsweek*, and *Elle Girl*; and in America, she has been interviewed on CNN and in *Time* magazine. She was also sponsored by Balmain watches.

Alexandra tells me that she does not have a personal style, and the thing she likes about fashion and modeling is that for each photo session 'a completely different look is achieved.' Her favorite shoot was for the December 2002 edition of Russian *Vogue*, in which she posed in Paris for fashion photographer Zhenia Minkovich in five different high-fashion outfits. Alexandra is pictured outdoors wearing a low-cut black couture dress and black leather boots with stiletto heels, her hair blowing. In another, Alexandra strolls down an indoor mall wearing a white dress, a brown suede belt, and brown cowboy boots. 'Unfortunately,' she said, 'I did not get to keep any of the clothes.'

In the noughties, Kosteniuk's website, which journalist Taylor Kingston called 'From Russia With Hype', was both provocative and prescient, functioning as a kind of proto-Instagram. It included extensive catalogs of Alexandra's photo shoots, including very sexualized images, with simple, descriptive captions.* A photo of Alexandra in a pink thong bikini is labeled simply, 'Alexandra is now in Miami!' or 'Alexandra is running toward the beach . . . and jumping in anticipation!' Another showed Alexandra naked from the waist up, with a digital Post-It covering both her breasts. Accompanying text reads, 'This picture is too sexy for the website.' She sold a collection of exclusive, high resolution photos called *Beauty and Chess*. Visitors to the site were urged to 'Buy it! Do a good action today!' A portion of the profits went to a fund to promote chess for children all over the world. Alexandra was firing on all promotional files: a sex bomb, a champion and a philanthropist.

Her books, *How I Became a GM at Age 14* and *Diary of a Chess Queen*, were originally written in Russian, and then translated into Spanish and English. She also sold photos and books with autographs, and as for inscriptions, she insisted on 'reasonable requests only'. One public school chess coach asked for a picture for a gallery of female chess stars in her classroom, and Alex sent an autographed one free of charge. It was a sultry shot of her in a bathing suit. Kind though the

---

* In an earlier edition of this book, I poked fun at these captions. Now they are another example of Kosteniuk's prescience, as they are quite similar to the now often mandatory alternative text for visually impaired website visitors.

gesture was, another (less-revealing) photo of Grandmaster Kosteniuk was downloaded, printed and posted on the wall.

In addition to her crowded schedule of photo shoots, chess tournaments and exhibitions, Alexandra also tried acting. She had a major role in the movie *Bless the Woman* by popular Russian director Stanislav Govorukhin. Alexandra is interested in performing in more movies, though she did not consider it challenging. 'It was too easy! I thought it was going to be so difficult because I'm always reading about actresses and actors who talk about how hard it is to act, and how long the hours are. Really, in comparison to chess, it was such a breeze.'

Kosteniuk reveled in her globetrotting, which she called a 'kaleidoscope of travel'. On one of her trips, to give an exhibition at a museum in Lausanne, Switzerland, she met Diego Garces, a Swiss-Colombian businessman and amateur chess player. According to her autobiography, *Diary of a Chess Queen*, Diego offered to show Alexandra and her family around the city, and encouraged them to send Alexandra to a British school to master English.

Alexandra Kosteniuk (photo by David Llada)

Two years later, on her eighteenth birthday, Diego proposed to Alexandra. She accepted, and they married later that year, in August 2002. Diego Garces was over two decades older than Alexandra.

I was curious about Alexandra's thoughts on her image and wondered if she was self-conscious about some aspects of her campaign. I got my chance to find out in a National Scholastic Championship in Chicago, where I was coaching IS 318, a national junior-high chess champion team from Brooklyn. Alexandra was there giving a simultaneous exhibition and a book-signing. I was eager to satisfy my curiosity about how she really felt about being a chess star/sex symbol. Assuming that Alexandra was charging the organizers exorbitant sums for her appearance, I was intrigued but also a little jealous, since a number of competent American players (myself, for instance) could make appearances too.

I watched Alexandra give a simultaneous exhibition to thirty children. She had to run around and defeat them all within a few hours. Susan Polgar was also giving an exhibition. I was surprised to see that Alexandra was wearing three-inch heels, but had to laugh when I noticed Susan wearing similar shoes. Apparently Susan and Alexandra were not aware of former US Women Champion Gisela Gresser's advice to women giving simultaneous exhibitions: 'Bring courage and a sensible pair of shoes!'

In chatting with an organizer, I found out that Alexandra was not only giving the simultaneous for free, she was paying for her own hotel room in addition to giving out prizes to the children. It was becoming clear to me that there was much more to Alexandra's campaign than money. Anxious to arrange some private time with her, I dropped by when she was signing *How I Became a GM at Age 14*. Alexandra was gracious and radiant, autographing books and chatting with her fans in the long line of young girls, doting parents, teenage boys and older men. When the crowd thinned out, I asked if she wanted to meet and maybe play a few blitz games later in the evening. She was enthusiastic, assuring me that although she had a dinner appointment, she would definitely keep our engagement: 'When I say yes, I mean yes!' Later that night, I came to her room and was greeted by Alexandra and Diego, her husband/manager.

Diego was propped up on the king-size bed, half watching an action movie, occasionally glancing at our blitz games, and mostly working away on Alexandra's website. He is the sole web designer, pointing out that 'it only takes a few months to learn how to do this properly.' Alexandra glowed with pride over her husband's computer prowess. When I asked her how much input she had into the website, she told me very little. 'Sometimes Alexandra does not agree with some of the photos I post there,' Diego teases her, 'like they are too sexy. For example the one on the beach. Alexandra must have thought her stomach looked big in it,' Diego said, as if Alexandra could not possibly doubt the appropriateness of a bikini-thong shot, and any objection she has must surely arise from vanity. When disagreements arose, Alexandra says, Diego always wins her over to his side. 'I listen to his thoughts on publicity and politics, and I always agree with him.' Diego, who is a strong player but much lower rated than Alexandra, says, 'I trust Sasha's chess evaluations.'[2]

In the first blitz game with Alexandra, I used one of my favorite openings for black, the Dragon, a risky set-up in which the pawn structure supposedly resembles a dragon. Midway through I became aware of how much I wanted to win. I may have come to her room primarily out of curiosity, but when the clocks started, I was a chess player. I outplayed her in the endgame and won a pawn. Alexandra fought back. She checked me, I moved my King to the only available square, and she checked me again, forcing me to return my King to its previous square. It was perpetual check, one of the paths to a draw. Afterward, she showed me a winning line I had missed. By now, the idea of winning the blitz match had completely seduced me. In the second game, I played a tricky, aggressive line, hoping to catch her off-guard and steal a quick point. It seemed as though it might work. Alexandra then spent nearly two minutes on three or four moves – a luxurious allotment for a five-minute game. She finally played the late World Champion Mikhail Tal's recommendation, which brought her victory. She visibly relaxed as we continued to speak about her career.

In their energetic lifestyle I sense Alexandra's and Diego's passion is more for the fame, fun and glamour than for the money: for shopping in Paris, lounging in Miami, having a quick vacation in Venice, and doing business in Moscow. Of course, money is required for such a lifestyle, but it seems merely the means for the jet-setting excitement that is the real source of pleasure for the couple. 'We always have a plane ticket in our front pockets,' says Diego. 'I can't stand being in the same place for too long,' Alexandra concurs. 'These days Alexandra gets about a hundred e-mails a day, and we try to answer each and every one of them.' Compared with those chess players who can't be bothered to show up for press conferences, Alexandra and Diego were refreshing in their enthusiastic quest for fame.

Alexandra and Diego don't comprehend feminist criticism of their campaign. When I asked Alexandra about her views on feminism, she tells me, 'I smile when I hear about feminism. I don't understand what feminists are fighting for now. Perhaps this was necessary some time ago.' Men's magazines, including *Penthouse* and *Playboy*, contact Alexandra, but Diego says, 'We will not allow them to photograph Alexandra, but they are free to choose any photograph from the site.' The two saw no problem in offering interviews or pictures to erotic magazines. 'What's the problem? The questions they ask are the same as usual.'

The 'Anna Kournikova of chess' was a journalist's moniker for Kosteniuk that quickly stuck. Both Kosteniuk and the Russian tennis star were central to debates about sexualization and lookism in their respective fields. Anna Kournikova appeared on the cover of *Sports Illustrated* in June 2000, causing heated criticism from feminists who pointed out that male athletes are not 'stuffed into tight-fitting uniforms that display their genitalia.' At first Kosteniuk did not mind the comparison to the tennis star, but as the number of championships Kosteniuk won grew, while Kournikova retired, it ceased to make much sense.

Alexandra is adept at combining her fame with serious chess play. She is a strong grandmaster with a peak rating approaching 2600. When she is not in a tournament, she trains for up to six hours a day. At chess tournaments she dresses professionally. She often wears thick glasses and expensive-looking business suits, dressed as if she is about to have a power lunch. In Alexandra's position, she will garner criticism no matter what she does. If she wore skimpy outfits, she would be criticized for dressing unprofessionally. People chided her for appearing so plain at tournaments and at the same time fancying herself as the Anna Kournikova of chess. I've heard people remark that Alexandra 'is no Kournikova.' Alexandra says: 'I am clever, so I can play chess; and I am not so ugly, so I can model.'[3] When I ask her if it is difficult to concentrate on chess with all her publicity, she denies a conflict, explaining that when she is playing chess, she is completely focused on the game.

Alexandra believes that 'chess deserves better' but that chess players tend to talk about promoting the game without doing anything. According to Kosteniuk, her initiatives have not been embraced by most chess players. She told me at the time, 'I have no female friends in chess anymore. They are all so jealous of me. I show people my photos and they say things like "Wow, it's amazing what photography, lighting, and make-up can do," as if the quality of the photos has nothing to do with my personality or style.' Alexandra says that she hears what others say behind her back, but no one in the chess world is brave enough to criticize her to her face: 'Not one person has ever said something straight to me.'

The Russian superstar would soon have even more for people to envy. In 2007, her daughter, Francesca Maria, was born. A year later Alexandra went to Nalchik, Russia to play in the 2008 Women's World Championship. The tournament was structured as a sixty-four-player knockout, and Alexandra tore through all her competitors, including several higher-rated foes, like Pia Cramling and Tatiana Kosintseva. In the final, she faced Chinese prodigy Hou Yifan. Kosteniuk won the first game with black, building a stronger position in a closed Ruy Lopez, and unleashing tactics only when it was too late for her fourteen-year-old opponent to defend. This game turned out to be decisive as she won the match by half a point. Kosteniuk became the twelfth Women's World Champion and the first Russian to claim the title since Bykova.* 'I was deliriously happy,' she later wrote, 'I had spent my whole life working toward this moment – and now, just like a fairy tale, it had all come true.'

Kosteniuk later remarried, to strong Russian Grandmaster Pavel Tregubov. She became more popular in the world of women's chess, finding a best friend in Almira Skripchenko. Her promotional activities, including bilingual streams as the Chess Queen on Twitch, are still active, but more subdued.

---

* Maia Chiburdanidze and Nona Gaprindashvili won World Championships under the Soviet flag but were Georgian by birth and nationality.

She still has that flair for fashion and its intersection with chess. At one event, I saw her wearing a black bracelet with customizable spikes shaped like chess pieces. She tipped me off on where to get it, and I ordered it immediately, choosing knights as the knives.

Alexandra was way ahead of her time, as social media, and especially Instagram, accelerated the pressure for female chess players to present themselves as both stunning and smart. Rather than allowing women the easy out of just playing up their looks, it can make many work even harder. In addition to preparing opening variations, there is pressure to do your hair and make-up, and wear a photogenic outfit.

I encountered this pressure when I started playing poker. An even more superficial world than chess, and just as male-dominated, most of the top female players were both brilliant and stunning. I felt totally out of place with my frizzy brown hair, bare face and flabby arms. Over the subsequent years, I spent a lot of time and money on my image to fit in. I'm sad to admit that it was probably worth it. In chess, poker and media, the number of invitations and connections I made after I started caring more about my appearance increased.

I now have a genuine interest in make-up, fitness and fashion, and see some of my previous discounting of it as a form of internalized misogyny that devalued traditionally feminine activities. And yet, what happens when the interest isn't genuine? When social media networks and their mysterious algorithms shape interests, rather than allowing users to shape their own images, dangerous trends emerge. For example, there is a strong correlation between increasing rates of depression and anxiety in young girls and social media usage.[*]

---

[*] There is less evidence that there is causation between depression, anxiety and social media use.

It's a lost cause to convince regular people, who aren't change-makers in tech, to stop caring about looks, beauty and hot selfies. The way forward, in my view, is to resist powerful advertising and online algorithms by limiting time on social media, or even opting out entirely. That's not always possible. For instance, in my career, I find it difficult to reject social media's opportunities for connection and amplification. So I try to focus and boost the things I value. In the attention economy, we are drawn to specific types of images. And they are too rarely chess positions or brilliant observations. If the algorithm doesn't feed you what you need, either leave, or find what truly nourishes you.

While the fixation on women's looks in chess is as intense as ever, it used to be even more shameless. ChessBase.com, the most popular chess news source in the noughties, with over 50,000 daily visitors, has always covered the top tournaments in the world. There also used to be a very heavy emphasis on photo galleries of female chess players. One old headline, 'Bikini chess championship in Ukraine', featured 'dazzling pictures of young women GMs and IMs in beachside circumstances.' In another news item, ChessBase profiled a teenage Siberian player, Ksenya Rybenko. Her master rating of 2260 FIDE was never mentioned in the report because her 'vital statistics' were determined to be her measurements, weight and height, which were duly noted. The picture gallery included a photo of Ksenya holding a gun and another of her lounging on a Thai beach in a bikini.

In the most pornographic example, ChessBase reproduced an interview with chess player Maria Manakova, who called herself a 'sex specialist' and posed nearly nude for the cover of a Russian tabloid magazine, *Speed*. 'I love to eat Bishops', reads the headline. This resulted in a spate of interviews, one of which, titled 'Sex and Chess', with questions about whether or not Maria travels with her husband so she can have sex during tournaments, and whether there are any 'real men' among the top male players. Another burning inquiry was, 'A chess game usually lasts for four hours or more – is there enough time for sex?' Maria's responses included: 'A woman should always be a woman,' 'Maybe I'm a bit perverted,' and 'We are not so strong as men, so we should cash in on our beauty, don't you agree?'

In an interview with a world-class grandmaster from Russia, Vladislav Tkachiev, ChessBase found a way to display its self-proclaimed 'sleaze alert'. Vlad has movie-star good looks and is proud of his bon-vivant lifestyle, including a love for alcohol and women. The interview ends with a discussion of the best-looking girls in chess, and with what ChessBase founder Frederic Friedel calls a 'humorously sexist note.'

> Among the girls who could compete for the beauty contest title are Kosteniuk, of course, and then the big favorites are [Dana] Reizniece,* a Latvian player who is a very spectacular woman, and Shirov's wife, Viktorija Čmilytė. Another big favorite is Regina Pokorna, who is a child-woman, an eternal girl. The reason there are so many beautiful women playing chess these days is because the game has become faster and faster. As Tal said, it was always too difficult for women to play chess because during the games they are forced to keep silent. Now the games are much quicker and it has become easier to shut up during the games [laughs uproariously].

Disclaiming his interview as 'humorously sexist' is typical. The presentations are done in such a light-hearted way that any critics are likely to be called 'Feminazis' – moral crusaders out to win an argument, while stunting the development of chess.

The spotlight moved offline in a 2002 match between

---

* Dana Reizniece is now FIDE's Managing Director.

Kosteniuk and German Elisabeth Paehtz held in Mainz, Germany. Officially the match between Elisabeth and Alexandra was the 'Duel of the Graces' but it was unofficially referred to as 'The Duel of the Cuties'. Most important to the press were the looks and sex appeal of the young players. If Kosteniuk is the pop star of chess, Paehtz is a rock star. She likes to go out, knows all the gossip, and dresses in funky outfits, including a signature black-leather hat pulled over her cropped red hair. Often blunt to the point of hilarity, she once complained to me about how her loose tongue got her into trouble with journalists: 'They made me look like an arrogant girl who parties all the time and only beats grandmasters who are drunk!'

The hairstyles and outfits of the attractive teens were scrutinized round by round, while their actual play was often dealt with as a sidebar – a shame considering how thrilling the games were. Both Kosteniuk and Paehtz have extremely aggressive chess styles and are most comfortable in wide-open games with lots of tactics, and in each round of the match, both girls played as if they might never get another chance to play a chess game. Both exchanged blows, each winning three games. The remaining two games were exciting draws. Since the match was tied, a blitz play-off determined the winner, who turned out to be Kosteniuk. A disappointed Elisabeth was unprepared for the surge of media attention the match got. She later complained to me that reporters would try to get her to say mean things about Alexandra to report in the papers the next day. In one instance, when Paehtz was asked what she thought of Alexandra's glamour photographs, she snapped, 'Anyone can look good with that much make-up.' Concurrent with the Kosteniuk–Paehtz match was a match between FIDE world champions Ruslan Ponomariov and Viswanathan Anand. This match was advertised as a serious match between grandmasters in which Ponomariov was never once asked what he thought of Anand's outfit.

The media frenzy over the Kosteniuk–Paehtz match is typical of the atmosphere at any chess tournament in which attractive females participate. Throughout the chess world, chatter about the looks of the top women players is constant, usually complimentary, but sometimes nasty and invariably inappropriate. Strong moderators on sites like Chess.com and Twitch have abated this in recent years, though the problem still festers underneath the surface.

Even the best female player in the world is vulnerable to criticism: one grandmaster criticized changes in Judit Polgar's figure, using gross gestures and language. Polgar is a much stronger player than he, and his comments sounded as though they were meant to put Judit in her place. I've personally been called every mean name under the sun, from 'Farmer's Body' to 'The Voice of Satan'. The mixed bags of insults and compliments can be the toughest to take, like one comment that described me as 'pretty, smart, but fat.' The 'but fat' caused me to scream, 'I'm not fat,' and then to ask, 'but so what if I were?' In an article titled 'Why I Chose to Look Ugly, and the Reasoning Behind it', Susan Polgar revealed that when she was a young chess star she 'consciously tried to look as plain and unattractive as possible.'[4] She wanted to avoid being harassed and hit on. And she did not have the money for expensive clothes and make-up anyway. 'Some male chess players cannot take NO for an answer, especially when they had too much to drink. Some tried to physically and sexually assault me.'

Excessive attention to the looks of female players, especially girls, can bleed into much more nefarious abuse and harassment. It normalizes reducing girls and women to their body parts. Girls may experience a disproportionate amount of abuse in the chess world, but chess players of all genders are vulnerable to misconduct. Some dangers are specifically intense in chess, considering the one-on-one nature of most chess lessons, which are often held in hotels at tournaments.

As a teenager I learned about the 'rule of four' in Rook endgames. That states that a Rook needs to be four files away to perpetually attack a King without worry. But the rule of three is even more important. That's a guideline that US Chess adopted in 2019, based on work done by the US Tennis Association and the US Center for Safe Sport, that no adult should be alone in a room with one child: there should always be at least three people to reduce the chances of abuse.

The debate on sexualization and chess reached a shocking peak in October 2021, when FIDE announced a new sponsor for women in chess: Motiva, a company that sells breast implants. FIDE argued that the sponsor would raise awareness for reconstructive surgery, as well as for breast cancer awareness month.

I think women's chess can get better sponsors, and don't think this one is worth the money. My opinion hardened after reading accounts from women who were grossly offended by the partnership.[5] One said, 'We chess women are already subject to endless comments about our appearance.' Another recounted her painful memories of having her breasts scrutinized at chess tournaments, as young as thirteen years old. 'I wore a new shirt to a club one day, and was feeling good about myself because it was a style I didn't usually wear; this changed when a man in his sixties came up to me when I was sitting with my friend, and said, "you're looking really good in that shirt," with a disgusting smile, as he looked at my chest.' I started hearing comments about my own breasts at a similar age. I heard the phrase 'rack' for the first time, about myself, at a chess camp when I was thirteen. Though some of these comments were from classmates of a similar age, others were from much older male professionals.

Breast implants aren't categorically bad, but the last thing chess needs is even more attention on women's bodies and looks. To move women forward in the game, we need to focus more on their minds and moves, not their boobs.

Grandmaster Susan Polgar points out: 'We all have different limits as to how far it is acceptable to promote chess through feminine beauty.' Promoting attractive chess players is not in itself objectionable. After all, much of Garry Kasparov's fame in the mainstream press is because of his confident swagger, good looks, and luminous energy. Magnus Carlsen, who became World Champion in 2013, is especially photogenic, and his chiseled jaw line was featured in advertisements for the fashion company G-Star Raw. However, there is a line with male players that is not crossed. Journalists and fans don't go around commenting on the size of Kasparov's cock. In the chess world, the sexuality of the top male players is private and implied, while discussion of a woman's sexuality is open to all.

Checkmate Around the World

'Some people call me "bitch" for playing with boys all the time. But it's the only way I can get proper training; so they can call me names until they get tired – they always do.'

Linda Nangwale, chess champion from Zambia

I am in Budapest, Hungary, losing game after game in the August 2003 edition of the monthly 'First Saturday' tournaments. I came in the hopes of earning my third norm toward the international master title. My living conditions are more suitable to socializing than competing against seasoned grandmasters. I am staying in a dingy hostel with college students on their summer breaks and Japanese teenagers on whirlwind tours of Europe. All-night revelers awaken me at all hours. I decide that since I can't sleep, I might as well join the fun.

I've become friends with a waiter in a nearby restaurant called Noa, which serves fancy salads and sandwiches to well-heeled tourists and stylish Europeans. In Hungary, chess is popular and the best players are national heroes, so when my waiter, Arpi, started talking with me, I mentioned that I was here for a chess tournament, and also to conduct some interviews. Arpi immediately began to gossip about the two top players in Hungary, Judit Polgar and Peter Leko. Arpi is tall and blond and has movie-star good looks. I can't help but think that this wild and charismatic twenty-four-year-old would be successful – even famous – if he lived in more prosperous circumstances. In Budapest he seems exhausted from working double shifts and he expresses his disquiet by self-destructing. When we go out, he tends to order a shot of tequila, a beer, and a double espresso. In between gulps of this fatal combination he puffs one cigarette after another. Arpi yearns to live in North America. He seems jaded by the sentiment that his beloved Budapest is irreparably corrupt. While waiting tables at a breakneck pace, he points out some muscled, tattooed men, who are sipping beers at a nearby table. Arpi whispers, 'They are part of the mafia that protects this place – they never pay for anything.'

Corruption can afflict chess tournaments too, especially when resources are limited. I had heard rumors that unscrupulous and desperate professionals sometimes buy the coveted final IM and GM norms, which will secure invitations and respect for them. Opponents with nothing special to gain from a win are sometimes willing to accept a fee to lose on purpose. When some of my American chess friends heard I was going to Budapest, one advised me not to play in the tournament because of its poor reputation, while another joked: 'Make sure to bring enough cash to buy your last IM norm.'

When in Budapest, I never once encountered anyone being offered the opportunity to buy or sell norms and suspect that it must have been the crooked practices of just a few chess players that gave rise to the myth that Budapest is a 'norm factory'. Several chess players from Iceland, the United States and Russia told me stories of another kind of Hungarian swindle. An Icelandic chess master was drunk at a bar when a beautiful Hungarian girl asked if he would buy her some champagne. He obliged. Thirty minutes later, he was shocked to find that the bill came to $500. When he explained that he didn't have the cash on hand, a few friendly members of the mafia escorted him to an ATM machine. An American chess player, who had fallen for a similar con, tried calling the police. They laughed and told him, 'There is nothing to be done.' Arpi just shook his head knowingly when I told him about the refusal of the police to intervene. 'To get any kind of justice here,' he said, 'you have to go back to the mafia.'

Hoang Thanh Trang (photo by Przemysław Jahr)

Budapest is a prime destination for ambitious young players. It is close to major tournaments in the Czech Republic and Germany and not too far from Russia, the Netherlands, and Spain. Every month, world-class tournaments are held on the second floor of a nondescript building on Budapest's antique row, where the Budapest Chess Club is housed. Players from six continents regularly come to the spacious club with big windows and sturdy furniture to chase their final grandmaster and international master norms. For Vietnamese Hoang Thanh Trang (Trang is the given name), a former Asian Women's Champion (2000) and European Women's Champion (2013),

Budapest is an ideal place to live. Hoang Trang earned two grandmaster norms in First Saturday tournaments in 1999 and 2000, and also reached a rating near 2500. She expected the GM title to follow quickly. But her rating soon dropped and the final norm was elusive. It took her another seven years to meet the grandmaster requirements, becoming the twelfth woman ever to do so.

Trang and I meet at Europa, a café on a bustling street in Budapest. Wearing small glasses, the petite chess champion arrives dressed in a trendy jean jacket and maroon dress decorated with printed elephants, which her mother brought from Thailand. She cannot devote much time to shopping since she spends four to six hours a day studying chess, and another few hours on the administration of her family's two businesses, in chess training and trade. 'My mother works in commerce between Vietnam and Hungary, and she always knows how to pick good clothes for me.'

From a sumptuous selection, Trang selects a slice of cake with raspberries along with peach tea. I am on my third cup of coffee of the day, at which Trang marvels: 'Coffee has always been repellent to me, though I wish I liked it.'

Hoang Trang is reflective about the differences between us. About fifteen minutes after settling down across a white marble table from each other, Hoang Trang confesses that she is bewildered by my note-taking. Apparently, I had not made my intentions completely clear. I felt slightly guilty that she did not understand I was eager to grill her on her life and opinions for my book. She thought I just wanted to hang out. Trang explained that I look like I go out a lot, shop a lot, lounge in coffee shops, lifestyle choices that are special treats for her: 'Usually I am too serious to meet up casually with friends, but my boyfriend urged me to come meet you. He said, "Hang out with the American girl! Enjoy yourself!"'

Hoang Trang met her first serious boyfriend when doing administrative work for her parents. A Vietnamese foreign-exchange student in architecture, who identified as an artist, Trang noted the differences between their perspectives on life: 'He is not as serious as I am. He only applies himself when he's really interested, in which case he will spend all day and night working. I, on the other hand, study chess every day, whether or not I feel inspired. He does what he wants to do, and I do what I need to do.' To Trang, being Vietnamese is as important to her identity as being a chess player. 'I need a boyfriend who is Vietnamese more than a chess player, because in any relationship, problems will arise. Being from the same culture makes them easier to overcome.'

The government supports chess in Vietnam. Trang describes a typical schedule for Vietnamese chess school as grueling. The morning begins at 6:00 a.m. with two hours of running, followed by eight hours of chess with a break for lunch. Trang thinks the system sometimes puts too much pressure on players, which can be detrimental to results. Her father, also her main coach, is more relaxed. 'My father understands that a chess player who is sitting down to play obviously wants to win.'

Trang's father, Hoang Minh Chuong, emphasizes the psychological aspects of the game. For a while, Trang experienced some difficulties playing against women. 'I realized at some point that my chess was suffering because when I played against male players I would work very hard, but against women players, even though I thought I was playing my best, deep down inside I thought that I should beat them pretty easily because I played so well against men. My father told me then that I have to add 100 points to a woman's rating in my mind when I play. I did this, and the problem was solved. Now I automatically respect women as serious, worthy opponents.'

Trang's career goals are as focused as her lifestyle. After earning the grandmaster title in 2007, Trang cast her eyes to the ultimate women's crown: 'A player of my level obviously dreams of being world champion. Without such high ambitions, I would not be where I am now.'

'I don't play as an Asian, or Vietnamese, or as a woman. I have my own personal style.' However, Trang describes her approach to chess as professional, and is baffled by the tendency of some players to drink and party after games: 'Asian players don't go out after the games. We stay at our hotel rooms, prepare for the games, and play. We take it more seriously, probably because of the government helping us.'

In Vietnam, which has a population close to 100 million, Hoang Trang is widely known. She has been elected one of the top ten sportspeople of the year six times. In 1998, when she became the Girls' World Champion, she was chosen as second sportsperson of the year, just behind a champion in wushu, a Chinese martial art. Whenever she returns home, customs officials stop her at the airport to inquire about her tournament schedule. She enjoys the recognition, but she assures me, 'I don't play chess with the goal of being famous.'

Living in centralized Hungary allows Hoang to compete with players from all over the world. In 2006, after winning a gold medal at the European Club Cup, she switched federations from Vietnam to Hungary. She thrives on the pressure of her career. Beneath her soft voice, small frame and polite manners is a character strong enough to withstand the demands to achieve from her country, her family, and from herself. 'When people around the world hear about Vietnam, they (often) hear about war or strife. It makes me proud to represent my country in a positive way.'

In Ecuador, recognition for Martha Fierro reached an unprecedented height. For three years in the late 1990s, her likeness, appearing in an advertisement for margarine, was plastered on buses all over the capital city, Quito. Ecuador is a small country on the west coast of South America, but for many years it claimed the strongest women's team on the continent, with Martha as its leader.

Although Martha grew up in Ecuador, with Spanish as her first language, she was born in Rhode Island, which allowed her automatic entry into the US and the opportunity to apply for citizenship. But Martha has never considered switching her allegiance. 'I have in Ecuador what I would never get in the United States: the love of the people.'

Martha has sparkling eyes and a warm smile. Charm seems to flow from her sing-song voice and graceful step. At tournaments she is always ready to laugh and talk with anyone from a grandmaster to a young novice. When I was just thirteen years old, I played in a tournament in Washington, DC, that Martha also attended. I admired Martha straight away. At the time I was just starting to take chess seriously and was competing in one of the lower boards of the tournament. I was excited when Martha, a master, came from the top boards to check out my games. Between rounds, she introduced herself to me and suggested improvements for my game. She told me stories about her international success and gossiped about the best players in the world. Martha couldn't get enough of the game. After rounds, she could usually be found playing casual blitz games with friends. She would tease her male opponents relentlessly. 'Oh no, you're going to lose to a girl! Has that ever happened to you before?' or announce, 'Time to attack!' before pounding down an aggressive move.

Martha Fierro (photo by Jennifer Shahade)

Martha did not always love chess so much. When she learned the moves from her mother as a thirteen-year-old, she was not so enthusiastic. But she liked to travel, and enjoyed the attention she got as one of just a few female players. After playing in more tournaments, she says, 'I began to become addicted to the game itself. I would play every day from six p.m. until one a.m. All I wanted was to win the Ecuadorian National Women's Championship.' She reached that goal in 1992, and went on to win the national title every year for the next decade.

In 1994 Martha began to represent Ecuador for the Pan-American Championships in which players from all over

North, Central and South America participate. She won the event and repeated the feat for the next four years. By the fifth time, Martha was becoming blasé about winning the title. This feeling was in direct contrast with that of her Ecuadorian fans, who hailed her as a heroine. The media hounded her for interviews, and fans clamored for autographs. 'For me it did not seem hard to win the Pan-American Championship. Though I was happy to give autographs to my fans in Ecuador, I felt guilty. Maybe if I won the World Championship I would feel as though I deserved all the attention.'

Martha was more proud of her international accomplishments. She won a silver medal for her individual performance at the 1996 Olympiad and became a WGM, one of only three women in South America to hold the title at the time. Martha was invited to an elegant banquet in her hometown of Guayaquil, a port city, the second most populous in Ecuador after capital, Quito. The Ecuadorian political and sporting elite was all there to determine the best sportspeople of 1997. Martha was delighted just to be invited, but was stunned when she was called to the stage to receive the award as number-one sportsperson of the year, ahead of Jefferson Perez, the 1996 Olympic gold-medalist in race-walking. Martha recalls, 'That evening was one of the highlights of my life. I was so happy when I went up to the podium, I could barely remember the names of the people I had to thank.'

Her new recognition resulted in sponsorship from the telephone company Bell South, which paid for her airline tickets and gave her a monthly stipend. A bank also sponsored her. With firm financial backing, Martha was able to travel around the world, playing in tournament after tournament.

Martha has a close friendship with Antoaneta Stefanova, with whom she shares a jet-setting lifestyle. Martha managed to take her games seriously while flitting around the tournament hall, keeping track of where the party was each night. Martha enjoyed the nightlife even more abroad than in Ecuador, where she was often recognized, even in the darkest clubs. 'And then they ask me: "Why aren't you studying chess?"'

'I play better when I'm happy. Going out and having a good time before the game and sleeping till the round time is far better than staying up all night worrying about the openings.' Martha claimed that she often won her best games after staying out late. In the 1996 Olympiad in Yerevan, Armenia, where Martha won a silver medal, she had a good time despite the Spartan conditions. 'The food was awful, the buildings were dark,' Martha said. Armenia, in the midst of political turmoil at the time, held its presidential elections during the Chess Olympiad. Protestors tried to storm the main square of Yerevan because of an irregularity in the counting of the votes. Tanks, which had been on display for Independence Day festivities, were used to block off the protestors. During the chaos, hotel guests were barred from the streets.

On that particular night, Martha Fierro and Antoaneta Stefanova, tired of the daily fare of bland meat at their assigned hotel, had gone out to dine at a better hotel. Because of the turmoil they found themselves locked inside: 'We only brought enough money to eat so we had to spend the night in the lobby. We had no idea what was going on outside. It was scary. But there was a bar so at least we had something to do.' The next day Martha won her game and went on to earn a silver medal.

In spite of Martha's frequent assertions that her freewheeling lifestyle has helped her chess, I get the sense that she herself is not entirely convinced. There were times in her life, says Martha, that she regrets not taking the game even more seriously. 'In Ecuador we call the years between seventeen and twenty-one the donkey (*el burro*) years, where young people go crazy. At this time (in the late nineties) I had so much support, I sometimes wish I had tried harder.' When I remind Martha of her claims that partying often improves her performance, she said, 'Well, maybe I did need to go out. I never learned to get that balance, where I could go out and prepare well.'

Martha admires Antoaneta's ability to balance the demands of having fun and preparing. 'If Antoaneta and I go out all night dancing, she will still be at her computer in the morning, even with dark circles under her eyes, preparing for the game.' When I ask Martha how good she might have become had she studied more, she gets philosophical: 'Who knows if I would have been in the (very*) top women players in the world? But at least if I had worked I would have a chance. Without working, there is no chance.'

Her fame in Ecuador brings with it pressure. Martha tells me that one of the reasons her chess waned for a few years was the overwhelming feeling that her fans in Ecuador would accept no less than first place. In 2001, at the age of twenty-four, she moved to Charlotte, North Carolina, where she taught chess to children for two years. Even there, she was recognized by one of the only Ecuadorian families living in Charlotte.

It didn't take long for Martha to become bored with Charlotte, where the Hispanic population is small, the nightlife limited. At the time, the opportunities to play top-level chess were non-existent. Since then, chess all over America has boomed, and Charlotte in particular boasts one of the top chess clubs and tournament series in the world.

Martha also lived in New York City, where her grandparents also lived, for several years. She taught, and often played in

---

* Martha did become an International Master (2005), a gender neutral title, and is perennially among the top 100 female players in the world. She also holds the International Organizer (2015) title.

the New York Masters, a weekly event held at the historic Marshall Chess Club, founded by my brother, Greg.* Martha has a voracious appetite for the game. Between tournament rounds she will play blitz games, and analyze late into the night. Greg, the founder of many projects to promote chess in America, wishes more women played. He finds Martha's attitude toward the game refreshing: 'Martha is so straightforward in her love for the game.'

Martha's father, Miguel, supported her chess wholeheartedly in the beginning, paying for her tournament expenses before she found a sponsor. Miguel was brought up in a working-class family, one of seventeen children. When attending university, he met Martha's mother, also called Martha, who was from a wealthy family and has an infectious personality that has clearly influenced the younger Martha. His burgeoning success as a naval engineer along with his wife's inheritance afforded the whole family a comfortable lifestyle. Unable to underestimate the importance of money, he ultimately wants Martha to have a career more lucrative than chess. Though her family is proud of her fame and success in chess, Martha points out, 'To be famous is not the same as to be secure financially. People in Ecuador assume that because I am always in the press, I am making a great living all the time.'

Although Martha has a strong allegiance to Ecuador, ultimately settling in her home country, she acknowledged the problems there, such as racism. Martha described her own skin as 'very light for Ecuador' and said that at the time, light-skinned models were usually used in Ecuadorian fashion magazines and advertisements. Martha acknowledged her privilege straightforwardly as she describes to me the fancy private

---

* Greg is also the founder of the United States Chess School and the commissioner of the PRO Chess League.

school she attended in her hometown, Guayaquil. Martha is a poster woman for Ecuador, but she is not representative of its average Ecuadorian. Because Martha is well-off and famous, she partially escapes rigid gender roles (an expectation to marry young and raise a family), which restrict many Ecuadorian women. Still, interviewers chide her about her non-traditional lifestyle. In one Ecuadorian radio show, the hosts insisted on discussing her love life: 'They even told me, "You better promise me you'll be married by age thirty!"' Martha, twenty-six at the time, was caught off guard: 'What could I do but laugh and agree?'

For Ecuadorians who are not as renowned or mobile as Martha, becoming an international chess player is harder. Martha's friend and Ecuadorian teammate, Evelyn Moncayo, won the World Girls' Under-10 Championship in Wisconsin in 1990. Despite this immense show of talent, Evelyn received few opportunities to compete internationally. Raised by a single mother (her father passed away when she was ten), her family could not afford to send her to tournaments, and Evelyn never managed to attract a regular sponsor or coach. Evelyn explained to me that Ecuadorian culture does not mesh well with her goals as an international chess star. 'In Ecuador women usually get married by twenty-three or twenty-four. After twenty-six, if you are not married, it is a problem. Before you get married, you should not be out after ten p.m. For a while, it was really difficult, because if I wanted to play in a tournament in a neighboring city or stay at the chess club until late, it was not possible. Now my parents are more accepting. But there is no struggle for boys who want to go to a tournament in a city far away. Their parents will say, "No problem!"'

Nadya Ortiz, born in Colombia, also had logistical quandaries in pursuing her chess dreams. Nadya was born in Ibagué, a city near Bogota. She explained to me the system of stratification in her country. Every family is assigned a number from 1 to 7, based on their income-level. Nadya was in group 1, the poorest group, along with approximately 16% of the Colombian population. Though Nadya thinks the system was created with good intentions, to streamline taxation and social services, it's also had a nefarious effect of making people in lower groups feel 'less than'.

Nadya's father taught her chess at six years old, and she picked up the game quickly, and started to get invited to represent her national team. The international invites were prestigious but expensive and she had to raise money for tickets. Her family allowed her to travel around the world by herself, because it was cost-prohibitive for them all to go. Her rating skyrocketed, and she became the first Women's Grandmaster ever in Colombia. Most importantly, her chess skills attracted the attention of American college recruiters. She went to University of Texas at Brownsville and later Purdue on full scholarships, where she studied computer programming, ultimately becoming a senior software engineer at Apple.

Nadya started to see a therapist while working in Silicon Valley. That experience gave her a new dream: to bring mental health services to lower-income children in her native Colombia. 'I feel I have so much privilege and so I have an obligation to help,' she told CBS News in 2021. And Nadya sees a connection between mental health and chess. Nadya explains to me that the impetus for sharing her story is to fight the taboo in many countries, including Colombia, about 'mental health, therapy and learning about emotional intelligence'. If she had to replay her career, she says that she would be kinder to herself when she made mistakes. Since starting therapy, she is more open with the girls she mentors, that 'It's not OK to treat yourself bad.'

I met Linda Nangwale at the 2002 Olympiad in Bled, Slovenia. She stood out from the crowd with her short braids dyed in green, yellow and red, the colors of the Zambian flag. The striking and confident Zambian woman with her wide smile and open, friendly personality attracted reporters and photographers, who clamored after her. Linda thinks little about her appearance and what she wears, and she told me that in Bled she was hoping to rid herself of vanity. 'I only brought along three pairs of trousers. Many women can't lay their hands on money without buying clothes. I think that emphasis in clothes in women is related to an inferiority complex, where what is inside is not enough. In chess, an inferiority complex will halt your progress.'

Linda Nangwale (photo by Jennifer Shahade)

Just getting someone to teach Linda the rules of chess was a struggle. Every night when her brother and his friends played chess in the backyard, Linda was distracted by the ruckus they made. She was also intrigued by their excitement and was anxious to learn the game. 'Chess is a man's game and you won't survive an inch on the board,' one of the crew told her. That was the night Linda convinced her brother to teach her the rules. He warned her that chess was boring, but Linda loved it. 'I joined the bandwagon of noisemakers behind the house every day. They hammered me easily at first, using [Scholar's] mate.' Scholar's mate is one of the quickest chess finishes possible, the same four-move checkmate that the chess whizz janitor in *The Queen's Gambit* used to defeat Beth Harmon in their first game. Like Beth, Linda wouldn't let it happen again.

'Some people,' Linda said, 'call me "bitch" for playing with boys all the time. But it's the only way I can get proper training, so they can call me names until they get tired – they always do.' When she became a strong player, boys from the neighborhood came to her for lessons. 'I don't forget to seek revenge Scholar's mate on the unlucky few!'

Linda's successes aroused considerable interest. After winning the 2002 Zambian Women's Championship, in which there were fifteen participants, Linda said that the local papers 'reported on my success, and many men came to my house to see if a woman could really beat them in chess. They lined up around the block.' Linda has a more feminist outlook than most of the women with whom I spoke, maybe because she had to fight so hard to get where she is. Linda's family life has been troubled. Her mother, Carolyn Tembo, divorced her father, Bebbington Nangwale, in 1989. 'My dad,' Linda says, 'was a selfish man who loved no one but himself. He hardly ever had time for us.' She describes her mother as an 'underpaid secretary', who worked tirelessly, dying soon after her divorce, leaving Linda and her older brother to take care of their two younger brothers. When Linda's successes were reported, her father 'wanted to play the proud papa', but Linda was unwilling to forgive his irresponsible behavior. 'In my country, men are always trying to take the credit for the accomplishments of their children, while women get the blame if they go astray.' Not reconciled with his children, Bebbington Nangwale died in 2001.

Linda had to tolerate sexist attitudes from society and from her friends, who frequently inquired about her marriage plans. Her experience with her father made Linda wary about jumping into a relationship prematurely. When we met in Bled, she told me: 'I'm twenty-one and have no boyfriend or prospects of a boyfriend. People are asking me: "What are you doing, girl?"' In response, she says, 'What kind of man is going to understand that I'd rather play blitz all night or study the Sicilian than hang out with him?'

Linda speaks Nyanja, one of more than seventy tribal languages in Zambia. She is also fluent in English, so our correspondence has been easy. She used to send me e-mails from a computer at an Internet café. They are filled with exclamations: 'YIPPEEE! Skirts up! Trousers down!' or 'Do men get angry when I beat them? OH YES!!! They actually go mad!' Telling me about the beauty of Zambia's wildlife and nature, she urges me to visit one day and with affection adds, 'It is super, just like you!' Lamenting about Zambian healthcare and finances, she says, 'It is a harsh situation, and many are afraid to speak out.' Linda, a positive person, couldn't bear to sign off on such a somber note and closes with, 'Despite all this, your brother is so cute!'

The top Zambian player, Amon Simutowe, has improved the visibility of chess in the country. He became the first sub-Saharan African and third Black grandmaster in history in 2009. Though Linda was sponsored to play in Olympiads and All-African tournaments, the Zambian chess federation did not have enough money to support her year-round. It is hard to get periodicals and chess books in Zambia. Linda complained, 'Once you have a good book it's best to hide it 'cause once someone borrows it the chances of it being returned to you are one in a thousand.'

Linda, who got married in 2008, loves Zambia and relishes mentoring youngsters. She spent many years coaching girls' chess, including a group of children with AIDS. Linda Nangwale counted many admirers among her students. She told me, 'I overheard one girl saying that I was her role model, and I felt so proud.'

Linda's chess heroes are Judit Polgar and Indian Grandmaster Viswanathan Anand, whom she admires because 'he proves that a player from the [developing] world can rise to the world-elite.'

Viswanathan Anand, a former world champion, is one of the best players in history, with an incredible longevity. Through his teens to his fifties, he maintained a position among the top players in the world, in both classical and rapid formats. A national hero in his country, he's been heralded as a 'one-man Indian chess revolution'. Partly because of the successes of Anand, chess in India enjoys an exalted status and is thoroughly covered in the sports sections of Indian dailies. Anand has given up to 100 interviews on busy weeks. When I remark how cooperative he is with the media, he tells me: 'Of course! You can't complain about the popularity of chess and then get mad when they want an interview.' In a report on an international tournament in Delhi, Scottish Grandmaster and author Jonathan Rowson observed, 'Chess had become a symbol of Indian national resurgence, or at least a vehicle for patriotism.'[1]

The Indian Chess Federation set a goal to produce 100 grandmasters by the year 2012. Even if they fell short, setting a lofty goal paid off. In 2004, there were eleven Indian grandmasters. In 2021, India boasted sixty-nine grandmasters and twenty women's grandmasters.[*]

The exposure and promotion of women's chess in India is growing, and the top women players are also national symbols. Much of this is credited to the success of Indian prodigy Koneru Humpy. Humpy's rise was fast and spectacular. She won the Girls' World Under-20 Championship at just fourteen.

Koneru's first grandmaster norm came as a huge surprise. She traveled with her family to Budapest, with a goal of earning a women's grandmaster norm. But instead, Humpy, who was fourteen at the time, started to win all of her games and earned the grandmaster norm. Just a year later Humpy became the ninth woman, and first Indian female, to earn the grandmaster title. She also broke Judit Polgar's record by three months and one day, becoming the youngest female grandmaster in history.[†] Humpy also became the second female in history to crash through the 2600 rating barrier, reaching a peak of 2623. Humpy explained to me that her rating was particularly high when she played in a lot of mixed gender competitions. 'When I played in women's events I felt more pressure. While when I played in open events, I felt totally free.'

Humpy's parents, Ashok and Latha, had designs for their child as soon as she was born in 1989. It was her father Ashok's idea to name her Hampi, which is derived from the word champion. Later, he was influenced by great Soviet chess players and changed his daughter's name to Humpy to sound more like a Russian name. When Humpy, at age six, showed a talent for chess, Ashok poured his extra resources of time and money

---

[*] Two Indian players hold both the grandmaster and the women's grandmaster titles.

[†] This record was later eclipsed by Hou Yifan, who got the title at fourteen years old.

into her development. Friends and relatives were surprised when Ashok and Latha used their savings to buy a laptop instead of a color TV, as most middle-class Indians would do. 'I still remember how people mocked our decision to buy a computer,' said Latha.

Koneru Humpy's quick rise made her one of the strongest female players in history. But Humpy was disappointed repeatedly in a tournament she desperately wanted to win: the Women's World Championship. Her attempts at the crown were stymied again and again, often by the Chinese prodigy and four-time Women's World Champion Hou Yifan.

Koneru got a taste of pure victory when she won the 2019 World Women's Rapid Championship, which she called the most memorable win of her career. 'It was quite a surprise for me,' she told me, 'I never considered myself a good player in the rapid format.'

In 2014, Koneru got married to Anvesh Dasari in a spectacular wedding. The marriage was an arranged pairing set up by relatives. In their first meeting, Koneru Humpy immediately agreed to the match after noting his soft and pleasant nature. In an interview with Indian chess journalist and International Master Sagar Shah, Anvesh revealed he felt similarly. As Shah wrote: 'It was the simplicity and understanding nature of Humpy that won his heart. He knew that she was a very famous chess player, but her behavior was very normal and down to earth.'[2] Humpy laughed when telling me that her husband's friends jokingly nicknamed him 'God', because he has a knack for helping his friends in need. The two had a daughter, Ahana, in 2017. Anvesh is very supportive of Humpy's undying chess ambitions. Humpy even told me that the little Ahana supports her, reminding her to study when she calls her from tournaments abroad.

Before Humpy came along, Subbaraman Vijayalakshmi, 'Viji'

for short, was the headliner in Indian women's chess. Viji is the first Indian woman grandmaster and the first Indian female to earn the international master title. She earned back-to-back silver medals for her first board performance in Olympiads in Bled and in Istanbul. Viji is forthcoming, willing to talk about her role in chess, women in India and the problem of poverty in her country. Viji says, 'I am quite patriotic and take the responsibility to represent India in team competitions very seriously.'

Koneru Humpy (photo by David Llada)

Viji is not satisfied with the status of women in India. She complains that the Indian culture 'worships the man. The woman is supposed to be of service to the man, and parents are disappointed when they have girl children.' Fortunately, Viji's parents were different: her father always encouraged his three daughters to be strong. 'He didn't care whether we were boys or girls. He wanted us to be good sportspeople.' Chess is an ideal sport for a woman in India, Viji points out, because 'women can study chess alone at home.' Traditional Indian values can actually help women in chess, Viji argues, since chess is an activity that can be pursued in private.

India has one of the strongest women's squads in the world – strong enough to compete for the highest honors at Olympiads. The team got even stronger and more popular with the rise of Harika Dronavalli, who became the second Indian woman to earn the grandmaster title in 2011. India also claims one of the most popular commentators in the world in the glamorous and charming International Master Tania Sachdev, who is sponsored by Red Bull and Air India.

My first trip to India was thrilling and emotional. The World Championships in 2000 were held in a luxurious five-star hotel in the capital city of Delhi. I had qualified by placing third in the US Women's Championship. Intent on seeing more of India, I had arranged to stay for three weeks, regardless of how many rounds I advanced in the knockout format.

The hotel had five gourmet restaurants, a nightclub, a fitness center, massage services and lush bars. It would be easy for a chess player to spend time in India sheltered in air-conditioned comfort. Many participants, serious about their chance to compete in the most elite tournament in the world, did not leave the hotel complex. To mix the chess world and the real world is difficult for some players. Former World Championship challenger Victor Korchnoi feels strongly that 'chess players should not be tourists.'[3]

For my first few days in Delhi, I followed Korchnoi's advice. I studied chess in my hotel room and ate at the delicious buffet. At night I sometimes went to the bar adjacent to the hotel, frequented by rich Indians and foreigners on business trips. An Australian rock band played U2 cover songs as customers drank eight-dollar martinis underneath flashing lights. This scene did not seem far from Manhattan. When Georgian

Ketevan Arakhamia knocked me out of the tournament, I switched from chess player to tourist.

I took an open-air taxi into Delhi's Old City, the ancient core of the now-sprawling metropolis where sacred cows and fornicating monkeys were out and about. The streets were in multiple zigzag lanes, and the permanent rush-hour traffic gave me the leisure to take it all in. I was bombarded by people, including many children, asking me for money, pencils and food. By the time I got out of the taxi, my face was covered in soot from the pollution. I had known about poverty in India, but to see it up close was unforgettable, and made the World Chess Championship back at the hotel seem extremely unimportant.

Phiona Mutesi (photo by David Llada)

As much as it can seem as if games are meaningless in the face of such huge problems, chess has created life-changing opportunities for many players. It can even be a vehicle out of poverty, like in the case of Ugandan chess champion Phiona Mutesi.

Phiona was born in Katwe, an impoverished area in the capital of Uganda, Kampala. Her father died at the age of three, leaving her mother in desperate financial straits. To help out, Phiona sold maize in markets at five years old, an age that many chess champions in this book start training their Rook endgames. Phiona and her siblings would wander around with saucepans on their heads, hoping to help their mother raise money for food.[4]

At the age of nine, while chasing after her older brother, she found him in a shack where a chess class was set up. She later recalled,

> I really wanted to go inside and touch the beautiful pieces. I thought 'What could make these kids so silent?' Then I watched them play the game and get happy and excited and I wanted a chance to be that happy.

The coach, Robert Katende, admired Phiona's fighting spirit right away, even if she mostly came to the classes for the free porridge at the start. Katende started the chess class with an American non-profit called Sports Outreach, which uses sports including chess to provide relief and religion.

Phiona's first coach was half her age. Gloria Nansubuga, aged four, taught Phiona the basic piece movements. Phiona advanced quickly, and in speaking to my girls' chess club years later at US Chess Women, she recalled the first time she defeated the strongest boy in the class. 'For him a girl could not beat him,' Phiona told me, 'so he quit and never played chess again because of that.'

Phiona's talent soon earned her a spot in national youth competitions, allowing her to travel at first to other African countries, and eventually all over the world. The ultimate underdog story caught the attention of *ESPN Magazine*, in which Tim Crothers wrote an in-depth profile, which turned into a book, *The Queen of Katwe*. Phiona was paid for the right to use her likeness in the book and eventual movie. She used it to buy her mother a house on a plot of land, which Phiona's mom now uses to grow food, to feed children and the homeless. 'It is one thing I am really proud of,' Phiona said, 'I have accomplished a lot (even) if only that.'

That book turned into a highly acclaimed Disney movie starring Lupita Nyong'o and David Oyelowo. Phiona loves the film, and feels emotional each time she watches it. The flood scene is particularly wrenching for her, as it makes her remember people she lost in the floods, including Adam, her best childhood friend, who she saw drown when he fell into the water after chasing a soccer ball.

Phiona got a college scholarship in Northwest University in Washington State, where she majored in Finance and Business Management. As Phiona acclimated to American college life, rapidly improving her computer skills and her English, she encountered another hurdle: racism. Phiona had already experienced classism when facing kids from private schools in Uganda, as captured in *The Queen of Katwe*. But she was now taken aback by racism she experienced at an American college. In a podcast interview, Phiona described how one of her professors told the class that Black Africans were lazy, due to the climate.[5] Phiona, who was the only Black person in the class, raised her hand and explained why he was wrong, insisting 'Africans are hard-working people.' The professor stopped that day's class, and Phiona never returned to it. She did speak to him personally, and the professor defended himself by explaining that he read about his opinion in a book. Beyond that horrific incident, she described ridiculous questions from classmates like 'Do you sleep with lions?'

Phiona was forgiving of her ignorant professor and class-mates. When speaking to my girls' chess club, Phiona shared her perspective to hundreds of young fans, from the United States to Kenya. 'I was raised to love myself.* I have dealt with worse things than racism,' Phiona said. She told us that if she made it through so many struggles, including being homeless, 'I don't think something like [racism] can stop me.'

After graduating from Northwest University in May 2021, Mutesi started the Phiona Foundation, where she helps Ugandan children with food, books, shoes and other critical supplies, like reusable sanitary pads. 'I wish to see that all the disadvantaged groups of people in the society are well catered for and given the opportunity to see the light and have a better piece of life.'

---

* Phiona spoke to a group of girls as part of a cross-cultural program co-hosted by US Chess, the Lighthouse Chess Club in Mombasa, Kenya, and Business Meets Chess & Kids. Girls from USA, Kenya, Colombia, Malawi, Uganda, Tanzania, Nigeria, Zambia, Botswana and Namibia participate.

Playing for America

'I hate anyone who beats me.'
Lisa Lane, 1959 US Women's Champion

In the fall of 2000 I was invited for the first time to play for America in the prestigious biennial team competition, the Olympiad, held that year in Istanbul, Turkey. After each Olympiad, the chess world buzzes for months about brilliant chess and lively gossip from the three-week-long event.

Arriving in Istanbul, I was immediately smitten. My first evening there, I walked around the main strip, my senses reveling in the aroma of beef kabobs, carts of mussels and mangoes and incense. The sounds of calls to prayer mingled with modern Greek music. I went to Turkish baths and toured ancient mosques. I remember thinking over and over, *I am in Istanbul, and this is so great*. Istanbul nightlife was diverse: when teammate Anna Hahn and I went out to a bar in a coastal suburb, the live Turkish music was performed by a man in drag.

The Chess Olympiad is a social occasion as well as a fierce competition. Most delegations include an equal number of men and women, so the male-to-female ratio is much more balanced than at most tournaments. Many couples meet at Olympiads. Lithuanian Camilla Baginskaite and the Russian-American Alex Yermolinsky met at the 1996 Yerevan Olympiad and later married and had two children, while John Donaldson and Elena Akhmilovskaya famously eloped in the 1988 edition. In the

2006 Olympiad, Arianne Caoili, a glamorous singer, economist and chess champion, danced with her future husband Levon Aronian, one of the top players in the world. This caused an international brawl when a jealous GM tried to intervene.[*]

Such relationships are instigated by social events at the Olympiad, like the historic Bermuda bash. The Bermuda team has one of the lower-rated line-ups in the event, but they make their mark each year with their party, held at every Olympiad since 1980. They rent out a huge space, hire DJs, and print out invitations for thousands of participants, along with arbiters, journalists, and chess tourists. Always held before a free day, even the most professional players abandon rigorous routines to stay out late and sleep in. 'I can't wait to see all these players, so serious over the board, shake it over the dance floor,' said Zambia's Linda Nangwale. Temporary social constellations form between players from all corners of the world, from Santiago to Oslo to Lagos. I met an Iraqi medical doctor, who asked me to dance: 'I don't like to talk about politics,' he said. I saw some of the best players in the world perform comically athletic dance moves, arms flailing, jumping up and down for some treasure on the ceiling.

Some non-players would be surprised at chess players' penchant for partying, but for me there are natural similarities between chess games and parties. Before either, I feel giddy over the numerous possibilities – perhaps this party will be one where I will have a transcendent conversation or perhaps this game will be filled with sacrifice and beauty, making the hours of small talk or technical study worthwhile. As the night or game goes on, anticipation dwindles into the reality of the present. You win or you lose, the lights are turning off.

---

[*] Arianne Caoili, one of the most intelligent and charismatic chess players I've met, died far too soon, from injuries in a car accident in 2020.

Not all of my memories from Olympiads are positive. In the 2002 event (held in Bled, Slovenia), in addition to playing, I was writing an article about the Olympiad for *Chess Life* magazine (the official magazine of the US Chess Federation). I wanted to interview two of the top young Russian players in the world, both of whom have been heralded as possible future world champions. I was nervous, especially because one seemed particularly cool – he had big blue eyes, dreadlocks and wore black leather. I was already familiar with his games, one of which had impressed me so much that I showed it to the junior high team I coached back in Brooklyn. 'That game was hot,' said one of my students, 'can I have a copy?' I approached him at the hotel's dining room and was pleased that he consented immediately to an interview. He wanted to do it right then and there, over dinner where his teammate, the other young grandmaster, was also eating.

It was the most disturbing interview I have ever conducted. One declared that he hated journalists, hated New York, and became annoyed when I asked him about his training routine. His teammate had even worse things to say. America was a horrible place, he said, because the rape laws were stricter than in Russia, where he was used to raping women who are 'too ashamed to go to the police.' He proceeded to use words like lesbian, fat and stupid to describe American women. As we left the dining hall, one of them asked me to join him and some friends for drinks later that night, as if their outrageous comments were part of a charming routine. I declined. Later, I found out that the two were bragging to their teammates about how much they upset me with their sexist, anti-American insults. Many years later, one of the players apologized to me, explaining that it was, indeed, not a serious conversation.

At my first Olympiad in Istanbul, I was feeling more American than I ever had. Competing for my country internationally certainly sparked my affections for the Stars and

Stripes. Because of this, chess at the Olympiad was even more intense for me as winning felt noble and losing shameful. At the Istanbul event, the US team began with a sensational upset in the third round, beating the higher-ranked German team 3-0. We were euphoric for a short time – the following day, we lost to the lower-ranked Vietnamese team.

Midway through the Istanbul tournament, I tuned into the BBC to watch the votes of the 2000 Bush–Gore election being recounted. I was nineteen at the time, so it was my first chance to vote in a presidential election. I knew I was going to be playing in the Olympiad on Election Day, and applied for an absentee ballot, but did not receive it before departing for Turkey. Feeling guilty, I lay down on the bed and watched the TV for hours until it became more and more clear who our new president would be. I yearned to be back in the States, commiserating with friends and family.

I often criticize the policies and customs of my own country – yet still I get defensive when I travel to tournaments and Europeans gleefully rip on America. It's like the difference between criticizing your family and hearing a stranger do so. Sometimes, I encounter foreigners who think that to be an American is to be stupid: 'I'm so surprised to have such an intelligent conversation with an American,' or 'I'm impressed you're doing so well! I heard it is very difficult for American girls to learn chess.'

Women's chess in America has, in fact, had a very rich history. True, there have not yet been any homegrown American women's world champions, or even direct contenders, but there have been many women who are deeply passionate about chess, just like their counterparts around the world.

The history of the US Women's Chess Championship in America had fortuitous beginnings. In 1934, Caroline Marshall was inspired to organize a women's event. Caroline was married to Frank Marshall, the world championship candidate and founder of New York's still-active Marshall Chess Club. For the next two years successful open women's tournaments were held at the West Village brownstone. In 1937, the tournament got an official boost from the National Chess Federation, which announced that the first official US women's title was at stake.

The tournaments began in a progressive spirit, through the impassioned efforts of Edith L. Weart (1897–1977), an energetic feminist born in Jersey City. She graduated from Oberlin College with a degree in chemistry. She learned to play chess late, at twenty-seven, and played in many US Women's Championships, though she was among the weaker players. A freelance writer, Weart penned many articles on the rise of female chess players in the world and in the United States.

To Ms Weart, the entry of women into the chess arena symbolized their acceptance into other fields. In one article she wonders why 'women have left undisputed men's claims to mastery of the royal pastime.' She responds, 'The answer lies, I think, in lack of opportunity.'[1] In another article she points out: 'As in practically every other sphere, woman is astir in the chessplaying world and bent upon emulating the activities and achievements of the male portion of the population. The doors . . . are beckoning our sisters to enter the portals behind which have been kept from them opportunities for delightful mental recreation and possible distinction at home and abroad.'[2] She organized a scrapbook of clippings on early women's chess in America, which is now part of the John G. White Collection at the Cleveland Public Library.[3]

There were ten players in the 1937 event, which was won by Belgian-born Adele Rivero. Rivero learned chess to disprove her Spaniard husband's assertion that women didn't have the brains for the game. Rivero won the 1940 championship also, but she faded as two women – Mona Karff and Gisela Gresser – established a nearly exclusive rivalry for the national title.

Refined, rich and redheaded, Gisela Gresser and Mona Karff were uncannily similar on the surface. Each won many national women's championship titles: Gisela won nine; Mona, seven. Both were multi-lingual, interested in the arts, and loved to travel. Mona had a degree in international affairs and in 1948 traveled through Europe in support of the One World movement. Gresser painted, sculpted and wrote. American player Dorothy Teasley, who knew both women, said, 'It was hard to mention Gisela Gresser without mentioning Mona Karff. The two went together . . . two very brainy, very savvy, very well-traveled, very sophisticated, and very cosmopolitan women of another era.'

Mona Karff was born in Eastern Europe and lived in Palestine as a teenager. She learned chess from her father, Aviv Ratner, a wealthy Jewish landowner, who moved the family from Russia to Tel-Aviv after the Bolshevik Revolution. Karff was described as 'a refined, elegant woman who loved opera, collected art, spoke eight languages fluently, traveled the world with confident ease, and made millions in the stock market.' She won the second US Women's Championship in 1938 and collected six more titles, the final one in 1974, thirty-six years after her first victory.

Karff was mysterious. Even good friends of hers were left in the dark as to the most basic matters concerning her life – her birthplace is to this day uncertain. The US Chess Federation listed her place of origin as simply Europe, while relatives attest that she was born in a Russian province, Bessarabia. It was not easy to ask her. Ms Teasley 'once inquired, innocently enough, where she had been born' and was disappointed: 'I got some kind of reply but it was definitely not a direct answer.'

Mona Karff vs US Chess Hall of Famer Hermann Helms (photo by Nancy Roos, courtesy of the World Chess Hall of Fame)

Soon after settling in Boston in the 1930s, Mona had a brief marriage with a cousin, Abe Karff, a lawyer. She kept even this a secret, and one good friend only found out about the marriage when she called Abe's house and Mona picked up the phone. Mona had a longer-lasting relationship with International Master Dr Edward Lasker, who was twenty-nine years older than she. Dr Lasker was sometimes nicknamed as 'a chest player' because he made bank by inventing a mechanical breast pump, which saved many babies' lives. When one female chess player innocently asked Karff's main rival and friend, Gresser, if Lasker and Karff were engaged, she responded: 'Miss Karff is much, much too sophisticated to be engaged.'

Lasker and Karff lived separately but were always together at tournaments and parties. Allen Kaufman, who was a rising young chess player at the time and was often a guest at their home in the 1960s, says, 'Lasker lived in a magnificent penthouse apartment overlooking the Hudson River, where he would host lovely soirées. He threw German lieder on the phonograph, and chess players would play and analyze for hours. Karff was always there – and she was a great conversationalist.'

Lasker died in 1981, leaving Mona single. Allen observed that 'she seemed heartbroken', but was still able to get on with her life. 'I saw her at restaurants dating guys when she was in her eighties – she was a go-getter, not the type to mope around for too long.'

Mona and Gisela were of approximately the same strength, but their styles were in direct opposition to one another. Karff was aggressive and 'never missed an opportunity to throw materialistic caution to the winds,' while Gresser had a patient style, preferring closed games.

Gisela Gresser was born in Detroit in 1906, with a silver pawn in her mouth. Her father, Julius Kahn, was the president of a steel company and an engineer who earned a fortune by inventing reinforced concrete. Though she had learned chess from her father as a child, her youthful passion was for Greek, of which she said in an interview in 1945, 'When the other children were out playing, I used to study Greek. I loved it just the way I love chess now.'

Gresser followed her love for ancient languages, earning an A.B. in classics at Radcliffe and a post-college scholarship in Athens. In 1927 Gisela found herself in New York City, where she married William Gresser, a lawyer and accomplished musician. They settled in a Park Avenue apartment, and her luxurious lifestyle allowed her to pursue many hobbies – horseback riding, sculpting, painting, and voracious reading in ten different languages.

Gisela and her husband went on a cruise to Europe in 1938, the same year the first US Women's Chess Championship was held. On the boat she met a man with a pocket chess set and a chess book and became hooked on the game. Thereafter, chess was her primary addiction. Gresser was quickly successful, winning her first US Women's Chess Championship just six years after her chance encounter on the boat. Gresser was a record-breaker on the US circuit: besides winning more US women's titles than any woman in history so far, Gresser was the first woman to achieve the national master title.*

Gisela Gresser (courtesy of the World Chess Hall of Fame)

In 1948, Gresser and Karff tied for first place in the US Women's Championship and were selected as the official US representatives to the first Women's World Championship held since the war. The event ran from December 1949 through into the New Year in Moscow. Both Karff and Gresser had dismal showings, scoring five points each from fifteen games, and finishing in a

* Grandmaster Irina Krush has won eight US women's titles as of 2021.

three-way tie for twelfth to fourteenth. One bright spot of Gisela's event was her victory over the tournament winner, Ludmilla Rudenko. Gisela was frustrated by her inability to communicate or navigate Moscow, and upon returning to New York, she began to study Russian. By the time Gresser won the 1955 US Championship, and was again selected to play for the World Championship in Moscow, she had a basic grasp of the language.

The 1944 US Championships. Immediately around the board
from left to right: Edward Lasker, Gisela Gresser, Reuben Fine,
Herman Steiner, Caroline Marshall, I. A. Horowitz,
Frank Marshall and Arnold Denker (photo by Nancy Roos,
courtesy of the World Chess Hall of Fame)

After her second journey, Gresser wrote 'Chess Queens in Moscow', a twenty-page, icy account of her thoughts on the tournament and the city. Gresser, a well-heeled Upper East Side socialite, was critical about the appearance of Russian women: 'There is no attempt at elegance or charm in the ordinary street dress,' Gisela observed coolly. 'The women appear resigned to their corrugated hair and crude cosmetics, their colorless knitted headgear and shapeless suits.' Her opponents did not escape her scrutiny either: 'The Russian ladies have all gotten very fat since I last saw them.'

According to Gresser, her hosts were gracious and intent upon showing her the best Moscow had to offer. 'In what other country would female chessplayers be fêted like traveling ambassadors and followed as though they were movie stars?' Upon her arrival at the airport, she was greeted with bouquets of flowers. The opening ceremony included ballerinas, marionettes, even 'a magician who extracted a bowl of live goldfish from a vest pocket.' The best seats at the opera and the ballet were arranged for her, and she was assigned a private translator and assistant, Tamara.

Despite such generosity, Gresser was struck by the difficulty of getting basic goods in communist Moscow. 'Toilet paper,' she noted, commenting on one trip to the restroom, 'must be a bourgeois luxury.' She was disappointed by the unavailability of jarred caviar to bring back to friends or glue to reinforce the soles of her shoes. In one particularly absurd episode, Gisela, overwhelmed by the jumbo pillow on her bed, asked for a smaller one, but Tamara deemed it impossible. 'We have some things, at other times, other things . . . This year we have only large pillows. A few years ago the pillows came small. But now it has been decided that Moscow people all like large pillows, so we have only large pillows.'

When Gresser left Moscow, Tamara was the last person she saw. 'I shall always think of her as a child, gentle and eager and obedient, never complaining and never questioning the authority of her guardians.' She condescendingly concluded, 'There must be many Tamaras in the Soviet Union.'

Women's chess didn't have the financial backing or support in the United States that it had in the Soviet Union. American women went to prestigious events without trainers, unthinkable for Soviet and European representatives. A trainer's, or 'second's', role, in a serious event was multiple. Up until the 1980s, adjournments occurred in major tournaments. The game would stop, and both players would have all night to analyze the position, resuming play on the next day. The advent of computer analysis killed adjournments, but seconds remain valuable. They can analyze openings while a player is sleeping, and even offer psychological support and companionship. To play in a foreign country can be a lonely, taxing experience, and a trainer psychs a player up before the game, then consoles or celebrates with her afterward.

Gresser was content to tackle the tournament solo. She was unimpressed with the attitudes of the Soviet and Eastern European coaches, many of whom were married to their students. Gresser overheard one trainer proclaiming loudly, in earshot of other players, 'Today my wife played like a dog.' Another said scathingly, 'Women can memorize mountains of opening theory, but can't win the simplest positions.'

Nearly ten years later, in the Georgian coastal town, Sukhumi, Gresser got a more positive impression of Soviet chess training. She played in the 1964 Candidates' Championship, which would determine a challenger to World Champion Nona Gaprindashvili. This time it appeared that a Serbian player, Milunka Lazarević, then representing Yugoslavia, would upset the Soviets. Lazarević had only one game left – against Gresser. Gresser recounts, with amusement, that a group of Russians bemoaned her chances of beating Lazarević. 'I heard a group of Russians discussing my gloomy chances . . . and was sorry that I had taken two years of Russian.' If Gresser won, it would pave the way for the victory of the Russian player, Alla Kushnir. Gresser was accosted on her way to the dining hall and asked where her trainer was. When Gresser responded that she had no trainer, the Soviet coach arranged an emergency lesson with her for the next morning. Gresser was blown away: 'In that hour I learned more about chess theory and chess psychology than I could have ever have thought possible. Next day, when I walked on the beach after winning the best game of my life, the bathers (all Russians, of course) were screaming *malodiez* (meaning bravo).' Gresser was ecstatic. 'One of life's great moments!'[4]

Gisela's dilettantish approach may have prevented her from cracking into the world chess elite. She was not so successful internationally as she was in the United States. She simply had too many other interests. Gresser never felt guilty for not spending more time studying chess. If anything, she seemed proud of it. She considered chess a dangerous addiction, and was sometimes wistful for the hours she had whiled away on the game. 'To spend so much time on something that's not really constructive hurts my conscience. I don't spend all my time on it, but I could.'[5]

Gresser had a vain streak. In one instance, she played in a senior championship, for players over sixty-five. She requested that the tournament director make a special announcement that she was playing under special consideration of her gender, and not because she was over sixty-five, which in fact she was.

Gisela played with verve till her last days. Ivona Jesierska was invited to Gisela Gresser's apartment to play blitz soon after she arrived in America from Poland. Under ordinary circumstances, a young immigrant with no knowledge of English would not find herself as a guest in a Park Avenue home. But in chess, such things are normal. Ivona was stunned by the comfort in which Gisela lived: 'I had never seen anything like it. We went up to her place in an elevator, where she had an entire floor to herself – the apartment was filled with antiques.' Even more surprising to Ivona was Gisela's blitz strength: 'I took one look at this old lady (Gisela was in her late seventies at the time) and thought, "No problem!" But I don't think I won a single game.'

In 1951, Hungarian-born Mary Bain interrupted the domination of the US Women's title by Karff and Gresser. Her stepfather had been captured in World War I and never reappeared: her mother died of a broken heart. In 1921, at the age of seventeen Bain travelled by ship from Europe to join her sister in New York City. Mary, who spoke no English at the time, spent most of the week-long trip to America playing chess with passengers. She showed remarkable talent for the game, and an audience of onlookers was delighted when she beat the captain of the ship. A highlight in Bain's career came in 1933, when, at twenty-eight years old, she defeated Jose Capablanca in a simultaneous game. The Cuban world champion missed a simple tactic, allowing Bain to grab his loose Bishop, after which he resigned – an ignominious eleven-move loss. As a prize, she received an autographed copy of Capablanca's book, *Chess Primer*. 'There was a bit of sardonic humour,' Capablanca said, 'in the thought that a player winning from the master should receive a primer.'[6] Bain's talent was recognized after this game by Hungarian Grandmaster Géza Maróczy, who hoped Bain would one day challenge his star student, Vera Menchik.

In 1937 Mary Bain sailed to Stockholm to play in the World Championship there. She was the first American woman to represent the US in an organized chess competition. Menchik won the tournament, but Bain came in a respectable fifth out of twenty-six players.

Mary Bain (photo courtesy of Cleveland Public Library)

Bain spent as much time at the Marshall Chess Club as she could, playing in tournaments or just hanging out and learning. Dr Frank Brady, author of *Bobby Fischer: Profile of a Prodigy*, called Mary a 'classic Village type . . . very liberal.' When a man addressed her as Mrs Mary Bain, she sharply corrected him: 'Just Mary Bain!' Another time, she waved her hand dismissively at the suggestion that women ought to wait till marriage to have sex – a strong declaration in the 1950s.

It was not until 1951 that Bain managed to capture a single title from the Gresser and Karff duo. This enabled her to take another stab at the world crown. She was thrilled to travel to Moscow, along with second-place Karff, to participate in the 1952 World Championship Candidates.

Bain was impressed by the generosity of her hosts, who invited her to the circus, the ballet and fancy banquets.

Distraught at being under-prepared, she did her best to relax: 'I am going to enjoy my stay, at least until the tournament starts. After, I'll be worried about my games.' Once the tournament began, she was overwhelmed, writing: 'The excitement is too much for me. The large crowd, the cameras, the large wall board . . . the importance of the scene is killing me.'

Bain did not play well. She lost game after game and finished with just 3.5 points out of 15. Elizaveta Bykova won the tournament and went on to defeat Rudenko for the world championship title. In a series of letters written to David Lawson – American organizer, chessplayer, and author of *Paul Morphy: The Pride and Sorrow of Chess* – Mary Bain reveals that her poor showing wrecked her emotionally. Depressed, she was unable to eat or sleep for days. 'I am not being outplayed, I simply beat myself.' Compounding her misery was news from America that Eisenhower had won the 1952 election over Democratic candidate Adlai Stevenson. After this, Bain was so despondent that she 'collapsed in my room and cried like a child,' signing one letter 'Good for nothing Mary.' But Bain didn't blame herself alone.

She was livid that the US Chess Federation offered her neither financial nor psychological support. 'My send-off was cruel. I was told that I was not going to represent the USA and USCF but Zone Number Four.[7] No use complaining . . .' She also had no second to help her analyze adjourned games, which usually resumed the following day: 'When I have an adjourned game I stay up all night and then make the worst move.' Ideally, Mary would be sleeping soundly, while her trainer would work through the night, and then supply her with a thorough analysis in the morning. Perhaps the worst insult was that the Soviet Federation had been willing to pay all expenses for her second, but Bain had not been told this until it was too late to arrange.

Bain and Gresser were both trounced by the Soviets, who were simply better players. Their reactions to their poor showings were diametrically opposed. Gresser looked at the chess world with detached curiosity and gentle derision. Happy to dip in and out of the elite chess world, Gresser was content with her position in the US chess circuit and comfortable in her Park Avenue penthouse. Her talent brought her to the top of the US women's chess circuit, but without assiduous work, she couldn't hope or expect to reach the top of the world. She never believed that losing a game reflected poorly on her character or intellect, both of which were nourished from other sources.

Bain was more focused on her own chess potential, which frustrated her because she was unable to unleash it. Bain may have overreacted, causing her to spiral downward faster.

Many players have trouble striking that fine balance between debilitating despair and nonchalance. 'If it doesn't hurt, there's something wrong,' said American Grandmaster Joel Benjamin, who expects to be in pain after losing a crucial game. However, professionalism requires that even the most distraught players pick themselves up after a tough loss and get ready to play their next game at full strength.

My own experience in finding the appropriate emotional involvement with the game has been an ongoing struggle. As a teenager, my identity was closely intertwined with my chess results and rating, so a poor result would set me back for days, or even weeks, leaving me in a state of near depression. I vividly remember feeling the world was over after losing a crucial game in the US Championship of 1998. A perceptive observer berated me: 'You put too much pressure on yourself,' suggesting, 'Your results will improve if you relax and allow your talent to show.' His advice was accurate, but it would take a while for me to implement it.

After winning my first US Women's Chess Championship in 2002, gaining my first IM norm and performing much better than even I expected, many people asked me how I had prepared. The truth was that I had not studied much chess, but instead had had four days of raucous fun celebrating the New Year with my friends in Brooklyn. We went to house parties, drank coffee all day, and planned decadent art projects. Entering the tournament in Seattle, I was happier than I'd ever been. I was more relaxed playing than I had been in the past, knowing that if I lost I'd still be happy. In retrospect, I see that the superior play I exhibited in that event had been hidden inside me for years.

The emotion attached to my chess results loosened after Seattle. I still feel pain when I lose, but it usually goes away within a few hours. This could have made me play worse temporarily. Fear of losing is a powerful motivation to study. But I don't think self-punishment is a sustainable cycle. I'd need to find a different source of inspiration.

How much a player identifies with results depends as much on disposition as chess strength. At weekend tournaments, it is common to see grown amateurs knocking their heads against walls or young beginners crying uncontrollably. Professionals, though, can often calmly pick up the pieces, even after the most excruciating losses. Some even channel their disappointment into renewed vigor for following rounds, like Garry Kasparov, who is renowned for recovering from losses by crushing his next opponent.

American chess pioneers Bain, Gresser, and Karff did not have professional approaches to the game, either in disposition or lifestyle. A further reason for their mediocre results may have been their ages. By the time all three were playing in the post-war world championships, they were in their forties and

fifties. The peak years of their careers would have been in the
1940s, but the war precluded international championships
during this time.

The grueling nature of contemporary chess rewards youth,
which is why most top players consider it a sport more than
an art or science. Women's chess is even more extremely skewed
toward youth. One reason may be that women are more likely
to retire after starting families. Another is that the bar for the
standard of the best female chess players is rising so rapidly
that young players begin with far higher ambitions than their
predecessors.

The next bright light of women's chess in America after Bain,
Gresser and Karff was an outspoken upstart from Philadelphia,
young enough to be the daughter of her competitors.

'Each move seems to be weighted with some cosmic significance
to her,' wrote Robert Cantwell, a reporter for *Sports Illustrated*.
'At such moments she seems . . . beautifully serious, or seriously
beautiful, a side of feminine loveliness that Hollywood has
rather neglected.'

Lisa Lane, the first chess player ever to appear on the cover
of *Sports Illustrated*, got hooked on chess as a nineteen-year-old.
She became US Women's Champion just two years later in
1959, edging out veteran players Karff and Gresser.

Lisa was not surprised by her success. Nor was she overwhelmed by the spate of journalists who began to call her for
interviews. Young, ambitious and arrogant, Lisa felt she was
entitled. 'I'm the most important American chessplayer. People
will be attracted to the game by a young, pretty girl.' Lisa
believed she deserved all the recognition and support she got,
since she was 'bringing publicity and ultimately money' to the
game.

Lisa Lane (AP Archive)

Born in Philadelphia, Lisa had a difficult childhood. She did not know her father, and her mother worked two jobs. Lisa had to stay with foster families as a schoolgirl: she did poorly in school and dropped out, and then she moved from low-paying job to low-paying job. Anxious to continue her education, after dating an older, well-educated man, Lisa enrolled at Temple University, where she began a special program in which she would complete her high-school diploma while beginning her college coursework.

At the same time, Lisa discovered chess while on a date in

the Artists' Hut, a bohemian coffeeshop in downtown Philadelphia. She began to play there regularly, and was discovered by an active player, who introduced her to Attilio Di Camillo, a charismatic Italian-American master, who was also a passionate and affordable coach. Di Camillo started to coach Lisa in the mornings. When 'Di-cam' was asked why he only charged his students two dollars an hour for lessons, he responded: 'When I teach, I learn more than my students.' Di Camillo was impressed by Lisa's talent and assured her that, with hard work, she could become US Champion in two years – a dead-on prophesy.

Lisa was soon a chess addict, dropping her studies at Temple to concentrate on the game. She worked up to twelve hours a day at chess, often staying up until three or four in the morning analyzing or playing at the club. Because of her volatile temper and fiery personality, Lisa was involved in scrapes and scandals. The details of one after-game dispute were murky, but Lisa was quoted in *Sports Illustrated* as saying, 'I never hit that guy with an ashtray!'

Lisa's defiant attitude made her all the more exciting to the press. Lisa declared, 'I hate anyone who beats me.'

'If talent alone won championships, I'd be world champion now.' Lisa was obsessed with chess and eschewed talk of politics: 'I don't care what's going on in the world.'

'Her main role in the chess world is social. She is pleasant to look upon,' was the backhanded compliment of one American master. Certainly, Lisa had scores of suitors, which seemed to amuse her: 'I get a lot of love letters from other chessplayers,' she said to a *New York Times* reporter. 'I read them, I laugh, and then I file them. Letters from grandmasters go on top.'

Lisa's victory in the US Championship in December 1959 earned her invitations to the Olympiad in the Netherlands and to the World Championship in Vrnjacka Banja, a mountain resort in Yugoslavia, both held in the fall of 1963. In preparation for these events and with the help of a public sports grant, Lisa moved from Philadelphia to Greenwich Village in New York City, then the center of American chess activity. She amassed a huge collection of chess books and studied day and night. She also studied Russian at the nearby New School so that she could read Soviet chess magazines.

The media hoopla over Lisa, articles in *The New York Times Magazine*, *Newsweek*, the dailies such as the *Post* and the *Sun*, along with chess magazines, scared her Russian opponents, who were reportedly just as afraid of Lisa as they were of better-established foreign contenders. Their fears were unjustified: Lisa only tied for twelfth out of eighteen players in Vrnjacka Banja.[8] It was becoming clear that Lisa had a way to go before she could be a serious competitor for the world crown.

Lisa stayed in Europe for the rest of the winter, having received an invitation to the prestigious Chess Congress (challengers' section) in Hastings, England. In a shocking move, Lisa dropped out midway through the tournament after two losses and a draw. Her explanation was that she was 'too much in love' to continue play. When Lisa left New York in October for her European chess tour, she had abandoned a burgeoning romance with Neil Hickey, a journalist who interviewed her for the *American Weekly*. Hickey wrote passionately about Lisa's 'lissome beauty', which 'confounds all customary notions of bookish, brainy females.' Clearly, Hickey's article reflected feelings deeper than the detached admiration of a reporter. Lisa was missing Neil and quit the tournament to return to New York. 'I could not concentrate – my thoughts kept wandering.'

Newspapers on both sides of the Atlantic had a field day with the story, joking that Lisa Lane had 'flipp[ed] her chessboard.' Another wrote that it was understandable for a brilliant girl to give up the game, 'especially if she really was in love.'

Lisa's return to supposed normalcy, where ladies put love above chess, elicited bemused pleasure from the public.

In fact, Lisa was not done with chess. Two years later she caused a stir when she was overlooked for the 1963 Olympic Team in favor of Mary Bain and Gisela Gresser.[9] The Associated Press ran a story on Lisa's reaction with the cheeky headline 'Scorned Woman Gets Something Off Her Chess'. Lisa had assumed that since she was the first runner-up in the 1962 US Championship (to Gresser) and the second-highest-ranked player in the country, she would be selected for the team. Lisa was only able to think of one explanation for being left out: 'They were sore from all the publicity I've been getting. Everywhere I go, people want to take my picture and get interviews with me.' The wealthy Gresser assured reporters that she was happy about any press coverage chess got, though she admitted that selection was based on factors other than merit, such as the player's being able to meet expenses. This explanation enraged Lisa. 'Since when did you have to be a millionairess,' Lisa fumed, 'to represent your country in sport?'

In a 2018 interview with *Sports Illustrated*, Lisa, now in her eighties, recalled mounting frustration with the meagre compensation for women's chess players.[10] The 1966 US Women's Championship first prize was $600, ten times less than the $6000 prize for the US Championship. Lisa Lane arranged a protest outside the chess club she opened in Greenwich Village, the Queen's Pawn. She recruited clientele to wear sandwich boards reading, 'One Man is Worth Ten Women?' and 'What Good is a King Without a Queen?'

The protest did not work. As Lane told *Sports Illustrated*, 'The other women were embarrassed', and the pay gap did not budge. In Lane's day, many female chess players were wealthy and didn't pay much mind to the meager prize purses.

Lisa's approach to chess had changed by the time she made

her next attempt in the Women's World Championship in 1964.
Lane played blitz chess for hours every night at the Queen's
Pawn, but gave up the grind of studying chess books: 'This
time I am preparing by not preparing.' Again she had a bad
result – twelfth out of eighteen. Soon after this, The Queen's
Pawn closed, and Lisa disappeared from chess.

Lisa has been called the 'Bobby Fischer of women's chess',
a tempting comparison. Both were good-looking, defiant, eccentric, and magnets for a press that till then was uninterested in
the chess world. Like Fischer, Lane suddenly dropped out of
chess and has not played since the late 1960s. Bobby did not
have kind words for Lisa or for any woman in chess. 'There
isn't a woman in the world I couldn't give Knight odds to and
still beat,' he said in an interview with Harper's. In *Newsweek*,
Bobby Fischer used different words to express the same sentiment: 'They can't concentrate, they don't have stamina, and
they aren't creative. They're all fish [an ineffective chess player].
Lisa, you might say, is the best of the American fish.'[11] Fischer
concluded that women should not be allowed in open tournaments. Lane retorted that adults like herself shouldn't have to
play with children like Bobby.

As similar as their personas were, Lisa and Bobby's accomplishments were not comparable. While Bobby's strength made
him one of the best players of all time, Lisa Lane's standard
did not even place her in the top ranks of women.

In 2004, I called Lisa at the health food store she ran in
upstate New York. Lisa, who was still married to Neil Hickey,
had not played chess in decades. Her competitive streak was
still intact – she commented that a young woman player had
bragged that she could easily defeat Lisa Lane. 'I think it's
absurd to compare the women players of today with those of
my generation. It's like comparing apples with oranges. Chess
was different then, women were different then.' I assured Lisa

that I was not the person who said that, but still Lisa did not want to meet me in person for an interview.

She no longer had any interest in fame and completely abandoned her former identity as a chess player. She seemed to have nothing but bitter feelings toward the game. What Lane values most in her life now is directly opposed to what was written about her in the press: 'I got a lot of attention from the press,' she reminds me, remarking wryly, 'I guess I was good copy.' 'I don't think the things I did in chess forty years ago are the most important things in my life.' Lisa quit chess partly because she was annoyed with being identified as a chess player. 'It got embarrassing – constantly being introduced as a chess champion at parties.' The fame brought on by Lisa's shockingly blunt speech, beauty and skill no longer seem important to her.

Diana Lanni (photo by Stella Monday)

Lisa Lane had a relatively short career on the professional circuit, but her passion for the game and glamorous lifestyle made an impression on girls and women who read about her in the press. Diana Lanni was one of these. Superficially, she was similar to Lisa. Both were born to troubled, working-class American families. Lanni, like Lisa, was beautiful, which proved to be a mixed blessing.

Diana's father showed her Lisa's press clippings, and Diana saw how much fun Lisa had had with chess. 'My dad pointed out that women were such novelties in the chess world, that if I spent a few good years of work, I could travel the world, and achieve rock-star status.' It wasn't until Diana graduated from high school and left home that she took her father's advice. Grateful to her father for introducing her to chess, Diana describes an otherwise terrible relationship with her dad. 'Having such a poor father figure and seeing my mom struggle so much made me a feminist very fast.'

Immediately after high school, Diana found herself in a series of unsavory jobs, including 'the drudgery of $1.60-an-hour retail work' at Lord & Taylor's. One night Diana went with a couple of friends to a strip club in Washington, DC. The owners encouraged the girls to audition, and they complied. Diana was offered a job. 'We dared each other to try it out for a while.' Diana did, and ended up making four times as much stripping as she did at her various day jobs. Setting up a Christmas display at Lord & Taylor's with a chess set, Diana remembered how her father had encouraged her to pursue chess. Soon thereafter she became friends with a strong player who was moving to Miami. Frustrated with all her jobs in DC, she went with him to Miami, telling all her friends that she was 'running away with chess.'

Her stay in Miami was disastrous. Diana got heavily involved in alcohol and cocaine. 'I drank my brains out.' In Miami, Diana took another job as a topless dancer, but she found that stripping in DC was far different from in Miami. 'In DC we stripped for government officials, but my job in Miami was far seedier. We were encouraged to hustle for drinks, ordering the most expensive drinks on the menu, and then charging men fifty dollars for them.'

At one after-hours party, a drunk Diana noticed three fat Italian men playing chess. She offered to play them for high stakes. The winner would receive an 'eight-ball' (an eighth ounce of cocaine). Diana, who was by then a strong amateur player, won easily, but the men refused to give her the drugs. 'I was so angry when they didn't give me the cocaine that I ran around the party complaining.' Her antics caused the men to threaten her. Shortly thereafter, Diana, scared for her safety, fled Miami.

She didn't know where to go, so her default plan was to drive back to DC, where her parents still lived. 'My father was abusing my mother at home, and I didn't want to go back, but I didn't know where to go.' On her way, Diana stopped off at a chess tournament in South Carolina, where she met a man who offered to put her up in Ann Arbor, Michigan. It was a fortuitous move for Diana.

In Michigan, Diana immersed herself in chess, playing as often as she could. When a few cocky masters teased her about her play, Diana was determined 'to get good and prove them wrong.' As she immersed herself in chess, Diana felt her self-esteem soar. Diana improved rapidly and realized how smart she was. 'Academically hopeless' in high school, Diana had assumed that she was dumb before she started playing chess. Her father had always given her that impression. 'He always told me how stupid I was and how ashamed he was of me.' Her success in chess gave her confidence to enroll at a community college in Ann Arbor, Michigan, where she got straight

As. After completing the two-year program, she pursued a BA at the University of Michigan, in which she investigated the psychology of female chess players, surveying dozens of American women chess players. Diana found that many women chess players had come from broken homes, and had 'messed-up' relationships with their fathers. She told me, 'Chess was a way for them to express their feminism, as well as gaining belated approval from their fathers.'

She won a tournament in Michigan in 1977, and qualified for her first US Championship to be held in Los Angeles. Her chess career was on the move. After finishing with the University of Michigan, twenty-three-year-old Diana moved to New York City to live with some chess friends. At the time, New York City was the closest thing to a chess Mecca in the United States.

In New York, Diana still had 'drug problems up the ying-yang,' especially with coke, to which she had developed a serious addiction. She was forthcoming about her most sordid moments in an interview in *Ms.* magazine, in which she said, 'I wound up living in a sleazy hotel on the Upper West Side of Manhattan, hooking for cocaine. I became increasingly suicidal.' After realizing how low she had sunk, she checked into Bellevue Hospital and entered a rehabilitation program. At this point, chess was a lifeboat for Diana. 'The logic of chess was an alternative system to the chaos of life.'

After Diana checked out of Bellevue, in 1980 on New Year's Eve, she began to take chess more seriously, earning an expert's rating and qualifying to play for the US women's team in the 1982 Olympiad in Lucerne, Switzerland, an event for which Diana has particularly fond memories. In Lucerne, Diana found the comforting social network she craved. 'We got drunk every single night and partied. It felt like having a family.'

Lanni tended to land in relationships with other games players, such as Grandmaster Roman Dzindzichashvili, a great chess talent and obsessive gambler, and Paul Magriel, a back-gammon champion. The guys she dated tended to be more successful than she, and in describing one such relationship, Diana said, 'He was the star. I was just the girlfriend who took too many drugs.'

Diana became a bookmaker in New York City, a job she excelled at immediately. In speaking with Diana over the phone, I could understand why. Diana's voice is both warm and author-itative, while her analytical mind is well suited to calculating odds and point spreads. 'Chess players make good bookies,' says Diana, who had a great time in New York in the games world, though 'it was hard to make ends meet in Manhattan.' She often wound up sleeping on the couch at the Barpoint, a game room where ping-pong, backgammon and chess were played till late at night. In the early eighties, rents on the Upper West Side skyrocketed, the club closed, and Diana realized she could not afford to live in the city anymore. In 1985, at the age of thirty, Diana moved to California.

In northern California, Diana worked as a poker dealer, 'a completely legitimate job.' Diana still speaks fondly of poker. 'Poker is a very deep game, and it's something you can use to make money all your life.' Diana feels that chess led her to more lucrative activities in poker and bookmaking and 'saved me from choosing between the drudgery of nine-to-five minimum-wage work and the humiliation of stripping and prostitution.'

Diana resumed bookmaking after she relocated to Santa Cruz some years later and soon got into trouble with the law. Since moving to California, she had been arrested for possession of opiates and driving under the influence. When her bookmaking ring was busted through an informant, she landed in jail.

Diana's time in prison was both wrenching and enlightening. She was incarcerated in the Dublin prison, the federal jail in California. There were three thousand prisoners, many of whom, Diana tells me, were young Hispanic girls. 'It was so sad. They were arrested as mules smuggling drugs across the border. They had been totally sacrificed by their boyfriends.' The atmosphere brought out Diana's progressive and feminist inclinations. She has always wanted to help other women, especially around issues of pregnancy.

For Diana, jail life was not so miserable. She took opera appreciation and Spanish, and attended ice cream socials. Diana worked forty hours a week, like all inmates, but acknowledged racial privileges in jail: 'Since I was white, the guards gave me a good job in the gardening department.' Diana even started a chess club in jail, hoping to introduce chess as a popular pastime like it is in men's prisons. Diana ordered chess sets for the inmates and advertised it in both English and Spanish. The club was given space in the pottery room. 'The recreation department was very supportive of my project.' Some of the women already knew how to play, and Diana gave lessons to the others.

She was incredibly relieved when her four-month sentence ended; it was the small comforts she missed most: 'I couldn't wait to get out and have a real cup of espresso instead of the awful coffee they serve you in jail.' Diana regrets the long-lasting repercussions. She is not allowed to vote, and her record puts off some employers. She is terrified of a future arrest, admitting, 'I am walking a very straight line these days.'

Now Diana teaches chess to kids, with a keen eye on her female students. She wishes she could play herself, but chronic back problems – the aftermath of a knee injury – preclude long periods of sitting.

Lanni is one of the most explicitly feminist chess players I spoke with, declaring, 'I think women play better than men. Chess is a language, and women are better at languages.' She rails on 'the testosterone baloney' saying, 'They still don't have a clue about how it affects people.' But in her work of teaching girls, Diana does observe differences: 'Winning is so important to men. Women don't play as hard to win. They sometimes feel bad to beat their opponents. I have to remind my girls: "Someone has to win, it might as well be you."'

In a 2020 interview with me, Diana Lanni spoke about the uncanny similarities she shared with the fictional Beth Harmon.[12] Walter Tevis used to frequent the same game arenas that Diana had, like the Game Room and Washington Square Park. Diana was the only strong female player in those clubs at the time, drawing huge crowds to watch her blitz prowess.

Diana and Beth also shared a deep passion for the game, that went beyond winning. Diana and Beth both talked about the beauty of chess – as she said herself in the April 1985 issue of *Sports Illustrated*, 'Chess is pretty, creative and artistic – all things women are supposed to be interested in.'

Elevated by *The Queen's Gambit* and online boom, chess has outgrown its reputation as a nerdy sport.

It might be that emphasizing the eccentric elements of chess, but with a positive spin, could further its popularity. Marcel Duchamp liked chess because, in comparison to the glitzy elite of the art world, chess players were 'madmen of a certain quality, the way the artist is supposed to be and generally isn't.' He believed that artists were often pressured to repeat their styles and successes in order to promote themselves and make money; chess players, on the other hand, were less likely to be corrupted.

One of my students, Venice Adrian, was an eccentric, glamorous woman, who managed a downtown New York City nightclub. Blond with plump lips, a Barbie-doll figure and feline gestures, Venice was described in a gossip-and-style glossy, *Paper*, as 'the chicest person in New York City nightlife.' I met Venice at the Man Versus Machine match between Garry Kasparov and Deep Junior. Venice attended with friends who were working on a documentary about the chess scene in New York City. 'I always had an attraction to chess, but never really got around to pursuing it,' Venice told me, 'and then one day I opened the phone book and looked up chess, and called the biggest number I saw.' For a while she took lessons with a Russian grandmaster. After watching Kasparov live, Venice's interest in chess was rekindled. She wanted to take lessons with me, and I wanted to teach her.

At ten o'clock on a Wednesday night, I met Venice at the Hotel Chelsea, what had been New York's bohemian epicenter in the 1960s and 1970s. This was where Dylan Thomas lived and Sid Vicious killed Nancy. Venice's apartment is decorated with her extensive taxidermy collection, but when I arrived, the centerpiece of the room was a wooden chessboard, set up between antique couches. Venice was just starting out in chess, so I showed her some basic checkmates. She was intensely interested in the positions I set up: sometimes she got up and pounced eagerly to the opposite side of the board to get a better look. Deeply involved in the media and nightlife culture, Venice was disenchanted with many of the fame-seeking New Yorkers she knew at her nightclub. She viewed chess as a purely intellectual activity, balancing her lifestyle.

Nearly a year after we had met at the Kasparov–Deep Junior match, I ran into Venice on a plane to Chicago. She was poring over horseracing magazines. We hadn't had a lesson in several months; her interest in chess had been replaced by a new obsession with horse-betting. I told her I'd read about her in some recent magazines, to which she responded, 'I hate fashion magazines. It's all superficial – all about being hip and beautiful.' She asked about my chess career, and at one point, grabbing my arm, she confided, 'I wish I could be as smart as you.' Usually, when people confuse skill at chess with intelligence, I take pains to explain that chess does not always correlate with general mental abilities. This time, I decided to let Venice's mistake go uncorrected.

Rachel Crotto was the first adolescent star of American women's chess – she played in her first US Championship as a thirteen-year-old in 1972, and five years later she tied for first at eighteen. As it was for Lanni, chess was for Rachel a route to higher self-esteem. The ideas of the two women on the subject are uncannily similar. 'I used to think I was stupid,' Rachel tells me. 'But when my dad taught me chess, I began to beat everyone during the breaks at lunch. Classmates and teachers told me, "You're such a good chessplayer. You must be really smart."' Rachel was on her own from the age of sixteen, when she ran away from home. She tried to make a living on her winnings from chess, giving up her studies at NYU to play in a tournament in Israel. 'My family was not very happy with my decision,' Rachel jokes, 'to become a chess bum.'

Rachel became a close friend of Ivona Jezierska. Ivona spoke only Polish and Russian when she arrived in New York, and Rachel, who spoke some Russian, became a close confidante. Ivona describes to me how tough it was for her at first: 'I would wait tables at a restaurant, and I spoke no English so it was hard to understand what the customers wanted.' The two played countless games of blitz and frequented chess clubs and roomed together at tournaments. Ivona has fond memories of late-night blitz marathons at Barpoint, a chess club in downtown Manhattan: 'Diana Lanni used to sleep on the couch there – people were up till three in the morning playing blitz, ping-pong, gambling. Lots of Russian was spoken. It felt like home to me.'

Rachel and Ivona were both in love with chess and the jet-setting lifestyle it offered. But with no independent means, they struggled to get by. Rachel says, 'I was always living on the edge. It was a struggle to pay the rent.'

At the 1986 Olympiad, held in Dubai, Rachel, at the age of twenty-seven, abruptly decided to give up the game. 'I had a bad tournament and realized that if I hadn't applied myself to studying by then, I probably never would.' I ask Rachel if she misses chess, and she tells me, 'I miss the traveling,' adding, 'and not having to work nine to five.' Ivona also quit semi-professional chess as she matured, because her minimum standard of living increased. Now Ivona makes a good living working as a chess coordinator and coach, but lacks the energy to play seriously. She told me wistfully, 'If I was wealthy I would play chess all the time.'

Ruth Haring, Rachel Crotto and Diane Savereide on the November 1979 edition of *Chess Life & Review* (courtesy of US Chess)

Rachel felt estranged from the male-dominated and often chau-
vinistic atmosphere at open chess tournaments. She once called
into a radio advice talk show, 'I am a woman chess player, and
every time I play a man they underestimate me, assuming that
I will play badly because I am a woman.' Rachel recalls that
the host advised her to 'dress very sexy, wear a low neckline,
and put on a lot of make-up to use my femininity against them.'
Rachel, a lesbian, says, 'Obviously, I was not about to do that.'
Rachel told me she never encountered any discrimination in
the chess world because of her sexuality, but said a lot of
American female chess players in the 1970s and 1980s were
incorrectly labelled as lesbians: 'Some players who were just
not particularly feminine got mistaken for lesbians.' There are
a number of top female chess players who are openly lesbian
or bisexual, but there are very few professional players who
are out as gay men, raising the question as to how we can do
more to welcome the LGBTQ community in chess. Many
important international events are held in countries that have
poor LGBTQ rights records.

Rachel's ego was boosted by the attention she got as a young
girl, but later, the scrutiny interfered with her relationship to
the chess itself. She wanted to concentrate on the game, but
was distracted by the attention she got. Despite lingering feelings for the game, Rachel hardly plays at all now. But she has
a comeback fantasy. 'I've always wanted to play chess as a man
– in one of those big open tournaments with 400 people.' Rachel
says, 'I would like to know how it feels to be invisible. To be
just one of 400 players. I always felt like I was on trial at tournaments. If I were to make a mistake, it would prove that I
really was a stupid woman.'

The most prolific champion of the era was Diane Savereide,
who won a total of five US titles from 1975 to 1984. Savereide
had a major influence on fellow US Championship contender

Diana Lanni also. 'She was my hero,' Lanni gushes. 'I remember being so psyched to ride with her each morning to the tournament hall on her motorcycle.' Savereide was the first American woman to maintain a national master rating, 'the first strong female master in American chess,' said IM Jack Peters, also from LA.

Savereide describes living in a positive chess environment as a young girl. She was nurtured by many prominent female players, most notably French-American philanthropist and organizer Jacqueline Piatigorsky. An heiress of the Rothschild banking fortune, Jacqueline fled Nazi-occupied France in 1940 with her husband, cellist Gregor Piatigorsky. They settled in Los Angeles after a brief stint in Philadelphia, where Jacqueline lived till the age of 100. Jacqueline was a strong player, earning a bronze medal in the first Women's Olympiad in 1957, but was most known for her patronage of events like the Piatigorsky Cup, and her support of talents like Diane.

Diane says, 'When I traveled to other parts of the country, I discovered that chess players were not always so hospitable to women, but it was too late to discourage me.'

In 1975, Diane won the first US Women's Chess Championship that she played in, earning her a spot in a world-title qualifier. Diane traveled from Hong Kong to Haifa to represent the US in international events.

In the summer of 1984, Diane tried to make a go of it as a professional chess player. She took time off from her job as a computer programmer to play in tournaments, but didn't make enough money. She quit. 'It came down to being thirty and deciding I had to make a living.' At the time, the first prize for the US Women's Champion was tiny. For becoming the best female player in the nation, Diane would get somewhere between $300 and $600.

Since then, Diane has not played much chess. She sometimes

misses the friends, travels, and its intensity. But she was too passionate about the game to play casually.

'The reason chess never became popular among women in America, while they broke barriers and proliferated in so many other fields,' Diana Lanni muses, 'is that women still needed money as an excuse to use their brains. Thinking for free was unacceptable.'

After Saveriede quit chess, Russian immigrants, who had strong chess foundations from Soviet training, won many US Women's Championships. However, many of these women came to the United States for a better life, hoping to make more money than they did as professional players. Irina Levitina, three-time US Women's Champion, gave up chess for bridge. Elena Donaldson, three-time champion, became a computer programmer. Anjelina Belakovskaia, another three-time champion, slowed her participation in her thirties to pursue a career in finance.

The opportunities for money in women's chess in America today are improving. The prizes for US championships have increased dramatically since the eighties, when the sums were in the three-figures. In 2008, chess philanthropists Dr Jeanne[*] and Rex Sinquefield founded the Saint Louis Chess Club, and the city became the epicenter of chess in the United States. In 2009, the club began to host richer editions of the US Chess and US Women's Championship. I chaired the organizing committee for the first few events, where I advocated for conditions for the players, from five-star accommodations to enticing prize funds.

The current US Women's Championship purse is $100,000,

---

[*] Dr Jeanne Cairns Sinquefield founded the 'Cairns Cup' an elite tournament for women in 2019, also hosted by the Saint Louis Chess Club. Russian Grandmaster Valentina Gunina won the 2019 edition while Grandmaster Koneru Humpy won in 2020.

a massive increase from the days that Lisa Lane complained about a $600 prize. But the US Championship has nearly double the prizes.* I used to think that was sensible, since women could qualify for both events. Now I see prizes for such events as compensation for time and entertainment as much as for skill. The richer purses and glamorous conditions have helped motivate young stars. Jennifer Yu, Carissa Yip and Annie Wang all started playing the US Women's as preteens then rocketed up the crosstables in their teens. Yu won two Championship titles, in 2019 and 2022, while Yip won in 2021, and Wang was runner-up in 2018.

Rochelle Ballantyne (photo by David Llada)

---

* In 2021, the prize fund for the US Championship was $194,000, while the prize fund for the US Women's Championship is $100,000.

Financial obstacles also prevent a lot of talented kids from pursuing the game. Many children learn chess in primary or elementary school programs but then lose access as they enter secondary school. Racism, and its intersection with class and gender, prevent many American chess talents from reaching their full potential. Rochelle Ballantyne, a chess expert featured in the award-winning documentary *Brooklyn Castle*, was interviewed by Kasparov Chess on how to make chess more welcoming to Black players. She suggested tournament organizers offer discounts to K-12 students that attend a school where over 65% of the students fall below the poverty line. 'Chess is incredibly classist, and any effort to increase chess participation from under-represented backgrounds has to look at the financial barriers.'

In the early 2010s, Rochelle's rating was bubbling up to the National Master level* and she represented the National team in the 2013 World Youth Championship in the United Arab Emirates. At the same time, her academic career was taking off. She received a full ride to Stanford University, and graduated with BAs in Political Science and African American studies. Ballantyne maintains a passion for the game and for speaking up about its racism and sexism. As Rochelle told Melinda Matthews:[13]

> I was always the odd person out. Always asked whether or not I was lost. Chess is supposed to be a battle of intellect and my intellect always seemed to be diminished or erased because I am Black and because I am a woman. Luckily, when I started playing chess I was too young to really process race and gender as a construct. I knew I was different but I didn't care because I wanted to win. And that drive continues to carry me.

---

* In 2013, Rochelle reached 2127, just 73 points from the National Master title.

Organizations and non-profits all over the world, from Chess-in-the-Schools in New York City, to Chess-in-the-Slums based in Lagos, Nigeria, aim to change lives through chess in education. In the United States such organizations have made a major impact in diversifying the game and giving opportunities for kids to learn and play. But I agree with Ballantyne that there are still many gaps. Some cities and communities don't have access to those programs, or age out of them when they need them most. For those starting out, chess is an inexpensive way to lose yourself in thought and build intellectual confidence. For those who take it more seriously, trips to play in state or national championships can be life-changing, leading to scholarships and deeper learning. And when we give kids the full support they need to follow their dreams, magical results are inevitable.

Jessica Hyatt, a student at Success Academy, an intensive charter school program in New York City with a robust chess program, told me she aims to be the first African-American female to earn the National Master title. Jessica revels in the chance to break new ground. She told me that it's important to show everyone that 'with passion and dedication you will succeed.' During the 2020 pandemic, Jessica amped up her chess training. And when live events started up again, her rating shot up. In one event at the King of Queens chess club, Jessica topped the field over several masters and an international master, inching her rating ever closer to the National Master title. In her favorite win of the event, an adult master complimented her aggressive style. Jessica told me that she found his flattery ironic, 'because I just played theory, and the game felt like a breeze.'

In 2020, at the age of fifteen, she earned the Daniel Feinberg Success in Chess award, which came with a $40,000 scholarship. Jessica's teacher, David Mbonu, a National Master himself, reminisces that when he was younger, he looked up to the one other Black child who frequented the same tournaments. 'Jessica doesn't currently have that person,' he told *BK Reader*, a Brooklyn local news source, 'but she has the ability to be that person for somebody else.'[14]

The most decorated American female player, Irina Krush, literally learned the moves between worlds, when her father taught her chess on the journey from Odessa to New York City. Irina is introspective about her split identity: 'I am half American, half Russian.' Even her voice contains a mix of accents from Brooklyn and Russia. She expresses the most fondness for the Russian language. 'I consider English a utilitarian language. When talking about emotions, I need to speak Russian – or at least English in a Russian accent.' Her early play was very strategic, marked by a keen understanding of the endgame. Her style changed as she became a professional: 'I used to always play against strong players as a kid, so I was used to defending.' Now her style is much more aggressive. 'No one could call me a passive player.'

Over the board, Irina enters another realm, one of deep mental focus, but she also seems to savor the physical process of making moves. She places her piece on the square with a determined yet tender touch, as if she is playing adagio piano. In immaculate handwriting, she records her move and then turns her concentrated gaze to the board. When playing Irina I feel particularly conscious of the illegible scribbles I use.

Irina is disturbed on a visceral level by lying and cheating. Irina once witnessed a competitor offer me a draw before a game that would affect the final standings of the tournament. I declined, but Irina was emotionally floored: 'I am so upset I had to see that.'

Irina was so precocious in chess – she earned the master title as a twelve-year-old, her first US_title at fourteen years old, and the IM title at sixteen years old – that she and her parents arranged for her to take half her classes at home in order to accelerate her chess career. After graduating from high school, Irina took a year off to devote herself entirely to chess. She had some major successes, but her results were inconsistent and, more significantly, Irina was not happy. 'I spent all day studying chess at home.' She felt alienated. 'I realized I wanted to go to college.'

She decided to enroll in NYU, because along with her passion for chess Irina wanted to learn about business, politics and writing. 'It takes me a while to write anything, because I have to choose just the right words.' Her perfectionist character was borne out by her record at NYU, where she earned a 4.0 average in her second semester, even though she was absent for two weeks to play in tournaments.

Irina worried about the limited financial resources in chess. 'I identify with a subculture of first-generation Russian-Americans,' she told me at the time, 'who aim to go to elite colleges and make a lot of money after graduation.' Her parents are successful accountants, and though they have encouraged her in chess, they wanted her to have a secure career. Irina, in trying to convey to me just how rich she would like to be, tells me, 'Remember the hotel we stayed at in Shanghai, Jen?' I tell her I do, an extravagant five-star hotel. 'I want to be able to afford to go on vacation to places like that without flinching.' Irina says she'd like to avoid 'degenerating into a materialistic parasite.' Chess is the counterpoint to all this, and what keeps her life creatively fulfilling. 'It's a panacea with which I combat the emptiness.'

When I ask Irina about her dreams in chess, I get a passionate response. 'My ultimate fantasy,' she says, eyes flashing, Russian accent on full, 'is to play e4 and d4 equally well . . . to be a two-headed monster. That's a dream with some soul in it.'

Irina Krush (photo by David Llada)

Beyond learning king pawn, Irina, never a fan of women's titles, wanted to make history and become the first American woman to earn the grandmaster title.* When she earned her first norm as a teen, the *New York Times* declared, 'Krush, 17, is on her way to a Grandmaster Ranking.' But her progress lagged and despite dozens of attempts over more than a decade, she was unable to meet the GM requirements.

* GM Susan Polgar earned her title while playing for Hungary.

In yet another try, Irina travelled to an event over 5000 miles from Brooklyn, but one she'd always dreamed of playing, the 2013 Baku Open in Azerbaijan. Irina craved playing in the challenging event, which was filled with grandmasters. Out of sixty-nine players, thirty-one were GMs. She didn't have any special expectations in this event – she didn't even feel that she was in particularly good form when she started. But she was ready to fight, even though she was the underdog in almost every game.

I know my opponent's rating, but it's just a number, not my sentence. For me, chess is a fight, sixty-four squares where you lay out everything you have.

After the grueling two weeks of play, Irina ended with three wins, one loss, and five draws, finishing in a tie for ninth place amongst dozens of heavyweight grandmasters. With this fine result, Irina won no trophies, not much money. She won something way more important: that final requirement for the grandmaster title. She became the first American woman ever to earn the title, and the thirtieth woman of all time. She earned the first norm close to home, in Queens, New York. The final one would take her twelve years, and halfway across the world. In Irina's case, the journey really was the destination.

12

Gender Play: Angela from Texas

'(S)he was a man; she was woman; she knew the secrets,
shared the weaknesses of each. It was a most bewildering
and whirligig state of mind to be in. The comforts of
ignorance seemed utterly denied to her. She was a feather
blown on the gale.'

Virginia Woolf, *Orlando*

In medieval chess, when a pawn reached the eighth rank and
became a Queen, a moral quandary arose. How could a
male foot soldier change sex to become a woman? In 1913, the
great chess historian H. J. R. Murray wrote about the dilemma:
'The pawn had to change its sex . . . the moral sense of some
players was outraged . . . the usual practice was to use a different
name for the promoted pawn from that of the original Queen.'[1]
The pawn promoted into a piece that moved like a Queen but
was given a masculine name, reserving the title of Queen for
the original.

In Texas a chess expert ushered in the twenty-first century
by transforming from a man, Tony, into a woman, Angela.
Angela Alston calls the day she got her sex-change operation
'the happiest of her life,' echoing what millions of pawns must
have felt when they reached the eighth rank. And like pawns,
Angela struggled against ranks of adversity.

'I was born aspected of both genders,' Angela says. 'I have
more testosterone than most women, but less than most men.'

Angela tells me, she has pseudo-hermaphroditism, in which a child is born with ambiguous genitalia. The incidence is estimated to be 1 in 20,000. In the rarer case (approximately one in a million) of 'true hermaphroditism,' a baby has tissues of both male and female sex organs.

Angela's wavering between the male and the female and eventual transformation has been painful, expensive, and ultimately redemptive. In my first e-mail communication with Angela, she referred to herself as 'two spirit.' In Native American culture, a two spirit is a revered person who has special insights into both the male and female psyches. Angela, who grew up in a traditional family in the fifties, feared that revealing her gender confusion would elicit more scorn than admiration.

Angela Alston (photo by Jennifer Shahade)

On a visit to Austin, Texas, I got a chance to speak with Angela face to face. We met in a dim, laid-back café, where Angela had driven from her home in San Antonio. She arrived dressed in white jeans and a black-and-white knitted sweater. She wore glasses and her long hair was crimped. She is self-conscious about her voice. 'My voice is the one thing I cannot change.'

Angela and I immediately felt comfortable with each other. We settled into couches on the smoking side of the café. Angela ordered a latte, lit up a menthol cigarette, and began to rhapsodize about the Texas capital. 'I love getting a chance to visit Austin – it's an oasis in Texas,' she raved. 'In this state, intellectual activity is like water in the desert.' Austin has a liberal, artistic community. The largest branch of the University of Texas draws 50,000 students, and the downtown is scattered with independent bookstores, country-music bars, and coffee shops. I spotted a vegetarian restaurant offering ten percent off to anyone with a mullet haircut. At that time George W. Bush's face was silk-screened onto T-shirts that read One-Term President, while Keep Austin Weird was the bumper-sicker slogan of choice. Angela thrives in such an accepting environment. 'In Austin you can do anything without being persecuted. Intellectual activity is what life is about for me.' Angela is drawn to chess for its challenge, pointing out, 'I could play this game for my whole life and never near the pinnacle.'

Born in Boston on 14 December 1955, with both male and female genitalia, Angela was quickly designated as a male and named Tony. 'After that, no one bothered to look for years.' Early on, Angela knew that she didn't fit in. 'As a six-year-old, I realized that something was very wrong. I did not fit in with the boys. I thought I was mentally ill.' A ten-year-old Angela would browse in the psychology section of the public library, hoping to find some clues. At thirteen, she chanced upon a copy of a book by Christine Jorgensen (1927–1989), a photographer who traveled to Denmark to get a sex-change operation. When the story leaked out to the press, the charismatic, multi-talented Jorgensen instantly became a public figure – an object of ridicule for some and an inspiration to others, like the young Angela, who said that finding Jorgenson's autobiography 'was like a revelation. Finally, I saw someone who was like me.'

Throughout her life, Angela has maintained a passion for chess. Learning the moves from her sister at the age of six, Angela played in her first tournament as a teenager. She quickly became hooked on the game, particularly attracted to its psychological aspects. Angela devoured the writings of her favorite player, the second world champion, Dr Emanuel Lasker. Lasker was well-educated in math, philosophy and psychology and was friends with major intellectuals, such as Einstein. Angela tells me, 'If I could be a fly on the wall, anywhere, anytime, it would be during the conversations between Lasker and Einstein.'

Alston had a frenetic lifestyle as a youth, switching from job to job: taxi driver, land surveyor, cook and Navy payroll officer. Throughout all of this, Angela was depressed. In her stint as a cab driver, passengers used to recount their woeful tales. 'I listened, and thought, I could live your life standing on my head.' She used to drive into the worst neighborhoods of San Antonio in the dead of the night, which Alston now sees as a 'subconscious suicide attempt.' Angela told me, 'Part of me just wanted my life to be over. When I was eighteen I thought I would never make it past twenty-one, and when I was twenty-one I thought I would never make it to twenty-five. But, somehow, I kept going.'

Alston's lack of comfort in her body led to reckless behavior from hitchhiking to alcohol and drug abuse. Reminiscing, Angela assures me, 'I did have fun.' But the troubles outweighed the good times. She didn't feel like a man, so she created a male persona 'imitating different aspects of dozens of the men I knew in my life – it was like making myself schizophrenic so I could fit in.' Alston lived in constant fear that the carefully constructed masculine identity would be unmasked: 'I some-times used feminine gestures – women tend to move their hands around a lot more when they talk, and one time, a tournament director told me, "You behave like a woman." I was terrified that I was going to be found out.' After such incidents, she'd retreat, desperate to iron out the kinks in her personality.

When she settled down in San Antonio, Alston set herself two goals: to become the top player in the city and the president of the chess club. Angela accomplished both feats in just four years. Instead of feeling joy, she felt only restlessness, wondering what to do next.

In order to truly fit in, she decided to start a family. Alston met Teri in San Antonio while employed as a land surveyor. They married and had two children, Ian and Sean. 'Doctors told me the chances of me having kids were very low, but it happened.' She kept her secret from Teri: 'She told me that I didn't look or feel like other men, but she didn't realize the extent of it.' During this time, Angela stopped using drugs, although she was drinking a lot. 'I replaced one vice with another.' The relationship was problematic and, she claims, 'We never really got along.' In 1993, after twelve years of marriage, they divorced.

Angela recalls being in a constant state of depression while living as a man. 'I used to be so jealous of people who were born into one sex, and did not have to go through what I had to go through.' In May 1996, a few years after her marriage with Teri fell apart, she became determined to pursue the dream she'd had since twelve years old. Angela yearned for an external body and social identity to match her internal female self. 'I had tried everything else. I had to either live as I really was or die.'

Alston was well aware of the obstacles she would face along the way. 'Some people thought I was just insane to give up being a white man in this culture. They did not understand why I would voluntarily descend the socio-economic ladder.'

Angela let it be known that she'd decided to let her female self emerge. As there were no laws in Texas to protect the rights of transgender individuals, employers cut back her hours as a cook and were openly nasty. In March 1998, she went to a medical doctor, who confirmed the existence of both male and female genitalia. Then she went to the courthouse, changed her birth certificate designation to female and renamed herself. 'When I was seventeen years old, I decided I liked the name Angela, and wanted it for myself. It took me twenty-five years.' Once she legally became a woman, her rights were protected at work, since she could claim sexual discrimination based on gender. This attracted the immediate attention of worried managers. Angela said they walked on eggshells once they understood her new legal rights. They gave Angela her hours back and were careful not to say anything offensive, at least not to her face.

A practical obstacle to Angela's transformation was financing her sex-change operation. To remove her phallus, she had to save for three years, working overtime as a cook. After saving approximately $10,000 for the operation and related drugs and therapy, Angela traveled to Montreal, where her surgery was scheduled.

The operation lasted two hours. Angela recalls, 'That day was the happiest day of my life.'

Born into a conservative family, Angela tells me, 'I was brought up on the idea that you don't just accept everything. No one ever talked about "celebrating diversity".' Her siblings (one sister and two brothers) and her late father did not support her transformation, but when her father was dying of cancer in 1998, Angela accepted the responsibility to take care of her ill mother, Mary, whom she moved in with. 'When my father was on his deathbed, I promised to take care of Mom,' she recalls. 'And I will keep my word.' Initially her mother was upset with Angela, but gradually began to accept her. Angela knew her mother was ready to love her as she was after receiving her forty-second birthday card. Her mother wrote, 'To my daughter.'

In San Antonio, Angela has settled into two stable, part-time jobs: teaching chess and working as a real-estate advisor. Teaching chess is Angela's favorite: 'I love to see the light in my students' eyes and realize I reached someone.' Angela's students, who range from six to twelve years old, sometimes ask her, 'Are you a man or a woman?' Struggling to answer the awkward question is worth it for Angela: 'I think it's good for young people to understand that some people are born different.'

The United States Chess Federation has considered Angela a female player since 1998. US Chess began to communicate with Angela, who was suddenly eligible to qualify for the US Women's Championship. Though some state delegates argued with Angela's participation in women's events, US Chess calmly accepted her changed status. According to Angela, Tim Redman, the president of the federation at the time, was well informed of precedent-setting cases such as that of Reneé Richards, a tennis player who was barred from playing in the 1976 US Open by the United States Tennis Association, because she could not pass the chromosome test. Richards – urged on by fans and supporters – fought the decision, resulting in a year-long battle that Reneé finally won in the Supreme Court, clearing the way for her to play in the 1977 US Open.

US Chess adopted an official transgender policy in 2018, allowing any member to change their gender identification with a single phone call, with the caveat that subsequent changes would require proof of identification. Prominent writer and influencer Charlotte Clymer, who has half a million followers on Twitter, called the policy 'outstanding', because it 'makes spaces welcoming for all players, regardless of gender identity.'

Lisa Willis (courtesy of Lisa Willis)

Lisa Willis, a transgender player from the Bay Area, told me the chess world has been extremely accepting of her, including clubs in San Francisco, San Gabriel Valley, Reno and San Diego. She legally changed her name in February 2021, but the Mechanics Institute in San Francisco, the oldest chess club in the United States, referred to her by Lisa long before that, in both crosstables and in commentary of her games online, which meant a lot to her. Lisa's worst experience so far was when she was kicked out of a women's online chess group because she is trans. 'I was annoyed, because they invited me – I didn't seek them out.' However, she turned the negative into a positive and she started her own club on the same site, 'Trans and CIS Women United', which quickly attracted dozens of members.

Angela Alston is also an online player, and especially enjoys e-mail chess, where she often juggled more than fifty games at once. In e-mail chess, the length of time between each move ranges from one day to two weeks, so games last anywhere from a month to a year.

Some of Angela's chess peers thought that her sex change would affect her play. One chess buddy warned her, 'Your rating will plummet after you change your sex.' Angela tells me she sees no difference between her style today and her previous style. In her first tournament game after her operation, Angela crushed a master – in twenty-nine moves. Selby Anderson, a friend of Angela's and a chess master, said the transition was 'a surprise, but not entirely out of character. I think she enjoyed being a lightning rod.' The most difficult thing for Selby was 'to stop calling her [by her dead name].'

Though she is talkative and candid, I gather that Angela is lonely and feels a little out of place in both the chess world and San Antonio. 'The person I'm closest to is my mother. I don't have a lot of friends, though my closest are from chess – we have a point of reference so we can all relate.' Angela is not optimistic about her future romantic prospects: 'At my age, it is hard enough to find a life companion, but (for me) I suspect it is nearly impossible.' However, the operation did leave Angela multi-orgasmic. 'After the procedure I was able to experience more pleasure than I could as a man.'

The misconception that irritates Angela most is the frequent confusion that arises between gender and sexuality. That Angela wanted to change her sex did not mean that she wanted to date men. She changed from a lesbian woman living in a man's body to a lesbian woman living in a woman's body. But many friends did not understand that, assuming that she changed her sex so that she could sleep with men. One woman even told Angela, 'If you want to find a man, you better stop acting so intelligent.'

Angela is suspicious of men. After the operation, the first thing she did was look to make sure 'it was gone.' Sometimes her rhetoric devolves into absurd invectives. 'Ninety percent of men ought to be flushed down the toilet immediately,' she tells me, adding that 'the other ten percent are very good people.' Angela said that, living as a man for thirty-five years, she heard things that men only say amongst each other. 'Many men really do think that women are stupid,' she told me. I press her for details, but she refused: 'If I told you, Jennifer, you'd want to become lesbian.'

Angela is not active in any LGTBQ or transgender activist groups. 'Being trans is not my life,' she says. Though she reads voraciously on topics like religion and history, she rarely reads about feminism or sexuality, though she does consider herself a feminist. Angela is happy to educate the curious, but she does not want to spend the rest of her life thinking or talking about her gender. 'I took care of my problem, so that I wouldn't have to think about it all the time.' Angela is so much happier after her operation that she swears if she ever became rich, she would set up a fund to finance sex-change operations for people who could not afford them.

Angela, often surprised by the reactions of her friends in the chess world, could not have guessed who would be supportive. 'At least I know who my real friends are.' Angela was shocked when one of her most liberal friends told her she was 'sick and perverted.' The friends who touched Angela the most were the ones who focused on her struggle, rather than on their relationship to her. One friend from the chess world looked at Angela and said, 'Oh my god, you must have been in so much pain.'

In San Antonio the population is conservative. 'Many people here only know about people who are trans from *The Jerry Springer Show*. They lack exposure – it's as if I'm the first person they met who was different. Hundreds of people, once they get to know me, say, "You're not like I thought."' It is Angela's belief and experience that people will often open their minds to her if she is patient with them.

According to Angela, specifying gender is not an effective way to classify people. In her view, gender expression lies on a flexible, non-binary continuum, pointing out commonplace examples. 'When a woman wears pants or when a man cries in public – these are transgressions of traditional roles,' and so, concludes Angela, 'if you really think about it, we're all a little transgender.'

13

Worst to First

'Every breath is a movement toward the endgame.'
Stacey Abrams, in *While Justice Sleeps*

In the spring of 2004, Irina Krush and I were invited to the Women's World Championship in Chess City, Russia. When I told my friends that I was going to Chess City, they thought I was joking, renaming my destination 'Chesstonia'. But this was for real. Irina and I were among sixty-four of the best female chess players in the world contesting the world title, up for grabs for the first time since 2001.

The tournament would be held near Elista, the capital city of Kalmykia, one of eighty-nine semi-autonomous regions in Russia. At the time, Kalmykia was led by the former president of FIDE, Kirsan Ilyumzhinov, who took his double presidency seriously, building a city in which to play chess on the outskirts of Elista. Since 1998, when the prestigious Olympiad was held there, Chess City has been a common site for world-class tournaments.

I usually love traveling, but I was not thrilled to visit Russia again. I had developed an irrational fear of the country two and a half years before when I was there in the dead of winter for the Women's World Championship. The first day I arrived, I walked around Red Square smiling, excited to be in Moscow. A tall, blond Russian laughed at me and asked if I was American. I asked how he knew and he said because of my manic smiling, which seemed demented to him. I had not brought sufficiently warm clothing, and knew only enough Russian to order food and read street names. There were things I liked about Moscow – the energy, the subways, the art museums, and the circus. Still, at the end of the tournament, walking through the security gate, I was happy to be going home.

The customs agent asked me where my visa was. I replied that it was inside my passport. She told me it wasn't and said that I should check my bags. After twenty minutes of fruitless searching, I still couldn't find it. She told me I would not be allowed to leave Moscow until I found it. I began to panic. I asked if I could pay a special fee to leave. She said no. I missed my plane, still looking for the god-forsaken piece of paper. After searching every crevice of my bag, I gave up and took a cab back to the city center. I spent the next four days waiting in lines at the police station, travel agencies, and photo shops in order to compile the mountain of paperwork required to obtain a new visa.

I relived all this four days before leaving for Elista when applying for my new visa at the Russian Embassy, located in uptown Manhattan. On my way from the diner where I had been filling out my application to the visa office it began to pour, soaking through my bag. When I tried to hand in my damp form, the visa officer screamed at me and called the application unacceptable, sending me to the back of the line to fill out a new one.

I traveled to Russia with Irina and Grandmaster Pascal Charbonneau, her boyfriend at the time and her 'second' during the tournament. I was glad to be with friends and also figured that Irina's fluency with the language would make my second trip to Russia smoother than the first.

When the three of us stepped off the plane in Elista, after the thirty-hour-long journey from New York City, a smiling woman dressed in a purple robe served us Kalmyk tea, black tea with milk and salt. She draped a gold-trimmed white scarf around my neck and handed me a single rose. Irina and I were besieged by interviewers. It seemed as though we had arrived in the fairytale land of Chess City, Kalmykia, where women chess masters are treated like queens. '[Gather] all the flowers of Kalmykia for Chess Queens' read posters all over the city. As it turned out, Elista was another world from Moscow. Kalmyk people have Asian features, their ancestry most closely linked with Mongolians. It is one of the few areas of Russia in which Buddhism is the predominant religion. One of the poorest areas of Russia, it is also considered one of the most hospitable.

Chess City is a fenced-off suburb of Elista with nothing much but lookalike cottages and an empty bar called Café Rook. I felt out of my element in the remote surroundings. During tournaments, I like to jog, play basketball and take long walks, but Chess City was so isolated that there was nowhere to walk except in half-mile circles.

We certainly didn't have to worry about our safety. There were about three security guards for each player, most of whom stood around smoking cigarettes and chatting all day. 'What's your name?' they would ask me as I walked to the dining or playing hall, 'Jennifer?' 'Jennifer Lopez!' they shouted, followed by uproarious laughter.

Irina, Pascal and I shared a large cottage, with a Western-style kitchen and bathroom. At first I thought our accommodations were simply comfortable, but then I learned how extraordinary they were compared to those of the residents of rural Kalmykia. Irina, Pascal and I traveled to a small town, Yashkol, to meet some Kalmyk players. We were treated like celebrities. We visited a school and were mobbed for autographs and given gifts by Kalmyk children who had never met foreigners. After playing chess with some local players, the three of us were invited to the mayor's house for lunch. Our gracious hosts had prepared a splendid lunch of fresh meat – 'the sheep was killed this morning' – cheese, pirogis and vodka. As we ate and drank, guests and hosts were all called on to give the customary lengthy toasts. Our hosts lavished praise on us – 'I can't wait to read about you in the papers in the coming years' – while Irina, Pascal and I declared in turn our affection for Kalmykia, chess and the most delicious pirogis of our lives. Despite the joyous pitch of the afternoon, we saw that the conditions of even the most powerful in rural Kalmykia were rough. The rooms in houses were tiny and there was no bathroom – even in the office of the mayor – only a rancid outhouse that seemed not to have been cleaned for months. Most Kalmyks, I later learned, do not have electricity.

After that afternoon I understood that, in contrast to the rest of the region, Chess City was a place of luxury. A few weeks after the tournament, a *New York Times* article, 'Where Chess Is King and the People Are Pawns', described the chess palace in which we played as a 'glassed-in biosphere on Mars, where the most brilliant minds of chess compete for diamond crowns. For miles around, 300,000 live in poverty in the barren plains.'[1] Upon walking just meters outside of Chess City, protesters pass out fliers in Russian and English denouncing Kirsan Ilyumzhinov and the chess championship. Roughly translated excerpts include: 'The citizens of our republic take the financial consequences due to these chess festivals', 'The majority of the children cannot eat to their heart's content while you are taking pleasure by the concerts of the poverty artists.' Though Ilyumzhinov claims that chess is a religion and a gift to humanity, he seems to believe it is a gift reserved only for the elite. Ordinary Kalmyk citizens need special permission to visit Chess City, and the only spectators at the event were the friends, families and coaches of the players.

As intrigued as I was by the politics and history of Kalmykia, I had to shift my thoughts to my first match. Two weeks before the start of the tournament I had learned that my opponent in Elista would be a young Georgian, Nana Dzagnidze. Busy with coaching my students, I had little time to prepare in America. Settled in Elista three days before the start of the tournament, I began to study Nana's games.

The other reason we decided to arrive early in Elista was to adjust to the nine-hour time difference, a change that affects some players more drastically than others. Irina can sleep soundly regardless of the time or location. Red-eyed and miserable on planes, I am jealous of Irina, who can go into REM sleep as soon as the plane takes off. Pascal and I have more trouble adjusting, so the night after we arrived in Elista, we stopped at the bar in the Chess Palace, hoping a glass of wine would help put us to sleep. One of the most active and popular women players, Bulgarian Antoaneta Stefanova, was there with her trainer and compatriot, GM Vladimir Georgiev. Antoaneta had just come from the Dominican Republic and looked tan and happy as she smoked a cigarette and sipped a whisky on the rocks. Chatting and drinking with them relaxed my nerves a bit.

Two days after settling in, we attended the opening ceremony, which was held in a field in the middle of nowhere; the bus to take us there was two hours late, and the drive itself took an hour. All the players were grumpy and hungry by the time we arrived. There were traditional Kalmyk dances, speeches, the Russian and FIDE national anthems, and Kalmyk models dressed in custom-designed black-and-white-checkered dresses. 'Why don't they give each player such a dress in their own size?' wondered Elisabeth Paehtz. 'That would be a really good present.'

Koneru Humpy, the Indian grandmaster, who was the

top-seeded player in the tournament, was invited up to the stage to determine the colors for each board of the tournament. Without cracking a smile, the serious teenager drew the colors: each odd-numbered player (which included me) would have the white pieces in the first game. As soon as I learned this, my mind started to focus on the next day's game.

The next morning, my sleeping schedule was still a bit out of whack – I woke up just before seven. Too early. The round was not until two. Too many hours to kill before game time. In preparing, I find it important to strike a balance between relaxation and study. Studying for six hours before a two o'clock start is dangerous, because it's important to save energy for the game. On the other hand, I am occasionally mad at myself for studying too little, especially when a position I only glanced at appears on the board. More often, I tend to overprepare, sometimes looking at games on my laptop until minutes before start-time. In Elista, I studied the Najdorf, the dynamic opening that my eighteen-year-old opponent had played since she was ten years old.

At two o'clock I sat down at my table, where the traditional wooden pieces were set up on a high-tech board that was wired to the Internet. Our moves would be instantly relayed to chess sites on the web. I began the game with confidence, expecting to improve on the play of a previous opponent of Nana's. Nana had played the Najdorf in more than fifty games, but against me she tried a different opening. My heart started to beat more rapidly. I had not prepared for this line, but had no choice but to pretend I was confident. I made a mistake on move eight and lost all the advantage that comes with the first move. After that, I began to calm down and play well. My position improved, but she was solid, and it was not easy to find ways to break through. I definitely did not want to get short on time – each player had only two hours, and I had already used more than one. I played a move and hit the clock. Instantly, my heart dropped. My move was a huge blunder, allowing Nana to win a Rook for a Bishop. The mistake would cost me the game and most probably the match. The only thing to do was pray that she would not notice. It was a vain hope – she won my Rook, and soon after, the game.

The tournament was single-elimination knockout, and the only way for me to advance would be to win the next game with black. I tried hard the next day, and even got a double-edged position in which I had full chances to play for the win. Unfortunately for me, Nana was determined to advance to the next round. She played well, rebuffed my activity, and gained an edge in an endgame. I had zero chance to win. We agreed to a draw. Nana advanced.

The pain was not all-consuming, but there was a lingering sense of incompetence that stayed with me for the whole week, and only began to dissipate when I returned to America. I stayed in Elista for a few days to watch the other games, and support my teammate Irina, who had made it to the second round. I both hoped and expected to see Irina go far. However, having just finished classes at NYU, she was rustier than usual, and missed some tactics in her second match. She was knocked out.

Irina and I were eliminated, but I still followed all the games of the tournament, hoping for a deserving champion who would be good for women's chess. I was therefore thrilled with the winner: Bulgarian bon vivant Antoaneta Stefanova.

In Elista, Stefanova abandoned her typically wild lifestyle to approach the tournament professionally. She brought a coach. Satisfied with ties in each two-game match, she relied on her superior nerves and tactical alertness to prevail in the tiebreaks. In the third round, Antoaneta was matched against a close friend, Ukrainian Natalia Zhukova. Antoaneta and Natalia made a controversial decision. Instead of playing out their match games, providing excitement for hundreds of spectators on the Internet, the two women agreed to draws after just ten moves, in less than fifteen minutes. Clearly, they had arranged this before the first game of the round. In the rapid tiebreak, Antoaneta won. But she had saved herself two days' worth of grueling games, giving her an edge over less-rested players. When I saw what Antoaneta had done, I was not particularly surprised: she was tired, needed rest to maximize her chances, and didn't care what people thought. Antoaneta described the tournament as 'exhausting mentally and physically.'

In the fourth round, Antoaneta beat my first-round opponent, Nana Dzagnidze, leading her to the semi-final match, where Antoaneta met her most famous victim in Elista, four-time world champion Maia Chiburdanidze. Stefanova clinched the match victory with a steady game in which she snatched a pawn and played actively to triumph against the Georgian legend.

In the final four-game match, Antoaneta played an underdog Ekaterina Kovalevskaya, two-time Russian Women's Champion. Ranked only twentieth going into the event, Kovalevskaya had climbed to the top by scoring upset victories over teenaged prodigies Katerina Lagno from Ukraine and the top-seeded Indian, Koneru Humpy. Antoaneta was convincing against Kovalevskaya. She won the first two games, and then drew the third to clinch the title. When the final game was over, she lit up a cigarette and called her family back in Sofia to tell them that she had become the ninth World Women's Chess Champion.

Antoaneta's jet-setting lifestyle became even more packed with publicity and tournament engagements. Just two months after winning the diamond-studded crown and $50,000 check, she had made stops in her native Bulgaria and also in Libya, Russia, Spain and Poland.

Pascal, Irina and I had intended to spend a few days in Russia after the tournament, visiting Moscow and St Petersburg. Those plans were waylaid because Irina and I had an appointment back in New York City: our second training session with number one in the world, Garry Kasparov. As thrilling as this should have been for me, I was not looking forward to it. At the session, I would have to show the games I had just played in Elista, which I dreaded. To show the world champion a game in which I'd blundered so horribly felt like a punishment fit for chess hell. Kasparov was easier on me than I was on myself: 'I understand why you blundered – you were better all game – this was the first moment of the game she had a threat.'

Despite the Kasparov training, I felt my confidence and spirit at a low point. My roommate, who was moving out, told me that the landlord would not allow me to take over the lease. I needed to find a new place to live. I was also anxious about the upcoming 2004 US Women's Chess Championship, which would assemble the strongest female field in US history. My performance would determine whether I would play on the 2004 Olympic team, for which I had trained all year. In a rotten mood, I enveloped myself with negative thoughts. What if I didn't make the team? What if I lost all my games?

I needed more training, so I called an old coach and friend, International Master Victor Frias, who lived in Chappaqua, New York, and asked if he could help me. 'Come on over!' he said. I showed up at Victor's home with my laptop, a dozen chess books and a bottle of red wine. The chessboard was already set up on his dining room table, where we immediately began studying my opponents' games. Victor was no longer an active player, but I have always admired his approach to chess, which is very different from my own. When I first look at a position I check for tactics and specific variations. Frias, on the other hand, goes straight to the pawn structure and attempts to decipher the essence of the position. This way of studying chess is good for me. After just a few hours of studying with Victor, I begin to look at chess in a more complete way.

Victor and I stuck to an intense regiment. Every morning I woke up at about seven in the morning, to study until about noon. Then we went to the gym for a couple of hours. After lunch we worked on chess until eight or nine in the evening. Most of the time we spent checking out the games of my opponents, or games with positions similar to the ones I expected to get in the tournament.

The training stopped after five days because I wanted to go back to Brooklyn to figure out where to live. I was also throwing a farewell party for my friend Ben, who was moving to California. Ben is my former high school teammate, who had recently given up chess for poker.* Many of my friends from chess, including my brother, had shifted their focus to poker, hoping that their intellectual skills (no doubt in part developed from their experience in chess) might make them rich at the card table. At the time, Greg was earning a good living playing online, giving lessons in his favorite game format, 'Sit and Go', and occasionally flying off to play in tournaments.

I later fell in love with poker too, and its beautifully embedded math and psychology. Before poker, I didn't understand much about finances and negotiation, but after several years of playing, I started to see how poker could be a prism to analyze important issues of class and gender, in the same way chess is. Women aren't nurtured to take risks in the same way men are. Poker

---

* Ben is now the host of the most popular chess podcast, 'The Perpetual Chess Podcast'.

made me realize that, whether it was chess, cards or writing, taking no risks is the biggest risk of all. In 2015, I joined Team PokerStars and travelled all over the world to play chess with cards, from Monaco to Prague. In 2021, I joined the board of Poker Power, an organization that aims to teach 1 million women poker to accelerate their progress in business, politics and finance, mirroring my own goals to lift girls and women through chess.

My father had also gotten into poker. When I was playing at the World Championship in Russia, Greg and Michael were in Las Vegas at the World Series of Poker – Greg as a player, Michael as a spectator. Greg still played blitz and rapid chess occasionally, but was more concerned with organizing tournaments and improving the state of chess in America than his own progress. 'It's very sad to compare the situation of poker players with chess players,' Greg said.* 'Chess will probably never be as big as poker, but it could certainly get more attention and sponsorship than it does now.'

After the party, my floors were littered with broken glass and covered in a sticky film from spilled drinks, a mess that seemed to symbolize the state of my life at that moment. I still didn't know where I was going to live. My bank statement recorded the lowest figure it had in years. Even after my hard work with Victor, I was nervous about the upcoming tournament.

The first sign that things were turning my way came when my landlord had a change of heart and I was allowed to sign a one-year lease for my loft, a big space with high ceilings and skylights in place of windows, located in the center of Williamsburg. Once an industrial haven with factories, populated by

---

* Greg's words were prescient, as the chess boom of 2020 brought unprecedented attention and sponsorship to chess. Among many of the new converts and fans were . . . you guessed it: poker players.

Polish and Dominican immigrants, in the late 1990s, Williamsburg gentrified. The rents went up, and the 'Burg was now filled with the young and hip – the streets lined with sleek bars, numerous Thai restaurants, and the occasional yoga center or art gallery. It was located right next to the subway, allowing me to arrive in Manhattan in ten minutes flat.

Relieved and in slightly better spirits, I invited my brother over to play some blitz. After a few games I confessed to Greg that I was a little jealous that he had found another subculture in which he could thrive. Sometimes I felt burned out by the chess world, frustrated by the lack of popularity of the game. Because of the glamorous TV coverage of poker events and the steady stream of Texas Hold 'Em cash games and tournaments on the Internet, it seemed as if Greg might have taken the better course. Also, I was so stressed out and nervous about the upcoming championship that my feelings toward chess were ambiguous. At that moment, chess was just not making me happy. My brother said, 'Jen, you have to figure out a way to play for fun.'

Greg was right. Too often, I played chess scared to blunder, as I had in Elista. Playing chess scared to make a mistake is the intellectual equivalent of walking around in the perpetual fear of falling.

A few months later, I found myself facing my fears at the 2004 US Women's Chess Championship, which was taking place in New York that year, so I could stay at home rather than having to travel. In the first round, I was due to play Rusudan Goletiani. Despite my brother's advice, I was extremely nervous all through the game. From time to time, I would remind myself, 'Play for fun!' but the tension was so high that the advice seemed absurd. I got a better position with an attack on her King, but Rusa defended well and I was unable to find a knockout blow. I sacrificed a pawn, a dubious decision. Rusa called my bluff and captured it. I fought back and found a drawish endgame. Rusa played on for the whole six hours, hoping to find a win. It wasn't there. She stuck out her hand and we split the point. I went home with my half point slightly relieved. It was now impossible for me to lose all my games!

Unlikely as it would seem, this game turned out to be the sole draw of the twenty-game tournament. In most prestigious tournaments, draws are as frequent, if not more common, than decisive results. Such gluts of draws (some of these are good fights, but many are dull and quick) detract sponsorship, galvanizing Grandmaster Maurice Ashley, the first Black grandmaster in history, to warn of 'Draw Death' and come up with ideas to counter it, from his high-end tournament series, Millionaire Chess, to a format he came up with, Clutch Chess.[*]

In the second game, I played against Tsagaan Battsetseg (Baagi for short), a cheerful master originally from Mongolia, where she had won seven national titles. I knew she was a tough player and a creative tactician, but her handling of the clock was impractical – she would often leave herself with less than one minute for more than ten moves. In such situations, it's nearly impossible for a player to hold on to all her pieces. Baagi and I played a theoretical line that had been played dozens of times by the best players in the world, and I instantly regretted not studying the position more thoroughly. I knew she might play this line, but I had spent most of my energy that morning on another opening.

Baagi played creatively, and I found myself up a pawn but in a terrible position. The only plan, it seemed at first glance, was to shuffle my pieces back and forth, forcing her to figure out

---

[*] Clutch Chess was a series of matches held in 2020, hosted by the Saint Louis Chess Club, with a format weighting 'clutch games' with more points and money for a win, reducing incentives to draw games.

how to break through. I started to look at a risky move, placing my Rook in the center of the board, where it could be taken by three pieces. After twenty minutes of analysis, I saw that the sacrifice was unsound, but I wanted to play it, because the move was funny and aesthetic. My fingers were itching. I played the move and took my hand off the piece. Is this a death wish?

Baagi thought for almost thirty minutes and captured my Rook. Her position was winning, but it was complicated. Luckily for me, she could only choose one move out of all the attractive possibilities. She began to run low on time and chose a second-rate line, allowing me to get back into the game. Her advantage was beginning to evaporate, and the best course for her was probably to take a forced draw. On move forty, we each got an extra hour. I got up from the board feeling as though my brain had been squeezed to the limit. I laughed nervously, had some water, and paced around. Baagi still had a good position – she was down two pawns, but my King was vulnerable. I would have to fight hard. She began to play too slowly, using nearly all the time she was allotted for the rest of the game in just a few moves. Her clock began to tick down. I was mesmerized, smelling victory. By the finish, I had a winning position, but really I was just waiting for her flag to fall. It did. The game lasted nearly six hours, the maximum time length.

I was happy, but there was so much unreleased tension in my body that I was longing for a jog. I got home and around ten o'clock I went to the nearby track. On my way, I passed several bars and cafés teeming with New Yorkers enjoying the delicious summer evening. It was Friday night. After jogging and listening to an hour's worth of pop songs on the radio, I went home to prepare for my next game.

In the next round I faced Armenian–American Tatev Abrahamyan, at the time a shy, sweet teenager, and now one of the strongest female players in the country. Uncomfortable with

all the variations against her favorite set-up, the French, Victor
and I had spent hours searching for the right way to play against
her. I still wasn't happy with any of my regular choices. Then I
remembered that my brother had told me her nickname on the
Internet Chess Club, 'axves'. Tatev, under 'axves', had played
hundreds of blitz games on the ICC, all of which are archived
into a database. I logged on to the server and searched her recent
history of games in the French opening. I felt sneaky using those
games as preparation, as if I were reading a private letter. Many
players didn't realize that their opponents would know how to
access their ICC matches, and often try out new ideas. Through
my last-minute online preparation, I saw that Tatev played very
badly against one pawn sacrifice. I made a snap decision. I would
play the same sacrifice.

Tatev was uncomfortable in the opening I chose. She used
too much time. I was very confident in this game and won in
less than thirty moves.

Now I was leading the tournament. With the title and my
spot on the Olympic team within striking distance, my urge to
win became intense, even animalistic.

I was most afraid of the game in the fourth round because
I had the black pieces against one of the strongest women
players in the world, Anna Zatonskih. Zatonskih had always
impressed me in analysis sessions: she calculates well, has an
extensive knowledge of opening and endgame theory, and is
assertive about her opinions on positions. Anna is a hard worker
with a professional approach to the game, studying all aspects
of the game year-round, often for up to six hours a day. After
giving so much time to chess, it is hard for Anna to understand
if she has an unsuccessful result. And this was, perhaps, the
only weakness I could sense in her – in very high-pressure
situations, Anna's nerves sometimes give way.

Anna played an opening I hadn't expected. It was a solid

choice for white and secured a small but steady advantage. I had to find an active plan or I would get slowly squeezed. I found a good idea, opened some lines for my pieces, and the game was balanced. I started to dream of mounting an attack on Anna's King. In fear of this, she traded Queens, and we reached a position that looked as if it would be a draw. Anna's position was still a little better, and she did want to win. My defense was sufficient, and as we neared the end of the sixth hour, it was clear that she would have to split the point.

Then Anna made a strange offer – a trade of Knights. I hadn't even considered the move. After thinking for a few minutes, I could hardly trust my calculations – Anna had just committed an appalling blunder. I took the Knight, simplified the position into a pawn ending, where I made a Queen after just a few moves. Anna was too upset after the game to analyze, but a few days later she seemed to have gotten over it or was at least able to joke about it, telling me with a laugh, 'I had nightmares about that move!'

This game happened to be on Father's Day, and my dad was in town to celebrate. He had left my game when Anna was still pressing for the win. When I called my father, he sounded excited. 'I hope you called to tell me you held the draw!' He was in disbelief when I told him I'd won – as a Father's Day present.

I was excited: with 3.5 points out of 4, I was leading the tournament. One more victory would probably clinch the title.

I entered the fifth round against Anjelina Belakovskaia, a three-time US Champion who had hardly played any serious chess in the past few years, having given up chess for a more lucrative career in finance. While I was invigorated by my great start, Anjelina was rusty, and I was hoping to take advantage of that.

This time my preparation paid off as the line I studied all morning appeared on the board. The game was close, and it was clear that it was going to be a long struggle. I played well in the first part of the game, gaining an edge. Anjelina made a mistake and lost a pawn. It was still tough to win – I had to muster all my energy and make sure that I successfully converted my material advantage. At some point during the endgame (Rusudan Goletiani had defeated the only person who could still catch me, Anna Zatonskih), I realized the title was at stake: if I won this game I would be the US Women's Champion. Nightmarish thoughts of blundering horribly entered my brain. I breathed deeply and ejected the bad thoughts, forcing myself to play confidently. After nearly two hours my extra pawn was on the seventh rank, ready to become a Queen. With just a few seconds left on her clock, Anjelina resigned.

I had clinched my second national title with a round to go.[2]

Jennifer Shahade on the August 2002 edition of *Chess Life*
(courtesy of US Chess)

Interviewing and profiling so many of the top women players in the world had diminished my own chess ego. Winning reacquainted me with my competitive streak. I was happy to see that part of myself again, the me who wanted to win so badly that I poured every shred of energy into my games and preparations.

I wandered around the streets and parks of the East Village, sipping an iced coffee. The weather that week was perfect, the type of weather that makes New York paradise. Why would I want to live anywhere else? A child jumped out of a newspaper bin and yelled, 'Boo.' It struck me as funnier than it normally would have. My victory made everything appear to be shot in Technicolor: the emotional content of every experience was heightened. Every joke became funnier, every conversation more satisfying, and every dessert sweeter.

Soon after my victory, I visited my hometown, Philadelphia, to celebrate with friends and family. Whenever I return to Philly, I feel comfortable: I settle easily into the rust-colored couches in my living room; my feet navigate by memory the streets and coffee shops downtown. At the chessboard, my mind senses the same kind of familiarity. In such a relaxed state, I can often enter a zone. Not even conscious of my name or how much money I have in the bank, at times of peak performance I just let go. My sense of time relaxes, which can be problematic when the time limit approaches, but is ultimately my favorite aspect of the game. I've often awakened from deep thought wondering, *Where am I?* Chess thinking at its most pure is a realm where gender is not relevant. This is in sharp contrast to the culture and politics of the chess world, where women are such a minority that their gender is extremely visible.

Chess has also given me a gallery of fond memories and an unusually flexible lifestyle. Great chess moves can pierce me with momentary but intense pleasure like a smile in a dream.

Then there are the worldwide travels and connections with people from Russia and China, half or twice my age. Still, I am distraught by how few women enjoy the freedom and pleasures that come with losing oneself in chess. To female readers, I pass the move to you.

Acknowledgements

Anna Baty at Hodder & Stoughton had a powerful vision in bringing this book to a broader audience from content to title to promotion. I didn't see it at first, and I'm very grateful that she did! Her incisive edits made this a more readable and current book too. This book is so important to me, and I am deeply grateful, over fifteen years after I wrote the bones of it, to bring it back to life in a stronger and better form.

Many thanks to my agent Elizabeth Sheinkman, whose passion for books and business is such a confidence booster. Her enthusiasm is so infectious, I get off every call with her excited to create. Thanks to everyone else on the team at Peter Fraser and Dunlop, including Tris Payne and Kim Meridja.

Many thanks to science journalist and poker player Alex O'Brien, who introduced me to Elizabeth Sheinkman. Thanks also to writer and decision-making coach Nell McShane Wulfhart for all her fantastic advice (please check out their 2022 books, *The Truth Detective* by Alex and *The Great Stewardess Rebellion* by Nell).

Thank you to my husband Daniel Meirom, who helped me revise chapters and gave suggestions on where and how to expand. And for being such a wonderful dad and husband relieving me of many worries during these updates. My five-year-old son Fabian also kept me motivated by constantly reminding me: Don't Fall Cup.

Thanks to my assistant and producer Charlie 'ChaeDoc' Docherty who helped me with many tasks on this book, on tight deadlines, from finding new sources to explaining Twitch jargon.

I'm grateful to historian and author Olimpiu G. Urcan of the Capablanca Project, and Lee Ka Yee for reading the manuscript on short notice and giving fantastic factual corrections and suggestions and making some archival photo arrangements.

Thanks to proofreader Sophie Bristow, cover designer Jo Myler, editor Izzy Everington, and publicist Maria Garbutt-Lucero.

For photos and rights huge thanks to David Llada of *The Thinkers*. Much gratitude to the devoted staff at the World Chess Hall of Fame, Saint Louis Chess Club and Spectrum Studios including Randy Sinquefield, Joy Bray, Tony Rich, Shannon Bailey, Emily Allred, Nicole Tessmer, Kevin Duggin, Austin and Crystal Fuller, Rebecca Buffington, and Brian Flowers. Thanks to Stella Monday, Macauley Peterson, Eric and Andi Rosen, Betsy Zacate, Mimi Hook, John Hartmann and Dan Lucas at US Chess and to Raymond Rozman at the Cleveland Public Library. Thanks also to Benjamin Portheault for his help in interviewing and photographing Isabelle Choko.

Thanks also to everyone who made the first edition happen, which this book was based on, including Jeremy Silman, publisher Gwen Feldman, who was so helpful in transferring the rights of this title, and to editor Marjorie O'Hanlon. My friend Elizabeth Spiegel was incredibly helpful in suggestions too.

I wish my mother, Dr Sally Solomon, were here to see this new incarnation, as she is a wonderful inspiration to me as a person, as a writer, and now as a mom myself. Thank you to my father, Michael Shahade, for always being my biggest cheerleader (now tied with Daniel!) and Alanna Kellon.

Greg Shahade was also incredibly helpful, and I am so proud of his accomplishments as a connector and innovator, and his infectious belief that it's never too late to learn something new.

I will always remember playing chess with my dad and younger brother Francois one Sunday. Fran: we miss you dearly.

Thanks to all my students from the US Chess girls club, and the Cross-Cultural Girls Club, for making this past couple of years so fun despite everything, and reinvigorating my belief in the connection between life skills and chess. And big thanks to all the visitors of the Girls Club, and to my partners who have given so much time and support in hosting and organizing them, including Judy Kiragu of the Lighthouse Chess Club, in Mombasa, Kenya, Grandmaster Pontus Carlsson of Business Meets Chess & Kids as well as Adia Onyango, Kimberly Doo McVay, Maureen Grimaud, Elizabeth Shaughnessy, Leila D'Aquin, Arthur and Krista Alton, Robin Ramson, Carolina Blanco, Katerina Nemcova, Sabrina Chevannes, Alisa Melekhina, Sabina Foisor, Uma Girkar, Kala Kanapathy-Bagley and Laura Smith. Thanks also to Jeff King and Baker Sound Studios, Josh Taylor, the artist Juga, Jason Andre and Quinn Waters.

Shout-out to all my friends who helped me with suggestions and inspiration including Yänjaa Wintersoul, Coren Apicella, John Papianou, Ben Johnson, Bonnie Friel, Martha Curren-Preis, Dylan Adams, John Foley, David Friedel, Gabrielle Revlock, Olivier Busquet, Rada Wilinofsky, Katie Stone, Robert Hess, Seth Stephens-Davidowitz, Maurice Ashley, Yasser Seirawan, David Lappin and Robyn MacDonald. Thanks also to the multi-talented chess champion Megan Lee for supplying an illustration in this book.

And to all the chess queens who inspired me to take this on, and to everyone pushing for women in empowerment and chess and games including Dr Jeanne and Rex Sinquefield and the Saint Louis Chess Club, Richard and Barbara Schiffrin, Carol B. Meyer at US Chess, Danny Rensch at chess.com, Frankie Butler, Jenny Schweitzer, Jean Hoffman and her prescient work with US Chess and 9 Queens, the ladies of the Madwoman

Book Club, Daniel Ginzburg and Jay Stallings, the Kasparov
Chess Foundation, David Heiser at Renaissance Knights,
Martin Colette and Justin Ennis at ASAP Philly and Gabrielle
Moshier and Jason Bui at the Philadelphia Chess Society.

Thanks to my supportive team at PokerStars: Rebecca
McAdam, Moya Wilson, Nikki Allan and to the inspiring
leadership of Poker Power including Jenny Just and Erin Lydon.

I'm grateful to everyone behind *The Queen's Gambit* series,
for making chess more mainstream and increasing interest in
a project like this one.

And for their help with the younger version of this title,
thank yous are in order to: Bernie Roswig, Jacob and Eva
Okada, Mark Ashland, Henk Chevret, Dr Lewis Eisen, Chris
Hallman, John Donaldson, Stephen Zeitz, Justin Phillips, Nina
Fried, Paul Hoffman, Carrie Jones, Michael Le Grand, Jonathan
Rowson, Aarvind Aaron, Mig Greengard, Dirk Jan Ten
Geuzendam, Jami Anson, Mike Klein, Mike Nolan, Yelena
Dembo, Ella Baron, Michael Negele, Gregory Braylovsky, Erin
Fogg, Diego Garces, Laszlo Nagy, Ron Young, Viktoria
Johansson and the American Foundation for Chess.

And to all the people mentioned in the book, for their candor
and their time.

Glossary

Adjournment. A game unfinished at the end of the playing session that is resumed at a later time; the last move is sealed in an envelope. Adjournments were gradually phased out in the nineties, partly because players could now use powerful computer programs.

Algebraic notation. System for labeling a chessboard so that each of the 64 squares is denoted by a number and a letter, from a-1 to h-8; files (left to right) are a-h and ranks (top to bottom) are 1-8.

Bishop. Piece that moves diagonally, as many squares as it wants. It's worth about the same as a Knight, and significantly less than a Rook.

Black. Player with the black pieces. Black moves second, a major disadvantage when playing an experienced player.

Blindfold chess. Playing chess without sight of the board, indicating the moves orally in algebraic notation. Usually played in friendly exhibitions for fun and publicity.

Bullet/Lightning Chess: Games with extremely fast time limits, usually one or two minutes per player.

Blitz. Chess games with fast time limits, usually five minutes per player in over-the-board chess, and three minutes when played online.

Blunder. A very poor move. Sometimes indicated on scoresheets or published analysis with two question marks; in contrast, an excellent move may be followed with one or two exclamation points.

Board one (also first board). The highest-ranked player on a team.

Castling. A special, composite move in which the King moves two squares toward the corner, while the Rook jumps to the square adjacent to the King. Castling brings the King to safety and centralizes the Rook, and experienced players castle in almost every game.

Check. The King is in immediate attack. The King must escape check by either capturing the attacking piece, moving, or blocking the check with another piece. It is not possible to capture an opponent's King.

Checkmate. A position in which the King is in check and cannot make any legal move to get out of check. Few professional games end in checkmate, because players tend to resign long before checkmate. Often abbreviated to mate.

ChessBase. Company founded in 1987 in Germany by Frederic Friedel. ChessBase developed software that organizes millions of chess games and allows players to sift through all games played by a particular opponent or in any opening.

Chess clock. A double push-button clock to keep track of the time each player spends on a game; after moving, players stop their own clocks and start the opponent's.

Closed position. Type of position in which there are few pawn trades and pieces are locked in behind pawn structures. Players who like long-term planning thrive in closed positions. See open position.

d4. White moves the Queen's pawn two squares on the first move. The second most popular first-move choice, most often the choice of strategic players. d4 is favored by top women players such as Susan Polgar, Antoaneta Stefanova, Irina Krush, Zhu Chen, Ju Wenjun, Aleksandra Goryachkina, the fictional Beth Harmon, and first Women's World Champion Vera Menchik.

Dragon. An opening set-up for black in which the pawn structure supposedly resembles a dragon. A very risky and aggressive system.

Draw. Result in which the outcome is undecided or deadlocked. A draw is worth half a point. There are many ways to achieve a draw, e.g. upon agreement, when there is insufficient material for either side to give checkmate, or when the position is repeated three times.

e4. Moving the King pawn two squares on the first move. e4, usually the choice of attacking players, is the most popular move by a small margin, just ahead of d4. Its practitioners include Judit Polgar, Almira Skripchenko, Alexandra Kosteniuk, Xie Jun, Anna & Mariya Muzychuk and Carissa Yip. And me!

Elo ratings. Rating system designed to estimate the relative strength of chess players based on their tournament results. Named after Professor Arpad Elo.

Endgame. The phase of the game in which the material is reduced (usually Queens are traded) and the result often settled; players memorize the most common ones.

English opening. White starts the game by moving the Queen's Bishop pawn two squares; commonly thought to be a strong and safe first-move option.

An exchange. A common material imbalance, involving the difference in value between a Rook (a major piece worth 5 points), and a Bishop or Knight (minor pieces worth 3 points each). Not to be confused with 'exchanging', which is synonymous with trading.

Expert. A US chess player with a rating from 2000 to 2199; the category just beneath national master.

FIDE (Fédération Internationale des Échecs). The worldwide chess federation, founded in Paris in 1924. FIDE assigns international ratings, awards titles and organizes the most prestigious tournaments, including the Olympiad and World Championships.

First board. See Board one.

Fish. Slang for a weak chess player

Flag. Indicator on a chess clock that drops when a time is reached (even when using digital clocks). Players often shout out 'flag' to announce a victory on time.

Fools' mate. Black checkmates white in two moves; very rare, since it requires white to play the worst moves possible. 1. G4 e5 2. F3 Qh4 checkmate

Gambit. Opening that involves the planned sacrifice of material.

GM. Grandmaster.

Grandmaster. The most distinguished title in chess. Awarded by FIDE, it is given to players who meet establised performance standards. A grandmaster usually holds a rating of 2500 or higher.

IM. International master.

International master. The second most distinguished title in chess. Awarded by FIDE, it is given to players who meet established performance standards. An international master usually holds a rating of 2400 or higher.

Kibitzer. Players who hang around post-mortems or skittles rooms, offering colorful – and sometimes unwanted – advice or comment.

King. The only chess piece that cannot be captured. The King moves one square in any direction. Because the King must be carefully guarded against checkmate, the King is rarely used as a fighting piece until the last stages of the game.

Knight. In many languages, the Knight translates to 'horse'. A short-range but tricky piece that moves in an L-shape, the Knight is the only piece that can jump over other pieces, making it particularly valuable in closed positions.

Knockout. Event in which a player is eliminated after losing a match so that the field is reduced by half after each round.

Line. Synonym for variation, often used when talking about various opening possibilities.

Master. A US chess master is a player rated over 2200, a FIDE master is a player rated over 2300.

Material. Pieces and pawns. Material is counted by a relative value system, which players use a guideline when deciding whether to trade one piece for another. A large disadvantage in material often prompts experienced players to resign, because extra material is often the means to inevitable checkmate. The pawn, the least valuable piece, is counted as the basic unit, 1 point. Other approximate values are Knight (3), Bishop (3), Rook (5), Queen (9). Because the King cannot be captured, he is not assigned a point value.

Middlegame. The phase of the game between the opening and the endgame, where a player must rely on creativity, intuition and calculating abilities.

Norm (grandmaster or international master). A prespecified rating performance against a specific number of internationally rated players. Three norms are required to become a grandmaster or international master.

Olympiad. Biennale team tournaments contested by teams representing the members of FIDE. The first Olympiad was held in London in 1927.

Open position. Positions in which there are many open files and diagonals, and fewer locked pawn structures. Often incites quick contact between enemy pieces, resulting in tactical play.

Open tournament. A tournament that is open to all comers, though there is often an entry fee.

Opening. The first phase of the game in which the pieces are developed. Strong amateur players have the basic ideas and moves of their openings memorized, while professional players memorize larger numbers of openings and variations, and often have new, never-before-played ideas, novelties. The names of openings can come from great players who invented or mastered the systems, such as the Najdorf Defense. Or they can refer to the opening's origin, such as the Berlin or English Opening.

Pawn. The weakest piece on the board. Each player gets eight at the beginning of the game. Pawns are the only chess pieces that cannot move backwards.

Pawn promotion. The exchange of a pawn that reaches the eighth rank (last row) for another piece, almost always a Queen.

Pawn structures. Locked formations that determine the pace of the game; often set up early in the game.

Performance rating. The rating level at which a player performs in a single tournament. For instance, a master (2200) level player has a 2500 performance rating if she has a tournament that would be average (e.g. three losses against 2500 players and three wins against 2500 players), and would not result in a rating point gain or loss for a player rated 2500.

Point. A unit used to give the result of a chess game; win 1; draw 1/2; loss 0; in a fifteen-round tournament, a player who wins eight games (8 points), draws five (2.5 points) and loses two (no points) has a total score that can be written 10.5/15 or 10.5-4.5.

Post-mortem. Analysis following a game.

Queen. The most valuable piece in chess, which can move on diagonals (like Bishops) and in straight lines (like Rooks). In medieval Europe, the Queen was the weakest piece on the board, and her sudden change in powers in the sixteenth century quickened the pace of the game. The presence of Queens allows for spectacular mating attacks and heightens the value of King safety. Trading Queens alters the nature of a game, usually transforming it into an endgame.

Rapid chess. Games with time controls that range from about twenty-five minutes a player to sixty minutes a player. This is in between the super-fast pace of blitz and the classical time controls, which range from a total of two to three and a half hours for each player.

Rating. Numerical values used to rank chess players; classifications according to the US Chess rating system include: senior master 2400+, master 2200–2399, expert 2000–2199, Class A 1800–1999, Class B 1600–1799, Class C 1400–1599, Class D 1200–1399, and Class E 1199–1000 down to Class J 100–199.

Resign. To give up by declaration. Often in view of inevitable checkmate or a tremendous disadvantage in material.

Rook. The most valuable piece besides the Queen. The Rook moves in straight lines and is particularly powerful in the endgame.

Round-robin. An event in which everybody plays everybody. Tournaments such as the US Chess Championship or US Women's Chess Championship are usually held as round-robins, and this is considered one of the best formats for determining the strongest player at a given time.

Sacrifice. Voluntary surrender of material in exchange for other advantages.

Scholar's mate. A four-move checkmate that shows up frequently in scholastic tournaments. 1. E4 e5 2. Bc4 Nc6 3. Qf3 (or Qh5) Nd4 4. Qxf7 checkmate

Score sheet. Where all moves made by both player and opponent must be recorded by each player; moves must be written as they are made unless a delay is allowed due to extreme time pressure.

Skittles room. Room for post-game analysis where players discuss their tournament games; a rich tradition in the chess culture.

Simultaneous (also simul). An exhibition in which a strong player is invited to take on many opponents at once. Can appear amazing to a lay observer, but depending on the strength of her opponents, simuls can actually be easy for a master chess player, who doesn't really think on each board as much as make an instant intuitive decision. This is usually enough for her to win. A more difficult version of this is the 'blindfold simul', which combines two challenging chess formats into one.

Strategy. Long-term planning and maneuvering.

Style. A commonality between the opening systems, tactics and strategies a player favors. Adjectives such as quiet, balanced, sharp and aggressive are common ways to describe style: e.g. A sharp style is one that favors tactics and risky openings and variations. Talk of style can be misleading, since in many positions all strong chess players would choose the same move.

Swiss system. A popular tournament format for large fields, used for most open tournaments. Before the tournament, players (or teams) are ranked according to their ratings, and assigned seed numbers. In the first round, players are paired according to their seeds. If there are ten players in a Swiss system, in the first round the number-one seed will play the sixth seed, number two will play number seven, and so on. In following rounds, players are matched with opponents with the same or similar scores. A player and opponent can meet only once.

Tactics. Short operations requiring proficiency in calculating that force checkmate or a quick win of material.

Three-move repetition. The same position appears three times with the same player to move; either player may claim a draw.

Time control. Predetermined time limit for a player to complete moves; if exceeded, the game is lost. Time controls range from blitz games, where each players has only three minutes, to classical games, in which each player has three hours.

Time pressure. When a player is forced to make a large number of moves in a short time, or else her time will run out and she will lose, regardless of how strong her position is. Time pressure often causes blunders.

Touch-move rule. Player who touches a piece must move or capture the piece.

Trade (pieces). Mutual agreement to give up pieces for opponent's pieces, usually of the same value: e.g. a Rook for a Rook or a Knight for a Bishop.

US Chess/USCF (United States Chess Federation). US Chess assigns national ratings and organizes national tournaments. US Chess used to be widely known as 'USCF'.

Variation. Long strings of projected moves.

White. Player with the white pieces. White moves first, a definite advantage for an experienced player.

WGM, WIM. Woman grandmaster, woman international master.

Woman grandmaster and woman international master: Gender-specific titles awarded by FIDE to women. The average performances and ratings are lower than the gender neutral equivalents, and therefore the titles are controversial. In the chapter about this, I recommend merging the WGM/WIM titles with gender neutral comps (IM/FM) to allow for players to choose between a gender restricted and gender neutral title.

Women's World Championship. World Championship in which participants are female. The first Women's World Championship was a round-robin held in London in 1927 (won by Vera Menchik), in conjunction with the first Olympiad. At the time of writing (2021), Ju Wenjun reigns as World Women's Champion, having defeated Aleksandra Goryachkina in a January 2020 match.

World Championship. Open to both men and women. The World Championship is currently structured as a biennial match. On the alternate year, an eight-player Candidates tournament is hosted to determine the challenger. During the first edition of this book, the World Championship was in flux, and was structured as a sixty-four-player tournament knockout. Although this event was extremely fun to follow, it was deemed too random for such a serious title. Now the same knockout is generally a qualifier for the World Championship itself.

Appendix: Games

This QR code will take you to an online library of the games below at chessqueensbook.com/games.

Menchik - A Becker (Karlsbad, 1929)
1.d4 d5 2.Nf3 Nf6 3.c4 c6 4.Nc3 e6 5.e3 Ne4 6.Bd3 f5 7.Ne5 Qh4 8.0–0 Nd7 9.f4 Be7 10.Bd2 Nxe5 11.dxe5 Bc5 12.Bxe4 fxe4 13.Qb3 Qd8 14.Na4 Be7 15.Bb4 b6 16.Bxe7 Qxe7 17.cxd5 exd5 18.Rac1 Bb7 19.Nc3 Qf7 20.Qb4 Rd8 21.Rfd1 Ba8 22.h3 Qe7 23.Qxe7+ Kxe7 24.b4 Rd7 25.Rd2 Rhd8 26.Ne2 Rc8 27.Rdc2 Rdc7 28.Nd4 g6 29.Nb5 Rd7 30.Kf2 h6 31.g4 a6 32.Nd4 Rdc7 33.f5 g5 34.Kg3 Bb7 35.h4 gxh4+36.Kxh4 Kf7 37.Kh5 a5 38.bxa5 bxa5 39.Nb5 Rd7 40.e6+, 1–0.

M Duchamp - Menchik (Paris, 1929)
1.d4 d5 2.c4 c6 3.cxd5 cxd5 4.Nf3 Nc6 5.Nc3 Nf6 6.Bf4 e6 7.e3 Bd6 8.Bxd6 Qxd6 9.Bd3 0–0 10.0–0 Rd8 11.Nb5 Qb8 12.Rc1 Bd7 13.Qe2 a6 14.Nc3 Qd6 15.e4 dxe4 16.Nxe4 Nxe4 17.Qxe4 g6 18.Qh4 Kg7 19.Ng5 h6 20.Qxh6+ Kxh6 21.Nxf7+ Kg7 22.Nxd6 Nb4 23.Be4 Bc6 24.Bxc6 bxc6 25.Rc4 Rxd6 26.Rxb4 a5 27.Rc4 Rad8 28.Re1 Rxd4 29.Rxc6 Rd2 30.g3 Rf8 31.f4 Rh8 32.h4 Rb8 33.b3 Rxa2 34.Rexe6 Rxb3 35.Rxg6+ Kf7 36.Rb6 Rd3 37.Rbd6 Rb3, ½–½.

Menchik - Capablanca (Hastings, 1930)

1.d4 Nf6 2.Nf3 b6 3.e3 Bb7 4.Bd3 c5 5.o-o Nc6 6.c3 e6 7.Ne5
d6 8.Nxc6 Bxc6 9.Qe2 Be7 10.Bb5 Qd7 11.Bxc6 Qxc6 12.Nd2
o-o 13.dxc5 dxc5 14.e4 Rad8 15.e5 Nd5 16.Nf3 Rd7 17.Rd1 Rfd8
18.Bd2 b5 19.Kf1 Nb6 20.Bf4 h6 21.Rxd7 Rxd7 22.Rd1 Rxd1+
23.Qxd1 Qe4 24.Bg3 Qc4+ 25.Qe2 Qxe2+ 26.Kxe2 Na4 27.Kd2
Nxb2 28.Kc2 Nc4 29.Nd2 Nxd2 30.Kxd2 c4 31.Bf4 a6 32.Be3
Kf8 33.Bb6 Ke8 34.Ke3 Kd7 35.Kd4 Kc6 36.Ba7 f5 37.a4 g6 38.f4
h5 39.axb5+ Kxb5 40.g3 a5 41.Ke3 Bc5+ 42.Bxc5 Kxc5, 0-1.

Menchik - Graf (Semmering, 1937)

1.c4 e6 2.Nc3 d5 3.d4 Nf6 4.Nf3 Nbd7 5.e3 c6 6.Bd3 Be7
7.0-o o-o 8.e4 dxe4 9.Nxe4 Nxe4 10.Bxe4 Nf6 11.Bc2 c5
12.dxc5 Qa5 13.Be3 Bxc5 14.Bd2 Qc7 15.Bc3 Be7 16.Qe2 b6
17.Ng5 g6 18.Qf3 Bb7 19.Qh3 h5 20.Rad1 Ng4 21.Rd7, 1-0.

Graf - Keres (Prague, 1937)

1.d4 e6 2.c4 Bb4+ 3.Bd2 Qe7 4.Bxb4 Qxb4+ 5.Qd2 Nc6 6.e3
Qxd2+ 7.Kxd2 f5 8.Nc3 Nf6 9.Nb5 Kd8 10.f3 a6 11.Nc3 f4
12.Nge2 fxe3+ 13.Kxe3 d5 14.Ng3 Re8 15.Rd1 Bd7 16.Be2
e5 17.Kf2 dxc4 18.dxe5 Nxe5 19.h3 Kc8 20.Rd4 b5 21.f4 Nc6
22.Rd2 Rb8 23.Bf3 Nb4 24.Nge4 Rb6 25.Nc5 Bf5 26.g4 Nd3+
27.Nxd3 Bxd3 28.g5 Ne4+ 29.Nxe4 Bxe4 30.Re1 Bg6 31.Bg4+
Kb7 32.Rxe8 Bxe8 33.Rd8 Bc6, ½-½.

Menchik - Graf (Women's World Championship,
Buenos Aires, 1939)

1.d4 d5 2.c4 e6 3.Nc3 Nf6 4.Nf3 Nbd7 5.e3 Bb4 6.Bd3 c5
7.0-o o-o 8.cxd5 exd5 9.Bd2 a6 10.Rc1 c4 11.Bb1 Re8 12.Ne2
Bd6 13.Bc3 b5 14.Ng3 g6 15.Re1 Bb7 16.Re2 b4 17.Be1 a5
18.Ng5 Ng4 19.Nh3 f5 20.Nf1 Qc7 21.f4 Ndf6 22.Bh4 a4
23.Ng5 Qe7 24.Re1 a3 25.b3 c3 26.Nf3 Qg7 27.h3 Nh6 28.Bxf6
Qxf6 29.Ne5 Qe7 30.Nh2 Rec8 31.Nhf3 Nf7 32.Bd3 Rc7

33.Qe2 Qd8 34.Rc2 Qc8 35.Nxf7 Rxf7 36.Bb5 Rc7 37.Bd3
Bf8 38.Ne5 Bg7 39.Kh2 Bf6 40.Rg1 Kf8 41.g4 Bxe5 42.fxe5
fxg4 43.Rf1+ Rf7 44.Rxf7+ Kxf7 45.hxg4 Qd8 46.Kg3 Kg7
47.Qf1 Qe7 48.Rf2 Rf8 49.Rf4 Bc8 50.Bc2 Be6 51.Rxf8 Qxf8
52.Qa6 Qe7 53.Bd1 Kf7 54.Kf4 h6 55.Qf1 Kg7 56.Kg3 h5
57.gxh5 Qg5+ 58.Kf2 Qf5+ 59.Bf3 Qc2+ 60.Qe2 Qxe2+
61.Kxe2 Bf5 62.hxg6 Kxg6 63.Bxd5 Bb1 64.Kd1 Bd3 65.Bc6
Kf7 66.d5 Ke7 67.e4 Kf7 68.e6+ Kf6 69.e5+ Ke7 70.Bb7 Bg6
71.Ba6 Be4 72.Bc4 Bg6 73.d6+ Kd8 74.Bb5, 1–0.

Gresser - Rudenko (Women's World Championship, Moscow, 1950)

1.e4 e5 2.Nf3 Nc6 3.Bb5 Bc5 4.c3 f5 5.d4 fxe4 6.dxc5 exf3
7.Qxf3 Nf6 8.Bg5 0–0 9.0–0 Qe7 10.Bc4+ Kh8 11.b4 a5
12.Bxf6 Rxf6 13.Qd5 Rf8 14.b5 Nd8 15.Nd2 c6 16.Qd6 Qxd6
17.cxd6 b6 18.Rfe1 cxb5 19.Bxb5 Nf7 20.Nc4 Ba6 21.Bxa6
Rxa6 22.Nxe5 Nxd6 23.Nxd7 Rc8 24.Rad1 b5 25.h3 Nf7
26.Re7 Kg8 27.Rde1 Nd6 28.R1e6 Rxc3 29.Ne5 h6 30.Rd7
Rc5 31.Nf7 Nxf7 32.Rxa6 Ne5 33.Rb7 b4 34.Raa7 Nc6
35.Rxg7+ Kf8 36.Raf7+ Ke8 37.Rb7 Rf5 38.Rg8+ Rf8
39.Rxf8+ Kxf8 40.Rb6 Ne5 41.Rxh6, 1–0.

Bykova - Gaprindashvili (Women's World Championship, Moscow, 1962)

1.e4 e5 2.Nf3 Nc6 3.Bb5 a6 4.Ba4 Nf6 5.0–0 Be7 6.Re1 b5
7.Bb3 d6 8.c3 0–0 9.d3 Na5 10.Bc2 c5 11.Nbd2 Nd7 12.Nf1
Nb6 13.Ne3 g6 14.Qe2 Be6 15.Bd2 Nc6 16.b3 a5 17.Nf1 b4
18.Bh6 Re8 19.c4 Bg4 20.Bd1 Nd4 21.Qe3 Bxf3 22.gxf3 a4
23.Ng3 axb3 24.Bxb3 Bg5 25.Bxg5 Qxg5 26.Kg2 Qh4 27.Rg1
Nd7 28.Kh1 Kh8 29.Ne2 Nxe2 30.Qxe2 h5 31.Qe3 Kh7 32.Rg3
Nf8 33.Qg5 Qxg5 34.Rxg5 Ne6 35.Rgg1 Ra3 36.Rgd1 Nd4
37.Kg2 Kh6 38.Rab1 Kg5 39.Rd2 Kf4 40.Bd1 Rea8 41.Bb3
Nxf3 42.Re2 g5 43.h3 Rg8 44.Re3 g4 45.Rc1 Raa8, 0–1.

Gaprindashvili - Chiburdanidze (Women's World Championship, Pitsunda, 1978)

1.Nf3 Nf6 2.g3 d5 3.c4 c6 4.Bg2 dxc4 5.a4 g6 6.Na3 Qd5 7.0–0 Na6 8.Ne1 Qh5 9.Nxc4 Bh3 10.Nf3 Bxg2 11.Kxg2 Bg7 12.d3 0–0 13.h3 Qd5 14.Bd2 Rfd8 15.Qc2 Rac8 16.Bc3 c5 17.Rad1 h6 18.Qb3 b6 19.e4 Qe6 20.Nh4 Nb4 21.Bxb4 cxb4 22.Rfe1 Nd7 23.Qc2 Nc5 24.b3 a6 25.Nf3 b5 26.axb5 axb5 27.Ne3 Na4 28.Qa2 Nc3 29.Qa5 Nxd1 30.Rxd1 Qxb3 31.Qxb5 Rc3 32.Qb7 Rcxd3 33.Rxd3 Rxd3 34.Nd5 Rxf3, (time), 0–1.

Chiburdanidze - Gaprindashvili (Women's World Championship, Pitsunda, 1978)

1.e4 d6 2.d4 Nf6 3.Nc3 g6 4.Nf3 Bg7 5.Be2 c6 6.0–0 0–0 7.a4 Nbd7 8.a5 Qc7 9.h3 Rd8 10.Be3 Nf8 11.Qd2 Bd7 12.Rfd1 Be8 13.b4 e5 14.dxe5 dxe5 15.Qe1 Rxd1 16.Rxd1 Ne6 17.Bc4 Qe7 18.Bxe6 Qxe6 19.Bc5 Nd7 20.Bd6 f6 21.Qe2 Bf8 22.Bxf8 Nxf8 23.Nd2 Qe7 24.Qc4+ Bf7 25.Qc5 Qxc5 26.bxc5 Rd8 27.Kf1 Rd4 28.Ke1 Ne6 29.Nb3 Rc4 30.Kd2 Nf4 31.a6 bxa6 32.Ra1 Nxg2 33.Rxa6 Be8 34.Rxa7 h5 35.Rb7 Nf4 36.f3 Kf8 37.h4 Ne6 38.Nd1 Nxc5 39.Nxc5 Rxc5 40.Ne3 Ra5 41.Rc7 Ra8 42.Nc4 Ra4 43.Ne3 Rd4+ 44.Ke2 Rd6 45.c4 Rd8 46.c5 Rd4 47.Ke1 Rd7 48.Rxd7 Bxd7 49.Nc4 Ke7 50.Kf2 Be6 51.Nd6 g5 52.Kg3 Kd7 53.Nb7 Bb3 54.hxg5 fxg5 55.Na5 Bd1 56.Nc4 Ke6 57.Kf2 Kf6 58.Na5 Ba4 59.Nc4 Bb5 60.Nd6 Ba6 61.Ne8+ Kg6 62.Nd6 Bd3 63.Ke3 Bc2 64.Nc4 Kf6 65.Kf2 Ba4 66.Nb6 Bd1 67.Nd7+ Ke6 68.Nb8 Ba4 69.Na6 Bb5 70.Nb4 Kf6 71.Kg3 Kg6 72.Nc2 h4+ 73.Kg2 g4 74.Ne3 gxf3+ 75.Kxf3 Kg5 76.Nd1 Bc4 77.Nf2 Bf1 78.Nh1 Bh3 79.Nf2 Be6 80.Nd3 Bg4+ 81.Kf2 Kf6 82.Nb2 Bd7 83.Kf3 h3 84.Kg3 Ke7 85.Nd3 Kf6 86.Nb4 Ke7 87.Nd3 Ke6 88.Kxh3 Be8 89.Kg3 Bg6 90.Kf3 Bh5+ 91.Ke3 Bd1 92.Nb4 Ba4 93.Nd3 Bb5 94.Ne1,½–½.

Judit Polgar - Chilingirova (Olympiad, Thessaloniki, 1988)
1.e4 c5 2.Nf3 Nc6 3.Bb5 g6 4.0-0 Bg7 5.c3 e5 6.d4 exd4
7.cxd4 Nxd4 8.Nxd4 cxd4 9.e5 Ne7 10.Bg5 0-0 11.Qxd4 Nc6
12.Qh4 Qb6 13.Nc3 Bxe5 14.Rae1 Bxc3 15.bxc3 Qxb5 16.Qh6
Qf5 17.Qxf8+, 1-0.

Sofia Polgar - Chernin (Rome, 1989)
1.e4 c5 2.Nf3 e6 3.d4 cxd4 4.Nxd4 Nc6 5.Nc3 Qc7 6.Be2 Nf6
7.0-0 Be7 8.Be3 0-0 9.f4 d6 10.Kh1 a6 11.Qe1 Na5 12.Qg3
Nc4 13.Bc1 b5 14.a3 Qb6 15.Rd1 Bb7 16.b3 Na5 17.Bf3 Rac8
18.Bb2 Rfd8 19.Nd5 Nxd5 20.Nxe6 g6 21.Nxd8 Qxd8 22.exd5
Rxc2 23.Rab1 Bh4 24.Qh3 Bc8 25.Bg4 Bxg4 26.Qxg4 Nxb3
27.g3 Be7 28.f5 a5 29.fxg6 hxg6 30.Qh3 Rxb2 31.Rxb2 a4
32.Rf2 Nc5 33.Rdf1 f5 34.g4 Ne4 35.Rg2 Bf6, 1-0.

Gaprindashvili - Xie Jun (Borshomi, 1990)
1.d4 Nf6 2.c4 g6 3.Nc3 Bg7 4.e4 d6 5.Be2 0-0 6.Bg5 Na6
7.Qd2 e5 8.d5 c6 9.h4 cxd5 10.cxd5 Qa5 11.Rb1 Bd7 12.Kf1
Rac8 13.h5 b5 14.a3 b4 15.axb4 Nxb4 16.Nh3 Rc7 17.Be3
Rxc3 18.Qxc3 Nxe4 19.Qe1 Bb5 20.Ng5 Nf6 21.hxg6 hxg6
22.Rd1 Bxe2+ 23.Qxe2 Nbxd5 24.Bc1 Rc8 25.g3 Ne7 26.Rh4
Nf5 27.Rc4 Rf8 28.Bd2 Qd5 29.Nf3 Nd4 30.Rxd4 exd4 31.Bc3
Qc6 32.Bxd4 Re8 33.Qd3 Ne4 34.Kg1 Bxd4 35.Nxd4 Qd5
36.Qb5 Re5 37.Qd3 Ng5 38.Kh2 Re4 39.Qb3 Qc5 40.Qb8+
Kg7 41.b4 Qe5 42.Nc6 Qf5 43.Kg1 Qh3, 0-1.

Yudasin - Susan Polgar (Pamplona, 1990)
1.e4 c5 2.c3 d5 3.exd5 Qxd5 4.d4 Nc6 5.dxc5 Qxc5 6.Be3
Qa5 7.Nf3 Nf6 8.Bc4 e6 9.0-0 Be7 10.Nd4 Bd7 11.Nd2 Nxd4
12.Bxd4 Bc6 13.Re1 0-0 14.Nb3 Qg5 15.g3 Rad8 16.f4 Qh6
17.Qe2 Ne4 18.Qe3 b6 19.Rad1 Nd6 20.Bd3 Qh5 21.Be5 Nf5
22.Qf2 Nh4 23.Be2 Nf3+ 24.Bxf3 Bxf3 25.Rxd8 Rxd8 26.h3
Bb7 27.Kh2 Rd3 28.Bd4 Qd5 29.Qe2 Bf6 30.Rg1 Bxd4

31.Nxd4 Qe4 32.Qxe4 Bxe4 33.Re1 f5 34.g4 Kf7 35.Re2 Rd1
36.Kg3 h6 37.Nf3 Rd3 38.Rf2 g5 39.fxg5 hxg5 40.h4 f4+
41.Kg2 gxh4, 0–1.

**Tolnai - Judit Polgar (Hungarian Championship,
Hungary, 1991)**

1.e4 c5 2.Nf3 e6 3.d4 cxd4 4.Nxd4 a6 5.Nc3 Qc7 6.f4 b5
7.Bd3 Bb7 8.Qf3 Nf6 9.Be3 Nc6 10.0–0–0 b4 11.Nce2 Na5
12.g4 d5 13.e5 Nd7 14.Kb1 Nc4 15.Bc1 0–0–0 16.h4 Nc5
17.b3 Na3+ 18.Ka1 f6 19.c3 fxe5 20.fxe5 Nc4 21.Nxe6 Nxe5
22.Qg3 Nxe6 23.Bf5 Kb8 24.Bxe6 bxc3 25.Nxc3 d4 26.Rhf1
Bb4 27.Na4 Rhe8 28.Bf5 Bc6 29.Bb2 g6 30.Bb1 Bxa4 31.bxa4
Bc3 32.Bxc3 Qxc3+ 33.Qxc3 dxc3 34.Rc1 Rc8 35.Rf4 Rc5
36.Rb4+ Ka7 37.Rb3 Rec8 38.Be4 R8c7 39.Rcb1 Nc6 40.Bxc6
R5xc6 41.Rb4 Rc4 42.a3 Rxb4 43.axb4 Rc4 44.h5 a5 45.hxg6
hxg6 46.Ka2 Rxb4 47.Rg1 c2 48.g5 Kb6, 0–1.

**Xie Jun - Chiburdanidze (Women's World
Championship, Manila, 1991)**

1.e4 e5 2.Nf3 Nc6 3.Bb5 Nf6 4.0–0 Nxe4 5.d4 Nd6 6.Bxc6
dxc6 7.dxe5 Nf5 8.Qxd8+ Kxd8 9.b3 Ke8 10.Bb2 a5 11.Nc3
Be6 12.Rfd1 Be7 13.h3 h5 14.a4 f6 15.Ne2 Bd5 16.Ne1 Kf7
17.Nf4 Rad8 18.c4 Be6 19.Nf3 Bc8 20.Re1 g5 21.e6+ Ke8
22.Ng6 Rg8 23.Nxe7 Kxe7 24.g4 hxg4 25.hxg4 Ng7 26.Nd4
c5 27.Nf5+ Nxf5 28.gxf5 Rh8 29.Kg2 b6 30.Rad1 Rdg8 31.Kg3
Rh4 32.Rh1 Rgh8 33.Rxh4 gxh4+ 34.Kh3 Rh5 35.Rd5 c6
36.Bxf6+ Kxf6 37.Rd8 Rxf5 38.Rxc8 Rf3+ 39.Kxh4 Rxb3
40.Rxc6 Rb4 41.Kg3, ½–½.

**Xie Jun - Chiburdanidze (Women's World
Championship, Manila, 1991)**

1.e4 e5 2.Nf3 Nc6 3.Bb5 a6 4.Ba4 Nf6 5.0–0 Be7 6.Re1 b5
7.Bb3 d6 8.c3 0–0 9.h3 Na5 10.Bc2 c5 11.d4 Bb7 12.Nbd2

cxd4 13.cxd4 exd4 14.Nxd4 Re8 15.b4 Nc6 16.Nxc6 Bxc6
17.Bb2 Bf8 18.Qf3 Rc8 19.Bb3 Qe7 20.Rad1 Bb7 21.Qf5 d5
22.e5 Nd7 23.Ne4 g6 24.Qxd7 dxe4 25.e6 fxe6 26.Qd4 Kf7
27.Qh8 Qh4 28.g3 Qh5 29.Qf6+ Kg8 30.Rd7, 1–0.

Chiburdanidze - Xie Jun (Women's World Championship, Manila, 1991)

1.e4 e5 2.Nf3 Nc6 3.Bb5 a6 4.Ba4 Nf6 5.0–0 Be7 6.Re1 b5
7.Bb3 0–0 8.d3 d6 9.c3 Na5 10.Bc2 c5 11.Nbd2 Re8 12.Nf1
Nc6 13.h3 h6 14.Ne3 Bf8 15.Nh2 d5 16.Nhg4 Nxg4 17.hxg4
d4 18.Nf5 c4 19.dxc4 bxc4 20.Ba4 Bd7 21.Bd2 Rb8 22.b3 cxb3
23.axb3 Ne7 24.cxd4 Nxf5 25.gxf5 exd4 26.Ba5 Qe7 27.Qxd4
Bxa4 28.bxa4 Qc5 29.Qd2 Qc4 30.e5 Bc5 31.Rac1 Qd4 32.e6
Rb2 33.Qxd4 Bxd4 34.exf7+ Kxf7 35.Rc7+ Kf8 36.Rxe8+ Kxe8
37.Be1 Bb6 38.Rc4 Rb1 39.Re4+ Kf7 40.Kh2 h5 41.g3 Kf6
42.a5 Bc7 43.Bc3+ Kxf5 44.Rc4 Bd8 45.Rc5+ Kg6 46.Rc6+
Kh7 47.Rxa6 Rc1 48.Bd4 Rd1 49.Bc3 Rc1 50.Ra8 Bc7 51.Bd4
Rc4 52.Be3 h4 53.a6 hxg3+ 54.Kg2 Bf4 55.a7 gxf2 56.Bxf2, 1–0.

Chiburdanidze - Xie Jun (Women's World Championship, Manila, 1991)

1.e4 e5 2.Nf3 Nc6 3.Bb5 a6 4.Ba4 Nf6 5.0–0 Be7 6.Re1 b5
7.Bb3 0–0 8.d3 d6 9.c3 Na5 10.Bc2 c5 11.Nbd2 Nc6 12.Nf1
Re8 13.h3 Bb7 14.Ng3 Bf8 15.Nf5 Ne7 16.Nxe7+ Bxe7 17.a4
Bf8 18.Bg5 h6 19.Bh4 Be7 20.d4 Qc7 21.dxe5 dxe5 22.Qe2 c4
23.Red1 Qc5 24.Nh2 b4 25.cxb4 Qxb4 26.Nf3 Nh5 27.Bxe7
Qxe7 28.g3 Qe6 29.Kh2 Nf6 30.Ra3 a5 31.Re3 Bc8 32.Qf1 Rb8
33.Rb1 Ba6 34.Qe1 Rb4 35.b3 Reb8 36.bxc4 Nd7 37.Reb3 Qxc4
38.Rxb4 axb4 39.Bb3 Qd3 40.Qd1 Qxd1 41.Rxd1 Nc5 42.Rb1
Bd3 43.Rb2 Bxe4 44.Nxe5 Nxb3 45.Rxb3 Bd5 46.Rb2 b3 47.Nd3
f6 48.g4 Bc4 49.Nc5 Rc8 50.Ne4 Bd5 51.Ng3 Ra8 52.Ne2 Rxa4
53.Nc3 53...Ra2 54.Rb1 Rxf2+ 55.Kg1 Rg2+ 56.Kf1 Rh2, 0–1.

Angela Alston - Rheanna English (San Antonio, 1992)

1.d4 d6 2.c4 Nf6 3.Nc3 g6 4.e4 Bg7 5.f3 c6 6.Be3 0-0 7.Qd2
Re8 8.0- 0-0 Qc7 9.Kb1 a6 10.g4 b5 11.Bd3 Rd8 12.Rc1 b4
13.Nce2 a5 14.Ng3 c5 15.d5 Bxg4 16.fxg4 Nxg4 17.Nf3 Nd7
18.Be2 Nxe3 19.Qxe3 a4 20.Bd1 Rdb8 21.Ne2 Ne5 22.Nxe5
Bxe5 23.h4 h5 24.Nf4 Bg7 25.Bxh5 Bxb2 26.Kxb2 Qa5 27.Rb1
a3+ 28.Kc2 Qa4+ 29.Rb3, 1-0.

**Ioseliani - Susan Polgar (Women's Candidates,
Monte Carlo, 1993)**

1.d4 d5 2.Nf3 c5 3.c4 cxd4 4.cxd5 Nf6 5.Qa4+ Qd7 6.Qxd4
Qxd5 7.Nc3 Qxd4 8.Nxd4 Bd7 9.Ndb5 Kd8 10.Be3 Nc6 11.h3
a6 12.Bb6+ Kc8 13.Na3 e5 14.Nc4 Be6 15.e4 Bb4 16.0-0-0
Bxc3 17.Nd6+ Kb8 18.bxc3 Nd7 19.Be3 Kc7 20.Bc4 Bxc4
21.Nxc4 f6 22.Rd2 b5 23.Nd6 Nb6 24.Bxb6+ Kxb6 25.Nf5
Rhd8 26.Rhd1 Rxd2 27.Rxd2 Ra7 28.h4 Rf7 29.h5 Kc7 30.h6
g6 31.Ng7 Re7 32.Rd3 Nb8 33.c4 bxc4 34.Rc3 Kd6 35.Rxc4
Nc6 36.Kd2 Rf7 37.Ke3 Rf8 38.g3 Rb8 39.f4 Ne7 40.Ra4 Ra8
41.f5 g5 42.Rb4 Kc6 43.Ne6 Rc8 44.Rc4+ Kd6 45.Ra4 Rc6
46.Nf8 Ng8 47.Nxh7 Kc5 48.Nxg5 Nxh6 49.Ne6+ Kb5 50.Ra3
Rc2 51.Kd3 Rg2 52.Nc7+ Kc6 53.Rc3+ Kb7 54.Nd5 Ng4
55.Rc7+ Kb8 56.Rf7 Rxg3+ 57.Kc4 Ra3 58.Nxf6 Nf2 59.Kd5
Rxa2 60.Kxe5 a5 61.Nd7+, 1-0.

Judit Polgar - Tiviakov (Madrid, 1994)

1.e4 c5 2.c3 d5 3.exd5 Qxd5 4.d4 Nf6 5.Nf3 Nc6 6.Be2 cxd4
7.cxd4 e6 8.0-0 Be7 9.Nc3 Qd6 10.Nb5 Qd8 11.Bf4 Nd5 12.Bg3
a6 13.Nc3 0-0 14.Rc1 Nf6 15.h3 b6 16.a3 Bb7 17.Bd3 Rc8
18.Bb1 b5 19.Qd3 Na5 20.Ne5 Nc4 21.Rc2 Nd6 22.f3 g6 23.Bf2
Re8 24.Ba2 Bf8 25.Re2 Bg7 26.Rfe1 Nd5 27.Nxd5 exd5 28.Qd1
a5 29.h4 Qc7 30.h5 Nc4 31.h6 Bxh6 32.Ng4 Rxe2 33.Nxh6+
Kg7 34.Rxe2 Kxh6 35.Qe1 Kg7 36.Re7 Qb6 37.Bxc4 bxc4
38.Qe5+ Kg8 39.Be3 f6 40.Qf4 Kf8 41.Rxh7 Ke8 42.Qh6, 1-0.

Judit Polgar - Kasparov (Linares, 1994)

1.e4 c5 2.Nf3 d6 3.d4 cxd4 4.Nxd4 Nf6 5.Nc3 a6 6.f4 e6
7.Be2 Be7 8.0–0 Qc7 9.Qe1 Nbd7 10.a4 b6 11.Bf3 Bb7 12.Kh1
Rd8 13.Be3 0–0 14.Qg3 Nc5 15.f5 e5 16.Bh6 Ne8 17.Nb3
Nd7 18.Rad1 Kh8 19.Be3 Nef6 20.Qf2 Rfe8 21.Rfe1 Bf8
22.Bg5 h6 23.Bh4 Rc8 24.Qf1 Be7 25.Nd2 Qc5 26.Nb3 Qb4
27.Be2 Bxe4 28.Nxe4 Nxe4 29.Bxe7 Rxe7 30.Bf3 Nef6 31.Qxa6
Ree8 32.Qe2 Kg8 33.Bb7 Rc4 34.Qd2 Qxa4 35.Qxd6 Rxc2
36.Nd2 Nf8 37.Ne4 N8d7 38.Nxf6+ Nxf6 39.Qxb6 Ng4 40.Rf1
e4 41.Bd5 e3 42.Bb3 Qe4 43.Bxc2 Qxc2 44.Rd8 Rxd8
45.Qxd8+ Kh7 46.Qe7 Qc4, 0–1.

Shirov - Judit Polgar (Buenos Aires, 1994)

1.e4 c5 2.Nf3 e6 3.d4 cxd4 4.Nxd4 Nc6 5.Nc3 d6 6.g4 a6
7.Be3 Nge7 8.Nb3 b5 9.f4 Bb7 10.Qf3 g5 11.fxg5 Ne5 12.Qg2
b4 13.Ne2 h5 14.gxh5 Nf5 15.Bf2 Qxg5 16.Na5 Ne3 17.Qg3
Qxg3 18.Nxg3 Nxc2+ 19.Kd1 Nxa1 20.Nxb7 b3 21.axb3 Nxb3
22.Kc2 Nc5 23.Nxc5 dxc5 24.Be1 Nf3 25.Bc3 Nd4+ 26.Kd3
Bd6 27.Bg2 Be5 28.Kc4 Ke7 29.Ra1 Nc6 0–1

Shahade - Fierro (World Junior Championship, Guarapuava, 1995)

1.e4 c5 2.c3 Nf6 3.e5 Nd5 4.d4 cxd4 5.Nf3 d6 6.cxd4 e6 7.a3
Bd7 8.Bd3 Bc6 9.0–0 Nd7 10.Nc3 Nxc3 11.bxc3 dxe5 12.dxe5
Nc5 13.Nd4 Qd5 14.Nxc6 bxc6 15.Be2 Qxe5 16.Bf3 Qc7
17.Bf4 Qc8 18.Rb1 Be7 19.Bd6 Nb7 20.Bxe7 Kxe7 21.Qa4
Nd8 22.Rfd1 Qc7 23.Qb4+ Ke8 24.Rd6 a5 25.Qd4 f6 26.Rd1
e5 27.Qg4 Qf7 28.Rxd8+ Rxd8 29.Bxc6+ Ke7 30.Rd7+, 1–0.

Susan Polgar - Xie Jun (Women's World Championship, Jaen, 1996)

1.g3 g6 2.Bg2 Bg7 3.e4 e5 4.Ne2 Nc6 5.c3 Nge7 6.d4 exd4
7.cxd4 d5 8.e5 f6 9.f4 0–0 10.0–0 Bg4 11.Nbc3 fxe5 12.fxe5

Rxf1+ 13.Qxf1 Qd7 14.h3 Rf8 15.Nf4 g5 16.hxg4 gxf4 17.gxf4
Qxg4 18.Qe2 Qg3 19.Qf2 Qxf2+ 20.Kxf2 Nxd4 21.Nxd5 Ng6
22.Nc3 c6 23.Be3 Bxe5 24.Rd1 Nxf4 25.Bxf4 Rxf4+ 26.Ke3
Nf5+ 27.Kd3 Rg4 28.Bh3 Rd4+ 29.Ke2 Rxd1 30.Nxd1 Nd6
31.b4 Kg7 32.a4 Kf6 33.Nf2 Bd4 34.Nd3 b6 35.Nf4 c5
36.Nd5+ Ke5 37.bxc5 bxc5 38.Ne7 a6 39.a5 Nc4 40.Nc6+
Kd6 41.Nb8 Kc7 42.Nxa6+ Kb7 43.Nxc5+ Bxc5 44.a6+ Kb6
45.Kd3 Nd6 46.Ke2 Kxa6 47.Kf3 Kb6 48.Be6 Kc7 49.Kg4
Kd8 50.Kh5 Be3 51.Bg8 h6 52.Bb3 Ke7 53.Kg6 Ne4 54.Bd1
Ke6 55.Bg4+ Ke5 56.Bd1 Bg5 57.Be2 Kf4 58.Bd1 Ng3 59.Ba4
h5 60.Bd7 h4, 0–1.

Susan Polgar - Xie Jun (Women's World Championship, Jaen, 1996)

1.e4 e5 2.Nf3 Nc6 3.d4 exd4 4.Nxd4 Bc5 5.Nxc6 Qf6 6.Qd2
dxc6 7.Nc3 Be6 8.Na4 Rd8 9.Bd3 Bd4 10.c3 b5 11.cxd4 bxa4
12.Qc2 Qxd4 13.Qxc6+ Kf8 14.Be2 Ne7 15.Qc2 f5 16.0–0 Qxe4
17.Qxc7 Kf7 18.Bh5+ g6 19.Bf3 Qc4 20.Qxa7 Qd4 21.Qa5 Nd5
22.Rd1 Qc4 23.Bg5 Rd7 24.Rac1 Qxa2 25.Bxd5, 1–0.

Xie Jun - Susan Polgar (Women's World Championship, Jaen, 1996)

1.e4 c5 2.Nf3 d6 3.d4 cxd4 4.Nxd4 Nf6 5.Nc3 Nc6 6.Bg5
Qb6 7.Nb3 e6 8.Qd2 Be7 9.f3 0–0 10.g4 Rd8 11.Be3 Qc7
12.g5 Nd7 13.0–0–0 a6 14.h4 b5 15.h5 Nb6 16.g6 Bf6 17.h6
fxg6 18.hxg7 Na4 19.Nd4 Nxd4 20.Bxd4 Bxd4 21.Qxd4 Nxc3
22.bxc3 Qxg7 23.Qb6 Qe7 24.e5 d5 25.Bd3 Bd7 26.Rdg1 Be8
27.f4 27...d4 28.cxd4 Rab8 29.Qxa6 Rxd4 30.f5 exf5 31.Bxf5
Qxe5 32.Be6+ Kh8 33.Kb1 Ra4, 0–1.

Judit Polgar - Kasparov (Dos Hermanas, 1996)

1.e4 c5 2.Nf3 d6 3.d4 cxd4 4.Nxd4 Nf6 5.Nc3 a6 6.f4 e6
7.Qf3 Qb6 8.a3 Nc6 9.Nxc6 bxc6 10.b3 Bb7 11.Bb2 d5

12.Bd3 c5 13.exd5 exd5 14.0–0–0 0–0–0 15.Na4 Qc7 16.Bf5+
Kb8 17.Be5 Bd6 18.Qc3 d4 19.Bxd6 Qxd6 20.Qxc5 Qxf4+
21.Kb1 Rd5 22.Rdf1 Qe5 23.Qc4 Rb5 24.Qxf7 Bd5 25.Qxg7
Rg8 26.Qh6 Bxb3 27.cxb3 Rxb3+ 28.Kc1 Qc7+ 29.Bc2 d3
30.Qf4 Rc8 31.Qxc7+ Rxc7 32.Rf2 Ne4 33.Rf8+ Ka7 34.Rf7
Rbb7 35.Rxc7 Rxc7 36.Rd1 Rxc2+ 37.Kb1 Rxg2 38.Rxd3
Rxh2 39.Rd7+ Kb8 40.Re7 Nd2+ 41.Kc1 Nb3+ 42.Kd1 h5
43.Re3 Nd4 44.Nc5 a5 45.Nb3 Nc6 46.Rc3 Kb7 47.Ke1 Kb6
48.Kf1 Rh4 49.Kg2 Nd4 50.Nxa5 Kxa5 51.Rc5+ Kb6 52.Re5
Kc6 53.Kg3 Rh1 54.Kg2 Kd6 55.Ra5 Rh4 56.Kg3 Rg4+
57.Kh3 Ne2 58.Rxh5 Rg3+ 59.Kh4 Rxa3 60.Kg4 Ke6 61.Rb5
Rg3+ 62.Kh4 Rg1 63.Rg5 Rf1 64.Ra5 Kf6 65.Ra8 Rg1
66.Rf8+ Ke5 67.Re8+ Kf4 68.Rf8+ Ke4 69.Re8+ Kf3 70.Kh5
Ng3+ 71.Kh6 Nf5+ 72.Kh7 Kf4 73.Rb8 Rg7+ 74.Kh8 Rd7
75.Re8 Kg5 76.Re6 Nd4 77.Re1 Kf6 78.Rd1 Rd5 79.Ra1
Ne6 80.Ra6 Kf7 81.Ra7+ Kg6 82.Ra8 Rd7 83.Rb8 Rc7
84.Kg8 Rc5 85.Ra8 Rb5 86.Kh8 Rb7 87.Rc8 Nc7 88.Rg8+
Kh6 89.Rg1 Rb8+ 90.Rg8 Ne8, 0–1.

Krush - Shahade (US Championship, Denver, 1998)

1.Nf3 Nf6 2.c4 d5 3.cxd5 Nxd5 4.Nc3 g6 5.Qa4+ Bd7 6.Qc2
Nb6 7.d4 Bg7 8.Bg5 Bg4 9.e3 Bxf3 10.gxf3 0–0 11.0–0–0 N8d7
12.h4 Nf6 13.Bxf6 Bxf6 14.h5 Kg7 15.Bd3 Rh8 16.Rdg1 c6
17.Rh3 Nd5 18.hxg6 hxg6 19.Bxg6 Rxh3 20.Bf5+ Kf8 21.Bxh3
e6 22.Bxe6 Nxc3 23.Qh7, 1–0.

Shahade - Kouvatsou (World Junior Championship, Yerevan, 1999)

1.e4 c5 2.Nf3 e6 3.d4 cxd4 4.Nxd4 Nf6 5.Nc3 d6 6.Be2 a6
7.a4 Nc6 8.Be3 Be7 9.0–0 0–0 10.f4 Qc7 11.Kh1 Re8 12.Bf3
Bf8 13.Qd3 Nb4 14.Qd2 e5 15.Nb3 exf4 16.Bxf4 Nd7 17.a5
Ne5 18.Ra4 Nbc6 19.Nd5 Qd8 20.Bg5 f6 21.Be3 Nd7 22.Qf2
Rb8 23.Bh5 Re5 24.Bg4 Nc5 25.Nxc5 Bxg4 26.Nd3 Re8

27.Qg3 f5 28.exf5 Be2 29.Bb6 Qc8 30.Rff4 Kh8 31.Nc7 Re7
32.Ne6 Ne5 33.Nxe5 dxe5 34.Rh4 Qxc2 35.Qg6 Qc1+ 36.Bg1
h6 37.Ng5, 1–0.

Zhu Chen - Krush (Women's World Championship, New Delhi, 2000)

1.e4 c5 2.Nf3 d6 3.d4 cxd4 4.Nxd4 Nf6 5.Nc3 Nc6 6.Bg5
e6 7.Qd2 a6 8.0–0–0 h6 9.Nxc6 bxc6 10.Bf4 d5 11.Qe3 Qa5
12.Be2 Bb4 13.Be5 Be7 14.exd5 cxd5 15.Bxf6 gxf6 16.Rhe1
Qc5 17.Qg3 Bb7 18.Bf3 Kf8 19.Kb1 Rc8 20.Rd2 Qb4 21.Rd3
a5 22.Red1 Ba6 23.Rd4 Qb6 24.Bh5 Bd6 25.f4 Rg8 26.Qh3
Bb4 27.Na4 Qc6 28.c3 Qxa4 29.a3 Bc4 30.cxb4 axb4 31.R1d2
Rb8 32.Bd1 Qa5 33.b3 bxa3 34.Ka2 Bb5 35.f5 Bd7 36.fxe6
Bxe6 37.Qxh6+ Ke7 38.Qe3 Rg5 39.Ra4 Qxa4 40.Qxg5 Qb4
41.Qe3 Kf8 42.g4 Qd6 43.Qh6+ Ke7 44.g5 fxg5 45.Qxg5+
Ke8 46.Bg4 Qb4 47.Bd1 d4 48.Rd3 Rc8 49.Qg8+ Ke7
50.Qg5+ Ke8 51.Qe5 Rc4 52.h4 Kf8 53.Qg3 Bf5 54.h5 Bxd3
55.Qxd3 Rc6 56.Qe2 Re6 57.Qc2 Qc3 58.Qg2 Qb2+ 59.Qxb2
axb2 60.Kxb2 f5 61.Kc2 Re3 62.b4 f4 63.b5 f3 64.Kd2 f2
65.Be2 Rb3 66.h6 Rb1 67.Kd3 Rxb5 68.Kxd4 Rb1, 0–1.

Sagalchik - Shahade (US Championship, Seattle, 2000)

1.e4 c5 2.Nf3 d6 3.d4 cxd4 4.Nxd4 Nf6 5.Nc3 g6 6.Be3 Bg7
7.f3 Nc6 8.Qd2 0–0 9.0–0–0 Nxd4 10.Bxd4 Be6 11.h4 Qa5
12.Kb1 Rfc8 13.Nd5 Qxd2 14.Nxf6+ Bxf6 15.Rxd2 Bxd4
16.Rxd4 h5 17.b3 Rc3 18.Kb2 Rac8 19.Bc4 Bxc4 20.Kxc3
Bf1+ 21.Kb2 Bxg2 22.Rhd1 Bxf3 23.R1d3 Bg4 24.Rc3 Kg7
25.Ra4 a6 26.Rb4 g5 27.hxg5 Kg6 28.e5 Rxc3 29.Kxc3 dxe5
30.Rxb7 h4 31.Rxe7 h3 32.Rxe5 h2 33.Re1 Bf3 34.Kd4 h1Q
35.Rxh1 Bxh1 36.c4 Kxg5 37.b4 Bc6 38.Kc5 38...f5 39.Kxc6
f4 40.b5 f3 41.b6 f2 42.b7 f1Q 43.b8Q Qxc4+ 44.Kb6 Qxa2
45.Qe5+, ½–½.

Kosteniuk - Zhu Chen (Women's World Championship, Moscow, 2001)

1.e4 c5 2.Nf3 d6 3.d4 cxd4 4.Nxd4 Nf6 5.Nc3 a6 6.Bg5 e6 7.f4 Qb6 8.Nb3 Be7 9.Qf3 Nbd7 10.0–0–0 Qc7 11.g4 b5 12.Bxf6 Nxf6 13.g5 Nd7 14.h4 b4 15.Ne2 Bb7 16.Bh3 d5 17.f5 Rc8 18.c3 dxe4 19.Qe3 Bc5 20.Nxc5 Nxc5 21.fxe6 fxe6 22.Rhf1 Rf8 23.Bg4 Rxf1 24.Rxf1 Qa5 25.Qd4 Qxa2 26.Kc2 e3 27.Bh5+ g6 28.Qh8+ Ke7 29.Qxh7+ Kd6 30.Bxg6 b3+ 31.Kc1 Na4 32.Rd1+ Bd5 33.Rxd5+ exd5 34.Kd1 Qxb2 35.Ke1 Qd2+ 36.Kf1 Rf8+, 0–1.

Zhu Chen - Kosteniuk (Women's World Championship, Moscow, 2001)

1.d4 f5 2.Nf3 Nf6 3.g3 e6 4.Bg2 d5 5.0–0 Bd6 6.b3 Qe7 7.c4 c6 8.Bb2 0–0 9.Qc1 a5 10.Ba3 Na6 11.Bxd6 Qxd6 12.c5 Qe7 13.Ne5 Nd7 14.Nxd7 Bxd7 15.f4 b6 16.cxb6 Qb4 17.Qc3 Qxb6 18.Nd2 Rfc8 19.Rfc1 c5 20.Nf3 Rc7 21.e3 Rac8 22.Qd2 a4 23.Ne5 Be8 24.dxc5 Nxc5 25.bxa4 Bxa4 26.Rab1 Qa7 27.Qd4 Be8 28.Rc2 Qa3 29.Qc3 Qa4 30.Qb2 Qa6 31.Bf1 Qa7 32.Qd4 Qa3 33.Qc3 Qa4 34.Qb2 Qe4 35.Re1 g5 36.Bg2 Qa4 37.Rec1 Qa5 38.Qc3 Qa7 39.Qd4 Qa3 40.Qc3 Nb3 41.Qxb3 Qxb3 42.axb3 Rxc2 43.Rxc2 Rxc2 44.fxg5 Re2 45.Nf3 Rxe3 46.Nd4 Kf7 47.Bf1 Bd7 48.Kf2 Rc3 49.b4 e5 50.Nf3 Ke6 51.Nh4 e4 52.g6 hxg6 53.Nxg6 d4 54.h4 Rc2+ 55.Ke1 Rc1+ 56.Kf2 e3+ 57.Kg1 Bb5, 0–1.

Zhu Chen - Kosteniuk (Women's World Championship, Moscow, 2001)

1.d4 f5 2.g3 Nf6 3.Bg2 e6 4.c4 d5 5.Nh3 c6 6.Qc2 Be7 7.0–0 0–0 8.Nd2 h6 9.Nf4 Qe8 10.Nf3 g5 11.Nd3 Nbd7 12.Bd2 a5 13.b3 Ne4 14.Nfe5 Bf6 15.Bc1 Be7 16.a3 Nxe5 17.Nxe5 b6 18.f3 Nf6 19.Bd2 Ba6 20.e4 c5 21.exd5 exd5 22.Qxf5 Kg7 23.Qd3 Rd8 24.Rfe1 dxc4 25.bxc4 Rxd4 26.Qc2 Bd6 27.Ng4

Qg6 28.Qb2 Nd7 29.Bc3 Kg8 30.Bxd4 cxd4 31.Kh1 Bxc4
32.Qxd4 Bb3 33.Re3 a4 34.Rd3 Nc5 35.Qxd6 Qxd3 36.Qxh6
Qf5 37.Qxb6 Qc2 38.h3 Ne6 39.Re1 Qc4 40.Kh2 Kg7 41.Re4
Qd5 42.Re5 Qd7 43.Qe3 Qe7 44.Nf2 Qf6 45.Ra5 Rd8 46.Ne4
Qb2 47.Rxg5+ Kf7 48.Qa7+ Ke8 49.Rg8+ Nf8 50.Rg7 Rd7
51.Qb8+ Rd8 52.Nd6 mate, 1–0.

Shahade - Sagalchik (US Championship, Seattle, 2002)
1.e4 e5 2.Nf3 Nc6 3.Bb5 a6 4.Ba4 Nf6 5.0–0 Nxe4 6.d4 b5
7.Bb3 d5 8.dxe5 Be6 9.Nbd2 Nc5 10.c3 Bg4 11.Bc2 Qd7
12.Re1 Be7 13.Nf1 Bh5 14.b4 Na4 15.Ng3 Nxc3 16.Qd2 Bg4
17.Qxc3 Bxb4 18.Qe3 Bxf3 19.Bf5 Qe7 20.Bd2 g6 21.Bxb4
Qxb4 22.Qxf3 Nd4 23.Bd7+ Kxd7 24.Qxf7+ Kc8 25.Rac1
Ra7 26.Qxd5 c6 27.Qe4 Rd7 28.e6 Rd6 29.Qg4 Kc7 30.e7
Re8 31.Qg5 Re6 32.Rxe6 Nxe6 33.Qd5 Nd4, 1–0.

Ambarcumjan - Shahade (US Championship, Seattle, 2002)
1.d4 Nf6 2.c4 g6 3.Nc3 d5 4.Nf3 Bg7 5.e3 0–0 6.Bd2 c5 7.dxc5
Na6 8.cxd5 Nxc5 9.Bc4 Bf5 10.0–0 Rc8 11.Qe2 Nfe4 12.Nxe4
Bxe4 13.Bb4 Na4 14.Ba3 Nxb2 15.Bxb2 Bxb2 16.Qxb2 Rxc4
17.Ne5 Rc5 18.Qd4 Qxd5 19.Nd7 Qxd4 20.exd4 Rg5 21.Rfe1
Rxg2+ 22.Kf1 Rxh2 23.f3 Rd8, 0–1.

Shahade - Stripunsky (US Championship, Seattle, 2002)
1.e4 g6 2.d4 Bg7 3.Nc3 c6 4.Nf3 d5 5.h3 dxe4 6.Nxe4 Nd7
7.Bc4 Ngf6 8.Qe2 0–0 9.0–0 b5 10.Bb3 a5 11.Nxf6+ exf6
12.a3 Re8 13.Be3 Nb6 14.Qd2 a4 15.Ba2 Be6 16.Bxe6 Rxe6
17.Rfe1 Qd5 18.Qc3 Qd7 19.Qd3 Bf8 20.Bd2 Nc4 21.Bc3
Rae8 22.Rxe6 Rxe6 23.Nd2 Nb6 24.Bb4 Bxb4 25.axb4 Qe7
26.c3 Re1+ 27.Rxe1 Qxe1+ 28.Kh2 Qxf2 29.Ne4 Qf5 30.Qe2
Nc4 31.Nc5 Kg7 32.Nxa4 bxa4 33.Qxc4 Qf4+ 34.Kg1 Qc1+
35.Kh2 Qxb2 36.h4 h5 37.Qxc6 a3 38.d5 a2, 0–1.

Judit Polgar - Kasparov (Russia vs The Rest of the World, Moscow, 2002)

1.e4 e5 2.Nf3 Nc6 3.Bb5 Nf6 4.0–0 Nxe4 5.d4 Nd6 6.Bxc6 dxc6 7.dxe5 Nf5 8.Qxd8+ Kxd8 9.Nc3 h6 10.Rd1+ Ke8 11.h3 Be7 12.Ne2 Nh4 13.Nxh4 Bxh4 14.Be3 Bf5 15.Nd4 Bh7 16.g4 Be7 17.Kg2 h5 18.Nf5 18... Bf8 19.Kf3 Bg6 20.Rd2 hxg4+ 21.hxg4 Rh3+ 22.Kg2 Rh7 23.Kg3 f6 24.Bf4 Bxf5 25.gxf5 fxe5 26.Re1 Bd6 27.Bxe5 Kd7 28.c4 c5 29.Bxd6 cxd6 30.Re6 Rah8 31.Rexd6+ Kc8 32.R2d5 Rh3+ 33.Kg2 Rh2+ 34.Kf3 R2h3+ 35.Ke4 b6 36.Rc6+ Kb8 37.Rd7 Rh2 38.Ke3 Rf8 39.Rcc7 Rxf5 40.Rb7+ Kc8 41.Rdc7+ Kd8 42.Rxg7 Kc8, 1–0.

Xu Yuhua - Krush (Olympiad, Bled, 2002)

1.e4 c5 2.Nf3 d6 3.Bb5+ Bd7 4.Bxd7+ Qxd7 5.c4 Nc6 6.Nc3 Nf6 7.d4 cxd4 8.Nxd4 g6 9.f3 Bg7 10.Nde2 0–0 11.0–0 Rfc8 12.Be3 Qd8 13.b3 Qa5 14.Qd2 a6 15.a4 Rab8 16.Rab1 Nd7 17.Rfd1 Qb4 18.Qc1 Qa5 19.Kh1 Kh8 20.Bd2 Qd8 21.Bg5 Nc5 22.Bh4 Nb4 23.Qd2 Qd7 24.Nd4 Ne6 25.Bf2 Nxd4 26.Bxd4 Qc7 27.Ba7 Ra8 28.Be3 Re8 29.a5 Qxa5 30.Nd5 Nc6 31.Qxa5 Nxa5 32.Nc7 Rac8 33.Nxe8 Rxe8 34.c5 dxc5 35.Bxc5 Bf6 36.Rd7 b5 37.f4 Rc8 38.b4 Nc6 39.e5 Bg7 40.Rbd1 Bf8 41.g3 Kg7 42.Rb7 e6 43.Rdd7 Nd8 44.Bb6 Nxb7 45.Rxb7 Bxb4 46.Ra7 Rc6 47.Bd8 Rc8 48.Bf6+ Kg8 49.Rxa6 Bc5 50.Ra2 b4 51.Rb2 Kf8 52.Kg2 Ke8 53.Kf3 Kd7 54.Ke4 Kc6 55.g4 Kb5 56.f5 gxf5+ 57.gxf5 Rg8, 0–1.

Shahade - Wang Pin (Olympiad, Bled, 2002)

1.e4 c5 2.Nf3 d6 3.d4 cxd4 4.Nxd4 Nf6 5.Nc3 a6 6.Bg5 e6 7.f4 Qb6 8.Qd2 Qxb2 9.Rb1 Qa3 10.Bxf6 gxf6 11.Be2 h5 12.0–0 Nd7 13.Kh1 Nc5 14.f5 Be7 15.Rf3 Qa5 16.Rg3 h4 17.Rg7 Bf8 18.Rg4 h3 19.fxe6 fxe6 20.e5 dxe5 21.Nb3 Nxb3 22.Rxb3 Bh6 23.Qd3 f5 24.Rg6 hxg2+ 25.Rxg2 Qd8 26.Bh5+

Ke7 27.Qe2 b5 28.Bf3 e4 29.Nxe4 fxe4 30.Qxe4 Bd7 31.Qb4+
Kf6 32.Qh4+ Kf7 33.Bh5+ Kf8 34.Rf3+, 1–0.

Socko - Zhao Xue (Olympiad, Bled, 2002)

1.d4 Nf6 2.c4 e6 3.Nc3 Bb4 4.Qc2 c5 5.dxc5 Bxc5 6.Nf3 Qb6
7.e3 Qc7 8.Bd3 b6 9.0–0 a6 10.a3 Be7 11.b3 Bb7 12.Bb2 d6
13.Rad1 Nbd7 14.Ne4 Rc8 15.Rd2 Qb8 16.Nxf6+ Bxf6
17.Bxf6 Nxf6 18.Rfd1 Bxf3 19.gxf3 Ke7 20.Qb2 g5 21.Bf1
Rhd8 22.Qd4 a5 23.Bg2 Qc7 24.b4 axb4 25.axb4 e5 26.Qa1
Qxc4 27.Bh3 Rc7 28.Qb1 h6 29.Kh1 g4 30.Bg2 gxf3 31.Bxf3
Qh4 32.Qf5 Rc4 33.b5 e4 34.Bg2 Rc5 35.Qf4 Qxf4 36.exf4
d5 37.f3 e3 38.Rd4 Kd6 39.Bf1 Rc2 40.Bd3 Rc3 41.Kg2 Kc5
42.Be2 Ra8 43.R4d3 Rxd3 44.Bxd3 Nh5 45.Bb1 Nxf4+ 46.Kg3
Ne2+ 47.Kg4 Rg8+ 48.Kf5 Rg1, 0–1.

Shahade - Stefanova (Andorra, 2000)

1.e4 d5 2.exd5 Qxd5 3.Nc3 Qa5 4.g3 c6 5.Bg2 Nf6 6.Nf3 Bg4
7.h3 Bh5 8.b4 Qc7 9.0–0 e6 10.Rb1 a6 11.a4 Nbd7 12.Re1
Bd6 13.b5 0–0 14.g4 Bg6 15.Nh4 axb5 16.Nxg6 hxg6 17.axb5
Nb6 18.Qf3 Nbd5 19.Bb2 Rac8 20.Nxd5 cxd5 21.Bxf6 gxf6
22.Qxf6 Be7 23.Qb2 Qf4 24.c3 Bc5 25.d4 Bd6 26.Re3 Rc4
27.Ra1 Bb8 28.Qb3 Qh2+ 29.Kf1 Rfc8 30.Ra4 Qd6 31.Rxc4
Rxc4 32.Qa2 Rc8 33.Qa4 Kg7 34.Qb4 Qxb4 35.cxb4 Rc4
36.Rb3 b6 37.Ke2 Rxd4 38.Ke3 Rc4 39.Kd3 Bd6 40.Bf1 Bxb4
41.Rb2 Bc5 42.f3 Rc1 43.Bg2 g5, 0–1.

Milov - Stefanova (Andorra, 2001)

1.c4 c6 2.Nf3 d5 3.e3 Nf6 4.Nc3 g6 5.d4 Bg7 6.Be2 0–0
7.0–0 a6 8.b4 dxc4 9.Bxc4 b5 10.Bb3 Nd5 11.Nxd5 cxd5
12.a4 bxa4 13.Bxa4 Bd7 14.Qb3 e6 15.Bd2 Ra7 16.Rfc1 Qb6
17.Rc5 Rd8 18.Bc3 Bf8 19.Ne5 Bxa4 20.Qxa4 Rb7 21.Qd1
Qd6 22.h4 Nd7 23.Rc6 Qe7 24.Nf3 Qe8 25.Rc5 Nxc5 26.dxc5
Bg7 27.Bxg7 Kxg7 28.Qd4+ f6 29.Rxa6 e5 30.Qc3 Qb5

31.Rxf6 d4 32.exd4 Kxf6 33.Ng5 Rxd4 34.Qf3+ Rf4 35.Qb3 Qc4 36.Qa4 Qc1+, 0–1.

Skripchenko - Atalik (Saint Vincent, 2001)

1.e4 c5 2.Nf3 d6 3.Bb5+ Bd7 4.Bxd7+ Qxd7 5.0–0 Nf6 6.Qe2 Nc6 7.c3 e6 8.d4 cxd4 9.cxd4 d5 10.e5 Ng8 11.Nc3 Bb4 12.a3 Bxc3 13.bxc3 Nge7 14.Rd1 Na5 15.Rb1 h6 16.Ne1 Rc8 17.Rd3 b6 18.Qh5 Rc7 19.g4 Qc8 20.Bd2 Nc4 21.Bc1 Ng6 22.f4 Ncxe5 23.fxe5 Rxc3 24.Rd1 Qc4 25.Ng2 Qa2 26.Be3 Qxa3 27.Ra1 Qe7 28.Rf1 Qc7 29.Ra2 0–0 30.Raf2 a5 31.g5 hxg5 32.Bxg5 Qc4 33.Be3 Qd3 34.Rf3 Qe2 35.Qg5 Rc2 36.R3f2 Qc4 37.h4 Rxf2 38.Rxf2 Kh7 39.h5 Nh8 40.Nh4 Qd3 41.Rg2 Rg8 42.Ng6 Qd1+, 1–0.

Kosteniuk - Paehtz (Duel of the Graces, Mainz, 2002)

1.e4 c5 2.Nf3 e6 3.d4 cxd4 4.Nxd4 a6 5.Nc3 Qc7 6.Be2 Nc6 7.0–0 Nf6 8.Be3 Bb4 9.Na4 Be7 10.f4 Nxe4 11.c4 0–0 12.Bd3 Nf6 13.g4 Nb4 14.g5 Ne8 15.Bxh7+ Kxh7 16.Qh5+ Kg8 17.Rf3 f5 18.Rh3 Nf6 19.gxf6 Bxf6 20.Nf3 Nd3 21.Ng5 Bxg5 22.fxg5 Nf4 23.Qh7+ Kf7 24.Rh6 Ne2+ 25.Kf2 Nf4 26.Rf6+ Ke8 27.Qxg7 Nh3+ 28.Ke1 Qa5+ 29.Ke2 Qb4 30.Qg6+ Ke7 31.Bc5+ Qxc5 32.Qg7+ Ke8, 1–0.

Paehtz - Kosteniuk (Duel of the Graces, Mainz, 2002)

1.e4 c5 2.Nf3 d6 3.d4 cxd4 4.Nxd4 Nf6 5.Nc3 g6 6.Be2 Bg7 7.0–0 0–0 8.Re1 Nc6 9.Nb3 a5 10.a4 Be6 11.Bf1 Bxb3 12.cxb3 e6 13.Bg5 h6 14.Bh4 Qb6 15.Bg3 Rfd8 16.Nb5 Ne8 17.Bf4 d5 18.e5 Nc7 19.Qd2 g5 20.Bg3 Nxb5 21.axb5 Nd4 22.Qe3 Bf8 23.Ra4 Bc5 24.Rc1 Rac8 25.Rxc5 Nf5 26.Rxc8 Nxe3 27.Rxd8+ Qxd8 28.fxe3 Qc7 29.e4 Qc2 30.exd5 Qxb3 31.Rxa5 exd5 32.Ra8+ Kg7 33.Bf2 Qxb2 34.Rb8 Qxe5 35.Rxb7 h5 36.Rd7 h4 37.b6 g4 38.g3 Qe6 39.b7, 1–0.

Shahade - Dzagnidze (Women's World Championship, Elista, 2004)

1.e4 c5 2.Nf3 d6 3.d4 cxd4 4.Nxd4 Nf6 5.Nc3 Nc6 6.Bg5 e6
7.Qd2 Be7 8.0-0-0 Nxd4 9.Qxd4 0-0 10.f3 a6 11.Kb1 Nxe4
12.Nxe4 Bxg5 13.Nxg5 Qxg5 14.f4 Qa5 15.Qxd6 b5 16.Bd3
Bb7 17.Qe5 Rac8 18.h4 Bd5 19.b3 Qc3 20.Qe2 b4 21.f5 a5
22.Rh3 Qf6 23.g4 exf5 24.Bxf5 Rcd8 25.Rhd3 Bb7 26.g5 Qb6
27.h5 Ba6 28.g6 Bxd3 29.gxh7+ Kh8 30.Bxd3 Rde8 31.Qg2
Re5 32.Rf1 Rfe8 33.a4 bxa3 34.Ka2 Qd4 35.Kxa3 Rxh5
36.Rxf7 Qa1 mate, 0-1.

Chiburdanidze - Stefanova (Women's World Championship, Elista, 2004)

1.c4 Nf6 2.d4 c6 3.Bf4 Qb6 4.Qd2 Ne4 5.Qc2 d5 6.f3 Qa5+
7.Nd2 Nxd2 8.Bxd2 Qd8 9.e3 g6 10.Bd3 Bg7 11.Ne2 dxc4
12.Bxc4 Nd7 13.Bb3 a5 14.a3 e5 15.0-0 0-0 16.Rad1 exd4
17.Nxd4 Qe7 18.Rfe1 Ne5 19.e4 c5 20.Nb5 c4 21.Ba4 Nd3
22.Re2 Nxb2 23.Rb1 Nxa4 24.Qxa4 c3 25.Be3 Bd7 26.Qc2
Rfc8 27.a4 Rc4 28.Bc1 h5 29.Ba3 Qe6 30.f4 Qg4 31.Bd6 Bxb5
32.axb5 Rd8 33.e5 Qxf4 34.Rf1 Qg4 35.h3 Qe6 36.b6 a4 37.Kh1
Rd7 38.Ra1 Kh7 39.Rf1 Rc6 40.Ref2 Qb3 41.Qe2 Rxb6 42.Qe4
Rc6 43.Rb1 Qc4 44.Qc2 b5 45.Rff1 Rcxd6 46.exd6 Rxd6 47.Rf2
Bh6 48.Rbf1 Rd7 49.Rf3 Bd2 50.Rf6 a3 51.Ra1 Ra7 52.Rd6 a2
53.Rd8 Bg5 54.Re8 b4 55.Qf2 Rc7, 0-1.

Kovalevskaya - Stefanova (Women's World Championship, Elista, 2004)

1.e4 e5 2.Nf3 Nc6 3.Bb5 a6 4.Ba4 Nf6 5.0-0 b5 6.Bb3 Bc5
7.a4 Bb7 8.d3 d6 9.Nc3 b4 10.Ne2 0-0 11.Ng3 h6 12.Nf5
Bc8 13.N3h4 Nd4 14.Nxd4 Bxd4 15.Qf3 Bg4 16.Qg3 Kh7
17.Be3 Bxb2 18.Rab1 Bc3 19.f3 Bd7 20.Qf2 a5 21.g4 Qe8
22.Nf5 Bxa4 23.g5 Nh5 24.Qh4 g6 25.Nxh6 Bxb3 26.Ng4
Qe6 27.Nf6+ Kg7 28.Nxh5+ gxh5 29.cxb3 a4 30.bxa4 Rxa4

31.Kh1 Ra2 32.Rg1 Re2 33.Bf2 Ra8 34.f4 exf4 35.Qxf4
Raa2 36.Rg2 Kg6 37.Qf3 Rac2 38.Rf1 b3 39.e5 Bxe5 40.d4
Bg7 41.Bg1 Rxg2 42.Qd3+ Kxg5 43.Be3+ Kh4 44.Rf4+
Rg4 45.d5 Rc1+ 46.Bxc1 Qe1+ 47.Rf1 Qe4+ 48.Qxe4 Rxe4
49.Kg2 b2 50.Bf4 Rb4 51.Bg3+ Kg5 52.h4+ Kg6 53.Rb1
Ra4, 0–1.

Shahade - Goletiani (US Championship, 2004)
1.e4 c5 2.Nf3 d6 3.d4 cxd4 4.Nxd4 Nf6 5.Nc3 Nc6 6.Be2
e6 7.0–0 Be7 8.Be3 a6 9.f4 0–0 10.Qe1 Qc7 11.Qg3 Nxd4
12.Bxd4 b5 13.a3 Rb8 14.Kh1 b4 15.e5 Ne8 16.exd6 Bxd6
17.Ne4 f6 18.Bd3 bxa3 19.bxa3 Be7 20.Rab1 Bxa3 21.Rxb8
Qxb8 22.Bc4 Be7 23.Qh3 f5 24.Ng5 Bxg5 25.fxg5 Qb4
26.Qb3 Qxb3 27.cxb3 Nd6 28.Bc5 Rd8 29.Bxd6 Rxd6
30.Rxf5 Rd1+ 31.Rf1 Rxf1+ 32.Bxf1 a5 33.Kg1 Kf7 34.Kf2
e5 35.Bd3 Bb7 36.g3 e4 37.Bc4+ Kg6 38.h4 Kf5 39.Bg8 Ke5
40.Ke3 Bd5 41.Bxh7 Bxb3 42.Bxe4 a4 43.h5 a3 44.Bb1 a2
45.Bxa2 Bxa2 46.h6 gxh6 47.gxh6, ½–½.

Tsagaan Battsetseg - Shahade (US Championship, 2004)
1.e4 c5 2.Nf3 d6 3.d4 cxd4 4.Nxd4 Nf6 5.Nc3 e5 6.Nb3 a6
7.Be3 Be6 8.f3 Be7 9.Qd2 Nbd7 10.0–0–0 Nb6 11.g4 0–0
12.g5 Nh5 13.Rg1 Qc7 14.Nd5 Bxd5 15.exd5 a5 16.Nc5 Rac8
17.c3 Nxd5 18.Qxd5 dxc5 19.Bc4 Rcd8 20.Qe4 g6 21.h4 Rd4
22.cxd4 cxd4 23.Bd2 Qxc4+ 24.Kb1 Qb5 25.a4 Qc5 26.Rc1
Qd6 27.Rge1 f6 28.f4 Qa6 29.Rc7 Bd6 30.Rd7 Kh8 31.fxe5
fxe5 32.Bc1 Ng3 33.Qd5 Nf5 34.Rxe5 Bxe5 35.Qxe5+ Kg8
36.Ka2 Qc6 37.Rc7 Qxa4+ 38.Kb1 Qb3 39.h5 gxh5 40.Qe4
d3 41.Rc3 Qb5 42.Qe6+ Kh8 43.Bd2 Qe8 44.Qd5 Qf7 45.Qxd3
Ng7 46.Qd4 Qf5+ 47.Ka2 Qe6+ 48.Rb3 b5 49.Bc3 Rg8
50.Bxa5 Ra8 51.Qb4 Qd5 52.Kb1 Qd1+ 53.Ka2 Qd8 54.Ra3,
0–1.

Shahade - Abrahamyan (US Championship, 2004)

1.e4 e6 2.d4 d5 3.Nd2 Nf6 4.e5 Nfd7 5.c3 c5 6.Bd3 Nc6
7.Ngf3 Qb6 8.0–0 cxd4 9.cxd4 Nxd4 10.Nxd4 Qxd4 11.Nf3
Qb6 12.Qa4 Be7 13.Qg4 Kf8 14.Bg5 Qd8 15.Qf4 Nc5 16.Bc2
Bd7 17.b4 Na6 18.a3 Kg8 19.Bd3 h6 20.Bxe7 Qxe7 21.Rfc1
Be8 22.Rc3 Rd8 23.Qd4 Nb8 24.b5 b6 25.h4 g6 26.Qb4 Qb7
27.Nd4 h5 28.Rac1 Rd7 29.Nc6 Kg7 30.Qf4 Rc7 31.Nd8,
1–0.

Zatonskih - Shahade (US Championship, 2004)

1.e4 c5 2.Nf3 d6 3.Bb5+ Bd7 4.Bxd7+ Nxd7 5.0–0 Ngf6
6.Nc3 g6 7.d3 Bg7 8.Ng5 h6 9.Nh3 0–0 10.f4 c4 11.Kh1 cxd3
12.cxd3 Qa5 13.Qe2 Qh5 14.Qe1 Nc5 15.d4 Nd3 16.Qd2
Nxc1 17.Raxc1 e5 18.fxe5 dxe5 19.d5 Rac8 20.Nf2 Rfd8
21.Ne2 Rxc1 22.Rxc1 Ne8 23.Rc3 Nd6 24.Rh3 Qg5 25.Qxg5
hxg5 26.g4 f6 27.Rc3 Rc8 28.Rxc8+ Nxc8 29.Nd3 Bf8 30.Kg2
Kf7 31.Kf3 Bd6 32.Ke3 Ke7 33.Nc3 Kd7 34.Nb1 Nb6 35.b3
Nc8 36.Nd2 b6 37.Nf3 Ne7 38.h4 gxh4 39.Nxh4 g5 40.Nf3
Ng6 41.Nh2 Ne7 42.Nf1 Ng8 43.Kd2 Nh6 44.Ne3 Kc7
45.Kc3 b5 46.a4 Kb6 47.Kd2 a6 48.Nf5 Nxf5 49.exf5 bxa4
50.bxa4 e4 51.Nf2 e3+ 52.Kxe3 Bc5+ 53.Kf3 Bxf2 54.Kxf2
Kc5 55.Ke3 Kxd5 56.a5 Ke5 57.Kd3 Kf4 58.Kc4 Kxg4 59.Kc5
Kxf5 60.Kb6 g4 61.Kxa6 g3 62.Kb7 g2 63.a6 g1Q 64.a7 Qa1
65.a8Q, 0–1.

Shahade - Belakovskaia (US Championship, 2004)

1.e4 e5 2.Nf3 Nc6 3.Bb5 a6 4.Ba4 Nf6 5.0–0 Be7 6.Re1 b5
7.Bb3 0–0 8.h3 Bb7 9.d3 d6 10.a3 Na5 11.Ba2 c5 12.Nbd2
Qc7 13.Nf1 Rae8 14.Ne3 Bd8 15.Nh2 Nc6 16.Nhg4 Nxg4
17.hxg4 Bg5 18.c3 Ne7 19.Qf3 Qd7 20.Nf5 Bxc1 21.Raxc1
Ng6 22.Rcd1 Rd8 23.d4 Qc7 24.dxc5 dxc5 25.Bd5 Bc8 26.g3
Be6 27.c4 Ne7 28.Ne3 Rd6 29.g5 Nc6 30.Bxc6 Qxc6 31.Nd5

Qd7 32.Qc3 f6 33.gxf6 gxf6 34.cxb5 Bxd5 35.exd5 Qxb5
36.Rd2 Rb8 37.Rc1 Rc8 38.Qc4 Qxc4 39.Rxc4 Kf7 40.b4
Rcd8 41.Rxc5 Kg6 42.Kg2 Kf5 43.Kf3 e4+ 44.Ke3 Ke5 45.a4
f5 46.Rc6 h5 47.Rxd6 Rxd6 48.f3 h4 49.f4+ Kf6 50.gxh4
Ke7 51.Kd4 Rh6 52.Ke5 Rxh4 53.Kxf5 e3 54.Re2 Kd6
55.Rxe3 Kxd5 56.Re5+ Kc4 57.b5 axb5 58.axb5 Rh6 59.Ke4
Rb6 60.f5 Rh6 61.Re6 Rh4+ 62.Ke5 Kxb5 63.Kd6 Ra4
64.Re5+ Kb6 65.f6 Ra7 66.Re7 Ra1 67.Re8 Rd1+ 68.Ke7
Kc7 69.f7 Re1+ 70.Kf6 Rf1+ 71.Kg6 Rg1+ 72.Kh5 Rh1+
73.Kg4 Rg1+ 74.Kh3 Rh1+ 75.Kg2. 1–0.

Yifan Hou - Kosteniuk (Mindsports, 2008)
1. e4 e5 2. Bc4 Nc6 3. Nf3 Bc5 4. c3 Nf6 5. d3 O-O 6. O-O
a6 7. Bb3 d5 8. Nbd2 Re8 9. h3 h6 10. Re1 Be6 11. Bc2 dxe4
12. dxe4 Qe7 13. Qe2 Rad8 14. Nf1 Bb6 15. Ng3 Qc5 16.
Nh4 Ne7 17. Qf3 Nh7 18. Nhf5 Nxf5 19. Nxf5 Bxf5 20. Qxf5
Qe7 21. Qf3 Rd6 22. Be3 Ng5 23. Qe2 Ne6 24. Bb3 Nf4 25.
Bxf4 exf4 26. Rad1 Red8 27. Rxd6 Rxd6 28. Rd1 Rxd1+ 29.
Bxd1 Qc5 30. Bb3 g6 31. Qf3 g5 32. g3 Qe5 33. Qh5 Qf6 34.
e5 Qg7 35. e6 fxe6 36. Qe8+ Qf8 37. Qg6+ Kh8 38. gxf4 gxf4
39. Qxe6 f3 40. Kf1 Kg7 41. Qg4+ Kh8 42. Qe6 Kg7 43. Bc2
Qd6 44. Qg4+ Kf8 45. Qxf3+ Ke7 46. Qe4+ Qe6 47. Qh7+
Kd6 48. Qd3+ Qd5 49. Qg3+ Qe5 50. Qg6+ Qe6 51. Qd3+
Qd5 52. Qg3+ Qe5 53. Qf3 Qd5 54. Qf6+ Qe6 55. Qf4+ Ke7
56. Qh4+ Qf6 57. Qe4+ Qe6 58. Qh4+ Qf6 59. Qe4+ Qe6 60.
Qf3 Qf6 61. Qe4+ Qe6 62. Qf3 Qf6 63. Qxf6+ Kxf6 64. Be4
c6 65. Ke2 Ke5 66. f3 Kf4 67. h4 Kg3 68. h5 Kf4 69. Kd3
Bc5 70. Kc4 Be3 71. Kd3 a5 72. a4 Bc5 73. Kc4 Be3 74. b4
Bb6 75. b5 cxb5+ 76. Kxb5 Bc7 77. Bxb7 Kg5 78. c4 Kxh5
79. c5 Kg5 80. Kc6 Bf4 81. Bc8 Be3 82. Kd6 Bf4+ 83. Kd7
h5 84. c6 h4 85. Kd8 Be3 86. c7 Bb6 87. Be6 Kf6 88. Bh3
Ke5 89. Kd7 1–0.

Haregeweyn Abera Alemu - Phiona Mutesi (Women's Olympiad, 2010)

1. e4 e5 2. Nf3 d6 3. h3 Nf6 4. Nc3 Be7 5. Bc4 h6 6. d3 O-O
7. O-O Nc6 8. Be3 Be6 9. Bxe6 fxe6 10. Qe2 d5 11. exd5 exd5
12. d4 Bd6 13. Rad1 exd4 14. Nxd4 Nxd4 15. Rxd4 c5 16.
Rdd1 d4 17. Nb5 Ne4 18. Nxd6 Nxd6 19. Bc1 Qf6 20. b3
Rae8 21. Qg4 Re7 22. Qg3 Ne4 23. Qd3 Nc3 24. Rd2 b6 25.
a4 Kh8 26. f3 Rfe8 27. Bb2 Re3 28. Qc4 Ne2+ 29. Kh2 Qf4+
30. Kh1 Ng3+ 31. Kg1 Nxf1 32. Kxf1 Re1+ 33. Kf2 Qxd2+
34. Kg3 Rg1 35. Kh4 Qf4+ 36. g4 Qg5# 0-1.

Yifan Hou - Judit Polgar (Gibraltar Masters, 2012)

1. e4 c5 2. Nf3 e6 3. d4 cxd4 4. Nxd4 Nc6 5. Nc3 a6 6. Be2
Nge7 7. Bf4 Ng6 8. Nxc6 bxc6 9. Bd6 Bxd6 10. Qxd6 Qe7
11. O-O-O Qxd6 12. Rxd6 Ke7 13. Rhd1 Nf4 14. Bf3 Rb8
15. R6d2 g5 16. Na4 d5 17. g3 Ng6 18. Re1 Kf6 19. Bh5 Rb4
20. Nc3 d4 21. e5+ Nxe5 22. Ne4+ Ke7 23. Nxg5 h6 24. Nxe6
Bxe6 25. Rxe5 Rd8 26. f4 Rb5 27. Rde2 Kf6 28. Bf3 c5 29.
a4 Rb4 30. Rxc5 Rxa4 31. b3 Rb4 32. Be4 Bg4 33. Re1 Rd6
34. Bd3 Bd7 35. Ree5 Be6 36. Kd2 Rbb6 37. Ra5 Rbc6 38.
Ra4 Rb6 39. Re4 Bf5 40. Rexd4 Re6 41. Bc4 Rec6 42. Ra5
Bc8 43. Bd3 Be6 44. Rd8 Bc8 45. Rad5 Be6 46. Rh5 Kg7 47.
f5 1-0.

Irina Krush - Azarov (Baku Open, 2013)

1. d4 Nf6 2. c4 e6 3. Nc3 Bb4 4. Qc2 O-O 5. a3 Bxc3+ 6.
Qxc3 d5 7. Bg5 c5 8. dxc5 d4 9. Qc2 e5 10. e3 h6 11. Bh4
Qe7 12. exd4 exd4+ 13. Be2 Qxc5 14. Bxf6 gxf6 15. Bd3 Nc6
16. Ne2 Qa5+ 17. Qd2 Qxd2+ 18. Kxd2 Be6 19. b3 a5 20. f4
f5 21. Rae1 Rfc8 22. Rhf1 Ra6 23. Rf3 Rb6 24. Kc2 a4 25.
b4 Bxc4 26. Bxc4 Nxb4+ 27. axb4 Rxb4 28. Kd2 Rcxc4 29.
Ra3 b5 30. Kd3 Kh7 31. Rc1 Rb2 32. Re1 Rcc2 33. Nxd4
Rxg2 34. Nxf5 Rxh2 35. Re7 Kg6 36. Ne3 h5 37. Ra1 Rb3+

38. Ke4 Rb4+ 39. Ke5 f6+ 40. Kd5 Rd2+ 41. Kc5 Rxf4 42.
Rg1+ Kh6 43. Reg7 h4 44. R7g6+ Kh7 45. Rg7+ Kh6 46.
R1g6+ Kh5 47. Ng4 Rxg4 48. Rxg4 Rf2 49. Kb4 Rb2+ 50.
Ka5 h3 51. Rg3 Kh4 52. R7g4+ Kh5 53. Rg8 Kh4 54. R3g7
1-0.

Bibliography

Find games and updates on https://linktr.ee/chessqueensbook

Books

Beauvoir, Simone de, *The Second Sex*, Alfred A. Knopf, New York, 1953.

Berger, John, *Ways of Seeing*, Penguin Books, New York, 1972.

Bykova, Elizaveta, *Vera Menchik*, Physiculture and Sport, Moscow, 1957.

Cabanne, Pierre, *Dialogues with Marcel Duchamp*, Da Capo Press, Cambridge, MA, 1987.

Cockburn, Alexander, *Idle Passion: Chess and the Dance of Death*, Simon and Schuster, New York, 1974.

Fine, Reuben, *Psychoanalytic Observations on Chess and Chess Masters*, National Psychological Association, New York, 1956.

Forbes, Cathy, *The Polgar Sisters: Training or Genius?* Henry Holt, New York, 1992.

Goldberg, Steven, *Why Men Rule: A Theory of Male Dominance*, Open Court, Chicago, 1993.

Graham, John, *Women in Chess: Players of the Modern Age*, McFarland & Co., Jefferson, NC, 1987.

Geuzendam, Dirk Jan Ten, *Linares! Linares! A Journey into the Heart of Chess*, New In Chess, Alkmaar, The Netherlands, 2001.

Graf, Sonja, *Asi Juega Una Mujer* (*Here Plays a Woman*), Editorial Sudamericana, Buenos Aires, 1941; *Yo Soy Susann* (*I Am Susann*), Piatti, Buenos Aires, 1946.

Hurst, Sarah, *The Curse of Kirsan: Adventures in the Chess Underworld*, Russell Enterprises, Milford, CT, 2002.

Károlyi, Tibor, *Judit Polgar: The Princess of Chess*, B. T. Batsford, London, 2004.

Kasparov, Garry with Donald Trelford, *Child of Change: The Autobiography of Garry Kasparov*, Hutchinson, London, 1987.

Kosteniuk, Alexandra, *How I Became a Grandmaster at Age 14*, AkyAS Publishing, Moscow, 2001.

Liu Wenzhe, *Chinese School of Chess*, B. T. Batsford, London, 2002.

Messner A. Michael, *Taking the Field: Women, Men, and Sports*, University of Minnesota, Minneapolis, 2002.

Murray, H. J. R., *A History of Chess*, Oxford University Press, 1913.

Nochlin, Linda, 'Why Have There Been No Great Women Artists?' *Women, Art and Power and Other Essays*, Harper and Row, New York, 1989.

Polgar, Zsuzsa (Susan) and Jacob Shutzman, *Queen of the Kings Game*, CompChess Consulting, New York, 1997.

Saini, Angela, *Inferior: How Science Got Women Wrong*, 4th Estate, London, 2017.

Tanenbaum, Leora, *Catfight: Women and Competition*, Seven Stories Press, New York, 2002.

Robert B. Tanner, *Vera Menchik: A Biography of the First Women's World Chess Champion*, McFarland and Co, 2016.

Xie Jun, *Chess Champion from China: The Life and Games of Xie Jun*, Gambit Publications Ltd., London, 1998.

Yalom, Marilyn, *The Birth of the Chess Queen*, HarperCollins, New York, 2004.

Newspapers, Periodicals, Internet, Other

Associated Press, 'Lisa Lane, Chess Player, Quits Tourney Because She's in Love', *New York Times*, 3 January 1962.

Beech, Hannah, 'Making All the Right Moves', *Asia Time*, 1 April 2002.

Benko, Pal, 'Match of the Century', *Chess Life and Review*, Vol. 34, No. 1, January 1979.

Braggioti, Mary, 'Queen Among the Knights', *New York Post*, 10 September 1945.

Cantwell, Robert, 'Queen of Knights and Pawns', *Sports Illustrated*, Vol. 15, No. 6.

Clarke, P. H., 'Vera Menchik: First Queen of Chess', *British Chess Magazine*, 1958.

Duffy, Pat, 'Diana Lanni: Chess Champion with a Checkered Past'. *Ms*, Vol.12, No. 7 (January 1984).

Eggers, Paul, 'Akmilovskaya, Donaldson in Olympiad Shocker', *Inside Chess*, Vol. 1, No. 25, 26 December 1988.

Flora, Carlin, 'The Grandmaster Experiment', *Psychology Today*, 1 July 2005.

Geuzendam, Dirk Jan Ten, 'Interview with Judit Polgar', *New In Chess*, No. 8, 1989.

Geuzendam, Dirk Jan Ten, 'Lion Queen Reaches New Heights', *New In Chess*, No.1, 2004.

Gilbert, Linda Carol, 'Chessplayers: Gender Expectations and the Self-Fulfilling Prophecy' Ph.D dissertation, California School of Professional Psychology, Los Angeles, 1989.

Gresser, Gisela, 'Chess Queens in Moscow'. Unpublished article.

Grimsley, Will, 'Scorned Woman Gets Something Off Her Chess', *The New York Sun*, 16 May 1963.

Hilton-Brown, Margaret, 'Vera Menchik', *British Chess Magazine*, 1944.

Kingston, Taylor, 'From Russia, With Hype', *ChessCafe.com*, 14 April 2002.

Lipsyte, Robert, 'Queen of Pawns, Etc.', *New York Times Magazine*, 4 June 1961.

New Yorker, The Talk of the Town, 'Chess Candidate', 19 September 1964.

Polgar, Susan, 'Susan Polgar on Chess', Monthly column on *ChessCafe.com*, from 2002–2004.

Savinov, Misha, Interview with Olga Alexandrova, *ChessCafe.com*, August 2003.

Glory to the Queen, directed by Anna Khazaradze and Tatia Skhirtladze, 2020, Berg Hammer Film, Amour Fou Vienna and Playground Produkcija.

Slater, Kathyryn, 'Women's Chess', *Chess Life*, October, 1966.

Sloan, Sam, 'Assembly Copes with Controversy', *Gulf News*, 1 December 1986.

Stevens, Tim, 'An American Champion Makes History Inside Cold-War Soviet Russia', *Chess Life*, January 2004.

Stix, Harriet, 'A Family Sees Its Road to Riches', *Los Angeles Times*, 18 December 1980.

Teasley, Dorothy, 'Mona Karff', *Marshall Chess Club News*, 25 January 2003.

Thrupkaew, Noy, 'The God of Big Trends', *Bitch*, No. 16 (Spring 2002).

Walsh, Nick Paton, 'I Play to Win', *Guardian*, 15 April 2002.

Weart, Edith, Collection of press clippings compiled at the Cleveland Library.

Woo, Elaine, 'Gisela Gresser: Chess Pioneer Won National Title Nine Times', *New York Times*, 16 December 2000.

Notes

Chapter 1: Playing Like a Girl

1 https://ratings.fide.com/download.phtml.
2 Saini, Angela, *Inferior*, 4th Estate, 2017.
3 H. J. R. Murray, *A History of Chess*, Oxford University Press, 1913, p. 530.
4 Nigel Short, *Vive Le Difference*, New in Chess, 2/2015.
5 Carlin Flora, 'The Grandmaster Experiment', *Psychology Today*, 1 July 2005.

Chapter 2: War-Torn Pioneers: Vera Menchik and Sonja Graf

1 *British Chess Magazine*, 1937.
2 Margaret Hilton Brown, 'Tribute to Vera Menchik', *British Chess Magazine*, 1944.
3 Eve Babitz, 'I Used to Be Charming', *New York Review of Books*, 2019.
4 There were no copies of *I Am Susann* available in US bookstores or libraries. Henk Chevret of The Hague Collection sent me a copy for Christmas.
5 R. H. Wood, 'Rolling Down to Rio', *Chess*, 20 September, 1939, pp. 18–19 (article was written before, but published after, the start of the War).
6 *British Chess Magazine*, August 1944.
7 Robert B. Tanner, *Vera Menchik*, McFarland and Co, 2016, p. 27.

8 Choko, Irwin, Kahan-Aufleger, Kalina and Lipski, *Stolen Youth: Five Women's Survival in the Holocaust*, Yad Vashem, 2005.

9 Thanks to Michael Negele, who encountered these stories in Max Euwe's writing in researching Sonja Graf's life for the German magazine *KARL*.

10 Manuel Azuaga Herrera, *The world champion who emulated Schindler*, Jan 5, 2020 https://www.diariosur.es/culturas/campeona-mundo-emulo-20200105223923-nt.html.

11 Ekaterina Bishard on L. Rudenko https://e3e5.com/article.php?id=1011.

12 R. Bilunova and S. Rosenberg, E3e5.com, Powerful Trio of Champions, September 2016.

13 Kathryn Slater, 'Women's Chess', *Chess Life*, October 1966.

14 John Graham, *Women in Chess: Players of the Modern Age*, McFarland & Co., 1987.

15 Nigel Short, 'Vive Le Difference', *New in Chess*, 2/2015.

Chapter 3: Building a Dynasty: The Women of Georgia

1 *New In Chess*, No. 8, 2003, p. 106.

2 CNN.com, 'Seven skinheads Await Sentences for 20 Killings', http://edition.cnn.com/2008/WORLD/europe/12/03/russia.skin-heads.conviction/index.html, December 2008.

3 Ellen Barry, 'Russian Mayor Walks into Chess Master's Trap', *New York Times*, April 2009.

4 *Chess Life & Review*, January 1979.

5 Graham, op. cit., p. 43.

6 The composition of women's Olympic teams started with two-player squads and expanded over the years. As of 2008, each women's team includes four players and one alternate, the same as Open teams.

7 *Inside Chess*, Vol. 1, Issue 25, pp. 4–5.

8 Olympiad Tromso 2014: 'A quick chat with Ana Matnadze' by Danny King.

Chapter 4: Be Like Judit!

1 Canadian Broadcast Channel, 1962, Interview with Bobby Fischer by Bob Quintrell on CBC-TV.
2 Jennifer Shahade, 'Make Way for the Queens of Chess' *Wall Street Journal*, 16 July 2021.
3 A. L. Chanin, 'Then and Now', *New York Times*, 22 January 1956.
4 ChessCafe.com interview between Misha Savinov and Olga Alexandrova.
5 Deja, Dominik and Karbowski, Adam and Zawisa, Mateusz, 'On the Existence of Optimal Level of Women's Intelligence in Men's Perception: Evidence from a Speed Dating Experiment' https://mpra.ub.uni-muenchen.de/60782/1/MPRA_paper_60782.pdf, December 2014.
6 Simone de Beauvoir, *The Second Sex*, Alfred A. Knopf, 1952, pp. 604–605.
7 *Melbourne Herald*, 1 April 1998.

Chapter 5: Bringing Up Grandmasters: The Polgar Sisters

1 Susan Polgar with Paul Truong, *Breaking Through*, Gloucester Publishers, London, 2005.
2 'Susan Polgar on Chess', ChessCafe.com March 2003.
3 Ibid.
4 Ruthe Stein, 'Banking on Their Teenage Chess Whiz', *San Francisco Chronicle*, 9 February 1980.
5 Jill Nelson, 'Ex-Queen's Gambit', *The Washington Post*, 17 January 1988.

6 Zsuzsa Polgar and Jacob Shutzman, *Queen of the Kings Game*, CompChess Cosulting, 1997, p. 17.

7 Ibid.

8 *New In Chess*, No. 8, 1989, p. 34.

9 Judit Polgar with Mihail Marin, *How I Beat Fischer's Record*, Quality Chess, Glasgow, 2012.

10 Tibor Károlyi, *Judit Polgar: The Princess of Chess*, B. T. Batford, 2004, p. 38.

11 *New In Chess*, No. 2, 1989.

12 Cathy Forbes, *The Polgar Sisters: Training or Genius?* Henry Holt and Co., 1992, p. 49.

13 Dirk Jan Ten Geuzendam, *New In Chess*, No. 4, 1994.

14 Dominic Lawson, '"I never wanted men's pity': Chess child prodigy Judit Polgar on the game's inherent sexism', *The Independent*, 24 November 2012.

15 Judit Polgar with Mihail Marin, *A Game of Queens*, Quality Chess, 2014.

16 Chesshistory.com, https://www.chesshistory.com/winter/winter-167.html#CN_10860.

17 Forbes, op. cit., p. 177.

18 Polgar and Shutzman, op. cit., p. 83.

19 Susan occasionally chose to develop her King's Knight on the first move (1.Nf3), the third or fourth most popular starting move, which often involves playing d4 later, thus leading to positions that would have come about after 1.d4 anyway.

20 Alexey Root, 'Checkmate', *La Leche League Magazine*, May–June, 1994.

21 Judit Polgar with Mihail Marin, *A Game of Queens*, Quality Chess, 2014.

Chapter 6: Women Only!

1 Jenny Schweitzer, 'Girls Who Slay at Chess', *The New Yorker Magazine*, 8/2/2018.
2 Graham, loc. cit.
3 Irving Chernev, *200 Brilliant Endgames*, Simon & Schuster, 1989.
4 Louisa Thomas, 'Hou Yifan and the Wait for Chess's First Woman World Champion', New Yorker Magazine 2 August 2021.

Chapter 7: Chinese Style

1 The quotes are from Xie Jun's book *Chess Champion from China: The Life and Games of Xie Jun*, Gambit Publications Ltd., 1998.
2 Sarah Hurst, *The Curse of Kirsan*, Russell Enterprises, 2002.
3 'Making All the Right Moves', *Asia Time*, 8 April 2002.
4 Ibid.
5 'God of Big Trends,' *Bitch* No. 16, Spring 2002.
6 *Asia Time*, op. cit.
7 Yu Nan's translations, found on his Internet site. At the time of writing, the book is only available in Chinese languages.
8 *New In Chess*, No. 1, 2003.
9 Louisa Thomas, 'Hou Yifan and the Wait for Chess's First Woman World Champion'.
10. Interview between Hou Yifan and Olimpiu G. Urcan in Singapore, Personal notes, 2012.

Chapter 8: Juno and Genius

1 Yakov Neishtadt, *Your Move*, Collier Books, 1990.
2 John Berger, *Ways of Seeing*, Penguin Books, 1972.
3 Edward Lasker, 'Letter from a Woman,' *Chess for Fun and Chess for Blood*, David McKay Company, Inc., New York, 1942.

Chapter 9: European Divas

1 Alexandra Kosteniuk, *Diary of a Chess Queen*, Newton Highlands, Mongoose Press, 2009.
2 In Russian, Sasha is a nickname for Alexandra.
3 Nigel Farndale, 'Blitzed by Russia's pawn star,' *Telegraph*, 14 August 2002.
4 Lichess, 'FIDE Picks Breast Implants as a Sponsor for Women's Chess', 30 September 2021. https://lichess.org/blog/YVWlhhIAACUAp9eF/fide-picks-breast-implants-as-a-sponsor-for-womens-chess.
5 Susan Polgar, 'Why I Chose to Look Ugly, and the Reasoning Behind it!' *Chess Daily News*, 13 April 2021 https://chessdaily-news.com/why-i-chose-to-look-ugly-and-the-reasoning-behind-it/.

Chapter 10: Checkmate Around the World

1 *New In Chess*, No. 8, 2003, p. 65.
2 Sagar Shah, 'Humpy's Spectacular Indian Wedding', Chessbase.com, 9/8/2014.
3 *New in Chess* No. 5, 1995.
4 Tim Crothers, *The Queen of Katwe: A Story of Life, Chess and One Extraordinary Girl's Dream of Becoming a Grandmaster*, Scribner, New York, 2012.
5 Grantley Martelly, *Above the Noise* podcast, 'The Queen of Katwe', October 2020.

Chapter 11: Playing for America

1 *New York Sun*, 16 April 1937.
2 *New York Herald Tribune*, 28 February 1937.

3 The Cleveland Public Library houses the largest collection of chess books and memorabilia in the world, and the Midwestern former steel capital is an unlikely Mecca for a small but zealous group of chess historians. Upon visiting the library myself, I was stunned by its wealth of materials, such as personal letters, original photographs, and rare books. The material in this chapter as well as in Chapter 2 is largely based on my findings there.

4 *Rank and File*, January/February 1993, pp. 16–17.

5 'Queen Among the Knights', *New York Post*, 10 September 1945.

6 *Brooklyn Daily Eagle*, 6 November 1941, p. 16; and 13 November 1941, p. 16; *American Chess Bulletin*, September–October 1941, p. 99

7 A preset number of World Championship invitations are awarded to zones consisting of several countries.

8 The winner was the young Nona Gaprindashvili, who later that winter defeated Bykova for the title.

9 Although many teams fielded two players and an alternate, the United States Federation only sponsored a two-player women's team.

10 *Newsweek*, 22 May 1961.

11 Emma Baccellieri, 'More Than Five Decades after Lisa Lane's Success, Equality Still Eludes Women in Chess', *Sports Illustrated*, 17 December 2018.

12 Jennifer Shahade, The GRID Bonus Episode featuring Diana Lanni, 24 December 2020.

13 Melinda J. Matthews, 'Q+A With Rochelle Ballantyne: Representation is Important', *US Chess*, 21 February 2018.

14 Jessy Edwards, 'Young Brownsville Chess Champs Wins $40K College Scholarship Award', *BK Reader*, 16 October 2020 https://bkreader.com/2020/10/16/young-brownsville-chess-champ-wins-40k-college-scholarship-award/.

Chapter 12: Gender Play: Angela from Texas

1 H. J. R. Murray, *A History of Chess*, Oxford University Press, 1913, pp. 426–427.

Chapter 13: Worst to First

1 Seth Mydans, 'Where Chess Is King and the People Are Pawns', *New York Times*, 20 June 2004.
2 In the final round, I lost against Irina Krush, who played a nice game. She ended up tying with Anna Zatonskih for second/third place.

Index

About the author

Jennifer Shahade is an Olympic chess champion, poker pro, speaker and award-winning host. She is a two-time United States women's chess champion and was the first female to win the US Junior Open. Jennifer works to bring more women, girls and gender minorities into the game through her advocacy and work. In 2023, she broke international news of #MeToo in chess, forwarding her mission to make the chess safe and fun for all. She has won two Global Poker Awards and is an ambassador for PokerStars and Poker Power. Her books include *Chess Queens* (previously published under the title *Chess Bitch*) and *Play Like a Girl!* She lives in Philadelphia with her family.